MW00906169

Life Beyond Death

Ramón Martínez de Pisón Liébanas

Life Beyond Death

The Eschatological Dimension of Christian Faith

NOVALIS

© 2007 Novalis, Saint Paul University, Ottawa, Canada

Cover design and layout: Pascale Turmel
Cover image: © Jupiter Images

Business Offices:

Novalis Publishing Inc.
10 Lower Spadina Avenue, Suite 400
Toronto, Ontario, Canada
M5V 2Z2

Novalis Publishing Inc.
4475 Frontenac Street
Montréal, Québec, Canada
H2H 2S2

Phone: 1-800-387-7164
Fax: 1-800-204-4140
E-mail: books@novalis.ca
www.novalis.ca

Library and Archives Canada Cataloguing in Publication

Martínez de Pisón L., Ramón
    Life beyond death : the eschatological dimension of Christian faith / Ramón Martínez de Pisón Liébanas.

First published 1993 in French under title: L'au-delà.
Includes bibliographical references.
ISBN 978-2-89507-901-9

    1. Future life–Christianity. 2. Eschatology. 3. Hope–Religious aspects–Christianity. 4. Judgment Day. 5. Salvation. I. Title.

BT902.M3713 2007   236'.2   C2007-903136-6

Printed in Canada.

All rights reserved. No part of this publication may be reproduced, stored in a retrieval system, or transmitted in any form, or by any means, electronic, mechanical, photocopying, recording, or otherwise, without the written permission of the publisher.

The Scripture quotations contained herein are from the New Revised Standard Version Bible: Catholic Edition copyright © 1993 and 1989 by the Division of Christian Education of the National Council of the Churches of Christ in the U.S.A. Used by permission. All rights reserved.

We acknowledge the financial support of the Government of Canada through the Book Publishing Industry Development Program (BPIDP) for our publishing activities.

5   4   3   2   1   1 1   1 0   0 9   0 8   0 7

In memory of
Sheilagh A. McGrath (1966–2002)

Table of Contents

Introduction

Hope for a better future is an essential dimension of the Christian faith. In fact, to hope for something better has always been one of the dreams of humanity. This tendency can be found in past history: one need only recall, for example, Plato (428?–347 B.C.), in *The Republic;* Saint Augustine (354–430), in *The City of God;* Thomas More (1478–1535), in his *Utopia*; and Tommaso Campanella (1568–1639), in *The City of the Sun*. Without hope for a better future, we would suffocate in this present life.

The question regarding our future is fundamental to our present condition and to its fulfillment. Hope for something better cannot ultimately be separated from concern for the present. However, such a separation has taken place often enough. This was in good part the result of a dualistic and Manichaean world view, with its negative conception of creation, which influenced Christian spirituality. Contempt for the world was considered the way to salvation. This pessimistic attitude both toward the present and to creation itself has been one of the principal reasons for the Marxist critique of religion, in which religion is considered the opium of the people.

Nevertheless, Christian faith alienates us neither from the present nor from creation. Faith brings us face to face with both the *already here* of salvation and the *not yet*. But the *not yet* is not a reality beyond this present life. It is, rather, its fulfillment. At the heart of this dialectic is Jesus Christ. The ultimate hope has already entered into history. Jesus Christ is the first fruit of what we are also called to be.

As a result, the new heaven and the new earth (Rev. 21:1-8) are not new states of life coming to us out of the blue, that is, from heaven. The new creation stands before us. It is a task to be accomplished.

> Therefore [says Piet Schoonenberg], when we speak about eternal life, we must again start with our earthly life. Eternal life is a fullness of what is earthly but without earthly limitations such as mortality, suffering, de-personification, the crumbling into bits and pieces of time (see, e.g., 1 Cor. 15:42-44).[1]

Life beyond death means the final fulfillment of our present faith in Jesus Christ. In this regard, as we will see later, we will have to take into account the already well-established difference between *eschatology*, namely, reflection about the final fulfillment of our *present* life—including our human participation in its attainment—and *apocalyptic*, that is, the belief that the future world is already established by God, without any human intervention and, consequently, without any connection with present history.

Human beings need not only bread to eat in the here and now, they also need a reason to hope. Along this line, an expression I heard several years ago, "If we knew that tomorrow we might not eat, then the bread we eat today would stick in our throats," holds a lot of wisdom. Does creation, therefore, have an ultimate meaning or is it just condemned to some sort of disintegration? Do our life and our history reach a final fulfillment or are they just condemned to futility? As Christians, we believe that life is not reduced to our own limited horizons without any relationship with any transcendence whatsoever. Questions regarding God and the final fulfillment of creation are endemic to the human heart.

In 1983, ten years before the publication of my book *L'au-delà (The Beyond)*,[2] I began teaching a course on Life Beyond Death in Santiago, Chile. Since then, I have continued offering this course at Saint Paul University, Ottawa. I taught it primarily in French. However, in the winter of 2005 I was asked to teach this course in English and realized that it was time to revise the 1993 French version for an English-speaking public. However, the present version is not simply a translation of the French text. Rather it is an elaboration and improvement on the overall problematic treated in

LIFE BEYOND DEATH

the earlier French text. Different from the French edition, this one is divided in two parts and contains three new chapters.

Part One, *Basic Presuppositions*, deals with some essential assumptions to be considered in order better to understand what our Christian heritage has to say regarding our final destination in God's kingdom. Thus, chapter 1 will introduce some present challenges affecting life beyond death. Chapter 2 will highlight the eschatological dimension of Christian faith in its historical developments. Chapter 3 will ask the question that lies at the core of any openness on the part of human beings and of history itself to the future, that is, the question concerning the meaning of hope in the Western world. Chapter 4 will emphasize the need for a renewed interpretation of assertions regarding life beyond death.

Part Two, *Beyond Death in Light of Christian Faith and Church Tradition*, will systematize the Christian message concerning the final fulfillment of all creation in God. Chapter 5 will show how we have become heirs to a great promise, taking into account the way in which this promise must be lived as we face life's painful realities. Chapter 6 will assess how this promise is fulfilled in Jesus Christ with whom we share a new life. Chapter 7 will draw a picture of the resurrection of the dead and of heaven as eternal life. Chapter 8 will highlight a more positive understanding of the final (general) judgment as liberation. Chapter 9 will deal with the difficult issue of the possibility of a final damnation, namely, of everlasting hell. Finally, chapter 10 will deal with the question of the relationship between our personal death and the final resurrection.

In writing this book I took into consideration some of my personal experiences. The first one is the presentation of the *last things*—death, particular (personal) judgment, purgatory, resurrection, final (general) judgment, heaven and hell—as found in the catechism of my childhood, and from some practices of the Church of my youth. The *last things* were used to make us behave according to the *correct* morality proclaimed by the authority of the Roman Catholic Church. The role of the *last things* then was very ideological: its purpose was to raise the fear of possible damnation within the faithful, and to stress punishments that would accompany that fear. I remember well my fear of fire because it reminded me of being burnt forever in hell!

Furthermore, we were told that we had a *soul* to be saved. Salvation was considered in a very individualistic and dualistic way. We lit little lamps on the eve of All Souls, which is a day dedicated in our Christian tradition to remembering the deceased and to praying for the souls of family members who have passed on. We would not forget any of them, because if we did, their souls would come back from purgatory during the night to remind us! I will never forget my fear of going to the washroom on the eve of All Souls. There was to be found the container holding all the lamps recalling our family dead. I was afraid the spirits of some of them might appear, asking for their lamps to lighten the darkness of their path into purgatory as well as having the burden of their debts, that is, the penance for theirs sins, reduced!

Another dimension of this way of understanding salvation was the idea that paradise was something we had to merit. It became a kind of mathematical retribution. If we were righteous God would accept us into heaven, but if we behaved badly we risked eternal damnation in hell, or at least some temporal punishment in purgatory.

With the decline of religious practice and liberation from this ideological use of fear, churches became silent concerning the eschatological dimension of Christian faith. Nonetheless, people still ask the question: What is the ultimate meaning of life? What is the future of history? A good example of the need to understand the final meaning of life can be found in the Indian Ocean tsunami of December 26, 2004 that caused such a disaster in Southeast Asia, affecting Sri Lanka, India, Indonesia, Thailand, Maldives, and the Seychelles. This disaster of course gave rise to a whole series of questions, especially to the question of why such a tragedy would occur.

We are participating in a major shift in thinking about the ultimate meaning of life. Christian churches no longer have a monopoly in the Western world on teaching about salvation. The kingdom of God is no longer the expected final destination shared by all of us. Why? Because the doctrine of reincarnation, for example, is presenting a major challenge to the faith we inherited from our ancestors.

It is for such reasons that I undertook to write this book, namely, in order to present the core of our Christian heritage regarding the eschatological dimension of Christian faith. Thus, this book represents an effort to confront some present challenges that Christians are facing concerning their understanding of the final destination of human life. I have situated myself within the Christian tradition. I am a Christian theologian who is a member of and identified with the Roman Catholic Church. It is within this context, then, that I will discuss the eschatological dimension of the Christian faith along with its ecclesiastical interpretation.

This book is dedicated to the memory of Sheilagh A. McGrath (1966–2002), a special friend, who died of multiple brain tumours, while she was still rather young. I would like to share here the most wonderful gift that I have ever received from another human being.

A few years before her death, we went to spend an evening at the house of one of our friends. I went to pick her up at the Bruyère Residence which is a hospice for those suffering from long-term, debilitating illnesses. After leaving Bruyère and while waiting in my car for her mother's arrival, Sheilagh shared with me an account of an intense personal experience.

"Ramón," she said, "one day I heard a voice. It was God's voice asking if I was able to bear his Son." I remained silent. However, for me, this was like a light that made me understand the mystery of Sheilagh's life. I did not ask her about the voice. In fact, I did not need to inquire about it. I was convinced not only of her sincerity but, indeed, about the reality of this experience. I began to understand something about which I had long wondered. How was it possible for her, while in full awareness of her own illness and of the challenges of pain and loss ahead, that she never once complained and yet continued to be so full of life?

She asked me to say nothing about this wonderful event. I have kept that promise till now although it has been very difficult for me to do so. But now that Sheilagh is in heaven, it seems to be the time to share her experience as a grace belonging to the whole Christian community.

The secret of Sheilagh's life is that she was visited by God's love in a particular way. I am not concerned at all to try to analyze what kind of spiritual or mystical experience she had. I leave this to other experts. The fact is that God filled Sheilagh's life in a very special way.

Since that moment, one passage in the Gospel comes immediately to mind: the Annunciation of the angel Gabriel to Mary (Lk. 1:26-38). Like the virgin Mary, Sheilagh had a "special visitation" by God, and like Mary, she was asked about bearing God's Son. Like Mary, too, Sheilagh's life was an example of the answer that Mary gave to the angel Gabriel: "Here am I, the servant of the Lord; let it be with me according to your word" (Lk. 1:38).

Like Mary, the gift that Sheilagh received from God was not only the wonderful experience that filled her life. There was also something to be shared with others. Mary gave birth to God's Son for the sake of humanity, and Sheilagh life's was a gift for all those who approached her. She was always ready to forget her own illness. In fact I never really knew whether or not Sheilagh was suffering at all because she never complained about anything. She was always smiling and making herself available to help others, despite her own limited physical condition. I remember so many times in her mother's apartment, or in our friend's house, or in my own apartment, when she was looking at us while we were preparing supper. She regularly asked: "May I help you?" It was always wonderful to hear this from her!

I must confess that sometimes, particularly from the moment she shared her extraordinary experience with me, I went to see her, not always for her sake, but for mine. I needed her presence, her smile, her prayer, her touch, her support and, during the last months, her silence—the silence of someone filled with the divine presence. She, the "favoured one," has transformed the life of every one close to her.

14

I could not keep this gift to myself alone. I kept my promise to Sheilagh to remain silent about her experience until her death. Now that she is in heaven I am sure that it is quite all right that I share this experience with others because, as I mentioned above, this is a grace that Sheilagh received for the whole Christian community.

Many times we believe that God has abandoned us, that God does not visit any more in a particular way, as God used to do in ancient times. Perhaps we too have the tendency to be sceptical with regard to those who have received a special gift from God. Perhaps for that reason Sheilagh was hesitant to let others know of her mystical experiences.

I deeply believe that she was a "holy woman," a holy woman in its deepest sense. In more classical ecclesiastical language these people are called "saints." I dare not use this word because it is not my purpose here to canonize Sheilagh. Nevertheless, it is important that we recognize and celebrate the special visitations that God freely grants to some people. She was one of these privileged ones, and now that Sheilagh belongs to the communion of saints we can continue to share with her.

Finally, I sincerely believe that Sheilagh, presently in paradise, is experiencing at least some of the things that she would have liked to have experienced here on earth: obtaining a driver's licence, so as to visit us all in a spiritual way; and having a boyfriend—the love of God that will be with her for all eternity!

This experience of having known and been with Sheilagh is for me the most existential example of what it means to live a full life. Sheilagh was able to enter "alive" into death, that is, to live a full life before death, in order to live fully for all eternity.

※

In the quotations, except where otherwise indicated, the italics and the capitals belong to the original texts. Jack McCann translated much of my original text into English. I am responsible for the balance of the translation and the adaptation of the French and Spanish sources for this new publication. The notes are located at the end of each chapter.

This book would not have been possible without the collaboration of my Oblate brothers who helped me put my ideas into correct English: Lorne MacDonald; Dale M. Schlitt; Claude Tardif; and, in a particular way, Jack McCann.

I also owe a debt of gratitude to my Saint Paul University colleague, professor John M. Huels, who corrected the manuscript and gave me useful advice.

The editor of *Theoforum* has granted permission to reproduce and develop my article "Does Hope Have Meaning in the Western World?" in chapter 3.

Finally, in April 19, 2005, a new Pope was elected. Cardinal Joseph Ratzinger succeeded Pope John Paul II and took the name Benedict XVI. However, in this work, I keep the name Cardinal Joseph Ratzinger when I cite works he wrote as a Cardinal. His book on *Eschatology*, often quoted in my work, was published many years before he became Pope Benedict XVI.

Notes to the Introduction

1   P. Schoonenberg, "I Believe in Eternal Life," in *Concilium*, 41 (1969), p. 107.

2   See R. Martínez de Pisón, *L'au-delà*, Ottawa: Novalis (L'horizon du croyant, [19]), 1993.

PART ONE
Basic Presuppositions

The study of what lies beyond death, an aspect of the wider question of eschatology, or the concern for the "end of times," has always made certain presuppositions, or assumptions. Until recently, several of these presuppositions remained implicit. This was the case, for example, with the common belief, in Western Christian society, in a God who is the creator and supreme judge of the universe.

A second presupposition concerned the ultimate destination of every human being. After death, one will be judged according to one's deeds. Heaven was reserved for the few very good. Hell was for committed sinners—those who were really bad, namely, the ones who had committed "mortal" sins. Purgatory was for those who were not completely bad but who, following death, did not merit immediate rejoicing in the vision of God. They needed to be purified of minor or "venial" sins before arriving at their final destination in heaven. Heaven, hell and purgatory were also conceived as physical places, since no distinction was made between a location in space and an existential state of being. In addition, time in purgatory was measured using our temporal categories of days, weeks, months and years.

A third important presupposition was the pastoral practice of fear used by Church authorities, theologians and preachers as a way of making people behave according to the norms and morality presented by the official teaching of the Church. This pastoral approach was present many centuries before the Protestant Reformation in the sixteenth century, and it continued in both

Reformed and Roman Catholic traditions. This use of the fear of eternal damnation to motivate people and, one could say, manipulate consciences, was a regular practice in many Christian churches until not so long ago.

A fourth presupposition consisted in an almost literal interpretation of biblical texts regarding what happens after death. In particular, this was reflected in the images of the final (general) judgment and the punishments that the damned would experience in hell for all eternity. Biblical and imagistic literalism also contributed to fear about one's condition after death.

A final presupposition is the vision of the world found in Roman Catholic theology and preaching. Church leaders' overall attitudes adapted only reluctantly to the emergence of a more scientific vision of the universe which began to appear in Modernity at the end of the fifteenth century.

Today we find ourselves in a completely different cultural and religious context. Part One of this book will address what I consider to be pertinent presuppositions necessary to understand the core of Christian eschatology. This will be presented in Part Two of this book. I consider it important to make these assumptions explicit so that readers will understand the perspective out of which I am working.

My first presupposition relates to the present challenges affecting our understanding of what lies beyond death. Contrary to what has been a common belief in Christian faith, the question of life after or beyond death no longer concerns heaven or hell alone, but for many, even some Christians, belief in life after death now concerns the possibility of reincarnation, that is, a new life on earth. Reincarnation is contrary to the basic Christian belief in life after or beyond death. We need to confront this difference head on. Furthermore, we can no longer accept the pastoral use of fear to persuade people to behave in an appropriate manner. Such a practice is contrary to the Gospel and to human dignity. In addition, another essential change regarding our understanding of life after death has to do with death itself. To a great extent, death has become a shameful dimension of life that needs to be hidden. For this reason it seems important to separate our consideration of death from the taboo that it has become in Western society.

My second presupposition is related to the importance of the historical development of the doctrine of a reality beyond death. This historical contextualization will help us understand the significance of this doctrine within our contemporary scientific view of the universe.

Despite any particular vision of the world, we should note that hope is a fundamental attitude necessary for living in the present, a present that is open to the future. The importance of rediscovering the place of hope in human life is the third presupposition which I will address.

Finally, we must take into account the role of hermeneutics, that is to say, the importance of interpretation. My fourth presupposition relates to the need for a new interpretation of assertions about life after or beyond death. I will address the importance of revitalizing our Christian imagination in terms of the language we use in speaking of life after or beyond death. This will help us to understand in a more creative way the eschatological dimension of Christian faith.

I

Life Beyond Death:

Present Challenges

Life is the greatest and most wonderful of all gifts. A gift is something received from another and does not acquire its full value until it is accepted. Furthermore, a gift-received is to be shared with others. A gift invites us to enter into a relationship that is characterized by grace. Can we speak of a more gracious gift than that of one's own life?

Life is an extraordinary adventure. It is a story whose plot unfolds as an existence highlighted by a two-fold fragility: that of our birth and that of our death. Everything reminds us of our contingency and finitude. We depend on others, on the world and, if we are believers, on God. Sooner or later, however, we will have to return the gift of life. Accepting this double fragility makes it possible for us to live life in its fullness.

Even if sin gives death a particular connotation, we no longer consider death to be one of the direct consequences of the sin at the origins.[1] Death is a constitutive aspect of what is means to be human. It is the last phase of life. Thus, death is a necessary stage in bringing our life as human beings to fulfillment, making it possible for us to experience the eternity that God offers us.[2] Consequently, it is difficult to understand why we try to repress the thoughts of death or transform it into a spectacle in order to relieve our boredom while we still think we are immortal.

It is true that the desire to live on beyond death, the ultimate sign of our fragility, is deeply rooted in our very nature. We have never ceased speculating on this desire.[3] In Christian tradition, this basic desire is reinforced by the promise of a life, through Jesus Christ and in the Holy Spirit, in eternal communion with God, as well as with other women and men in a transformed universe. Death is in fact the point of departure either for eternal communion with God or its definitive refusal.

Nevertheless, today we are facing some special challenges regarding this belief in our final destination, even if life beyond death continues to be an issue discussed by so many of us. First of all, unfortunately, even in this discussion death itself tends to become a taboo, a shameful dimension of life. Second, not every aspect of the current discussion is bad. For example, ending the pastoral practice of fear makes it possible for us to rethink what occurs after or beyond death in a more positive way. We cannot use the fear of eternal damnation to make people behave appropriately. Third, the illusion of immortality, the doctrine of reincarnation, and possible communication with the dead are of great interest even to Christian believers. We are witnessing the emergence of a religious syncretism according to which salvation is acquired through knowledge (a new kind of Gnosticism). The traditional systems of Christian beliefs are in decline.[4]

The understanding of life after or beyond death that has been presented by our Christian churches is being challenged. This chapter will deal with some of the changes resulting from this challenge. Faith in our Christian heritage invites us to face this challenge and come to terms with these changes.

1. Death: From a Familiar Event to a Shameful Dimension of Life

In the past, death and dying were considered family events. In North American culture today, death and dying have been transformed into a taboo. As a result, many people feel ill at ease when they have to face these realities and prefer to repress or deny the feelings generated by them.[5]

Silence Regarding Death

As Cardinal Joseph Ratzinger once remarked, "the family home frequently seems no more than a sleeping-bag. In the daytime it effectively dematerializes. No more can it be that sheltering space, in sickness and dying. Indeed, sickness and death are becoming purely technological problems to be handled by the appropriate institution."[6] Today, in the family, in the hospital milieu, and often in other therapeutic environments, we do not speak clearly about the imminence of death to a dying person. We try to avoid the process of mourning as well. According to Hans Schwarz,

> We have managed to shut away death into the sterile white walls of the hospital room and the intensive care unit. What was normal for the patriarchs of the Old Testament—dying in the midst of their families, with both parties saying farewell to each other—is hardly any longer a possibility for us. We have no immediate encounter with death, except through its trivialization in TV programs, its facticity in news services, or in the euphemistic version offered by the funeral home, where the diseased [sic] often look better than they did during their lifetime. Thanks to cosmetology and embalming practices, perpetual care will be extended to the dead in our cemeteries.[7]

Death as a Spectacle

At the same time, death has become a spectacle to be observed, a sort of entertainment, but not something that really happens to oneself. The violence which is unfortunately present in society also diminishes the overall meaning of death for us. These attitudes contribute to our tendency of avoiding "to ask ourselves regarding [the] metaphysical implications [of death]."[8] Death and dying are for other people. We are only spectators!

Integrating Death into Life

Accepting the reality of death makes possible living one's life fully, for here below the fullness of life is closely bound up with mortality. Though death is the obverse of the supreme grace that is life, it lends value to life and to each of life's moments. It stimulates life and pushes one to achieve things, to create before death arrives. In this way, we can fulfill our vocations as persons, that is, we overcome death by integrating it into our human existence without letting ourselves be beaten by it first.[9] The only reason we could have for considering our life as a failure would be to die without having really lived.

Death sets us before what is irrevocable and irreversible in our existence. To hide it is to deny the possibility of our fulfillment as persons. The end of life gives fullness to life. Death invites us to give our actions a special weight and to examine the real significance of existence. Thus wisdom is born, and it does not die. In addition, to integrate death into our human development obliges us to end the pastoral practice of fear. To use fear as a primary way of bringing people to personal conversion is no longer acceptable in our day.

2. *Ending the Pastoral Practice of Fear*

According to some already well-established, even perhaps one could say by now "old-fashioned," interpretations found in some psychoanalytic theories,[10] religion has reinforced the neurotic consciousness of many people because religious preaching has frequently centred around the idea of sin; transgression; the fear of being punished in hell for all eternity; hatred of oneself, one's body and sexuality; and the image of a vindictive God.[11] In Western society the pastoral practice of fear is not a recent phenomenon. Its presence in Christianity can be traced back to the Middle Ages (5th-15th centuries), and has led to a denaturalization of human existence and death, according to the French historian Jean Delumeau.[12] The ideological use of death was accompanied by an image of God as a ruthless judge rather than someone who loves us, a judge who closely watches all our movements and keeps a record of our bad actions in order to hand us the bill on the day of our death, during the so-called particular judgment.

LIFE BEYOND DEATH

The Ideological Use of Death

We can easily agree with Marc Leboucher when he describes how "the Church has frequently used the fear of hell to bring people to conversion, to live in better conformity with the [officially established] faith."[13] Older people, familiar with the religious milieu of earlier times, can remember this situation very well. The sermon about the eternal truths: death, particular judgment, purgatory, resurrection of the dead, the last (general) judgment, hell and heaven all constituted the focus around which popular missions were organized. After the sermon was finished, priests would spend several days hearing people's confessions. The criterion for determining the success of the mission was precisely the fact that everyone went to confession!

Jean Delumeau, who has studied the theme of sin, fear and guilt in Western society, stresses the Church's role in this process: "The church played a key role in the gradual erasure of a 'tame' image of death and the 'natural' way of experiencing departure from life when it proposed meditation on death as a prime method of moral pedagogy."[14] This ideological use of death was accompanied by the description of the punishments that the souls of the deceased experienced in a transitory way in purgatory or for all eternity in hell.[15] Analyzing past sermons on eternal truths, and in particular on the punishments being suffered by people in purgatory or in hell, we see a lack of originality. Most of those sermons repeat stereotypes about the eternal punishments suffered by the damned in hell: "The almost invariable structure of these sermons on Hell," says Delumeau, "reveals three major, stereotyped emphases concerning the pains experienced by the damned. They suffer both spiritually and physically, and this double punishment will last forever. The order in which these three elements are presented matters less than their constant presence."[16]

A False Image of God

The attitude expressed in these sermons and elsewhere is rooted in and reflects a false image of God. It comes, in large part, from the theocracy of the Middle Ages. As Maurice Zundel said in 1937:

"God has been stereotyped, the divine face hardened. God has been objectivised and turned into a prefabricated persona, so strange to our heartbeat that, from the moment someone pronounces the name of God, we have the desire to run away."[17] This concept of God is representative of the patriarchal culture that kept so many passively obedient in an infantile state.[18] Today, however, "the ghost of biblical apocalypses and the terrors of hell have disappeared from our culture."[19] Nevertheless, the eternal truths concerning life after death have been so linked to fear that with the disappearance of the pastoral practice of fear the eschatological dimension of Christian faith also seems to have vanished from our horizon. For this reason we need to rethink those truths in a completely different context. Three tasks are especially important as we confront these new challenges.

Confronting New Challenges

The first task is to discover and proclaim a different image of God—the God of our biblical tradition.[20] This God is not an invention but a discovery: the most marvellous and greatest discovery, and also the most gracious. In this discovery we find a God who invites human beings into a new covenant through a new life with others and in harmony with the universe. This personal and liberating God calls women and men to become themselves.

Memory plays an important role in the lives of nations and of human beings. Through memory, women and men recall the founding events that constitute them as a nation, a society, a family, a religious community or even as individual persons.[21] People celebrate religious festivals by remembering the liberating events of their past, as the Bible shows. The experience of a liberating God, in the Old Testament as well as in the New, was the beginning of the whole biblical reflection. God is not a rival, an enemy who overwhelms women and men and from whom they would like to be freed. God is the liberator of the people. The experiences of the liberation from Egypt became the centre of Israel's creed:

> When your children ask you in time to come, "What is the meaning of the decrees and the statues and the ordinances that

LIFE BEYOND DEATH

the Lord our God has commanded you?" then you shall say to your children, "We were Pharaoh's slaves in Egypt, but the Lord brought us out of Egypt with a mighty hand. The Lord displayed before our eyes great and awesome signs and wonders against Egypt, against Pharaoh and all his household. He brought us out from there in order to bring us in, to give us the land that he promised on oath to our ancestors. . . ." (Deut. 6:20-23)

This was a faith repeated from father to son through generations (see Deut. 26:4-10; Josh. 24). The people did not meet an abstract and distant divinity, but a personal and liberating God who was present in their suffering. Centuries later, when Israel was forced into the Babylonian exile (from 597 to 538 B.C.), Deutero-Isaiah used the theme of the exiles' liberation in relation to a new creation: permanent salvation. In the same way that God created heaven and earth, God shall free the people from exile and lead them to the Promised Land (see Isa. 40:3-5; 41:17-20; 43:16-21). On the basis of these salvific experiences, commemorated particularly during liturgical celebrations, some believers reflected theologically about the different dimensions of their lives. Concrete liberating experiences were the starting point of subsequent theological systematization.

Our ancestors' God comes into our lives in Jesus Christ. Fear is no longer a valid force able to cause human beings to be obedient to God, nor even to be obedient to the commandments of the churches. On the contrary, the Gospel is the revelation of the love of God which is at the opposite extreme of constraint (1 Jn. 4:7-21): the Good News is the manifestation of the compassion of God.[22] The first Christian communities reflected on life's ultimate meaning from their experience of liberation, commemorated in their liturgies. Jesus Christ is the giver of new life, as the apostle Peter proclaimed in one of his addresses to the people in the Temple of Jerusalem:

While he [the man lame from birth who was healed] clung to Peter and John, all the people ran together to them in the portico called Solomon's Portico, utterly astonished. When Peter saw it, he addressed the people, "You Israelites, why do you wonder at this, or why do you stare at us, as though by our own power or piety we had made him walk? The God of Abraham, the God of Isaac, and the God of Jacob, the God of our ancestors has glorified his servant Jesus, whom you handed over and rejected in the presence of Pilate, though he had decided to release him. But you rejected the Holy and Righteous One and asked to have a murderer given to you, and you killed the Author of life, whom God raised from the dead. To this we are witnesses. And by faith in his name, his name itself has made this man strong, whom you see and know; and the faith that is through Jesus has given him this perfect health in the presence of all of you. . . ." (Acts 3:11-16)

For the different Christian communities, the incarnation, life, death and resurrection of Jesus Christ became the starting point of their creed. God's plan of salvation is accomplished in Jesus Christ: human beings are called to live forever. Hence freedom and eternal life, before being a human realization, are the fruit of a divine gift.

Indeed, the newness of Jesus Christ's revelation consists in the presentation of a different image of God. Rather than a God conceived as a despotic monarch, proposed in medieval ecclesiastical tradition, the Gospel manifests a trinitarian monotheism. God is unique but not solitary. The notion of God as Trinity represents a decisive new step in our comprehension of divinity. This signifies a rupture with the theocratic God who gave final meaning to the universe by imposing God's will without any further consideration of human beings. Conceiving God as Trinity provides us with a very different idea of the divine grandeur, one that is opposed to narcissism:

No one can be offended, no one can feel diminished if he learns that God, understood as a Presence interior to ourselves and always already there, that this God is God because he possesses nothing. No one can be offended by a God on his knees, by a God who proposes himself without ever imposing himself. The Trinity revealed by Jesus Christ gives us the understanding of the gesture of the Washing of the feet. If Jesus is on his knees,

LIFE BEYOND DEATH

if He introduces a new scale of values in the world, he bases it precisely on the heart of the Trinity.[23]

The Christian's God does not oppress us. God grounds our freedom, and we are invited to discover the real divinity which lies in human hands. In our day, as we experience the crises of institutions, Christian churches must learn to recover their original mission, namely, to be a sacrament of Jesus Christ. The Church will be an efficient sign to the extent that it continues to be the transparency of Jesus Christ. Thus the mission of the Church consists in proclaiming the compassion and tenderness of God whom the Gospel reveals. "The originality of Christianity," says Maurice Zundel, "is, precisely, to present a Person, much more than a doctrine, and to offer us a Light without any mixture through a Humanity without any frontier."[24] At the heart of the Church's mission there is always the same question: What God is the Church speaking about? Only in discovering a loving God, as presented by Jesus Christ, can we understand the importance of Christian community as a place of sharing, life and freedom.

The second task in rethinking certain eternal truths concerning life after death consists in the recognition of the importance of social and especially political laicization for ending the pastoral practice of fear. Laicization contributed to the rupture of the link between religion and State—the end of the official religion of a State.[25] For us, religion is no longer something we inherit, so to speak. Religion has often been put at the service of constraint exercised by the group on the individual, making it a collective rather than a personal phenomenon, whether this collective be family, a clan, a country, a race, and so forth. In order to subsist, a group requires the individual's obedience. In that regard, however, a very significant turning point occurred. Religion served to warn us about the Divinity through a series of customs, precepts and traditions, which were to be internalized by individuals who might be tempted to cheat when no one was watching. As a result of this divine guarantee, individuals embrace fear as the essential attitude to display before the Omnipotent-God. Thus, the religion of the group became an obstacle to freedom. Unfortunately, this outlook and approach had very negative consequences:

> To attach religion closely or distantly to fear, to feed our fears in order to establish ourselves in God, is at the same time to deny God and to deny man, and we know that this tendency exists in us: a catastrophe is almost always interpreted in the sense of a warning from Providence that brings us back to order and asks us to put ourselves back in line with its requirements.[26]

Today, as women and men who are living a new spirituality that is the manifestation of their deepest desires and possibilities, and who are discovering a God who is a liberating Presence, Zundel invites us to rid ourselves of dualistic attitudes. "There is no longer any duality between the flesh and the spirit, nor between the earth and heaven, nor between time and eternity, nor between the visible and the invisible. All that is one, one in the unique Presence which is the Life of our life."[27] Attitudes that still bring or imply fear or terror are being rejected as contrary to a more existential, evangelical, and liberating spirituality and religion.

The critiques of Ludwig Feuerbach (1804–1872), Karl Marx (1818–1883), Friedrich Nietzsche (1844–1900) and Sigmund Freud (1856–1939) against religion find their foundation in people's desire to be liberated from external constraints. Their critiques of religion, and in particular of Christian morality, are rooted in human beings' desire to become their own creators, and to claim autonomy for the self, particularly if, in a given situation, God is presented in an oppressive way. For this reason, the pastoral practice of fear has had disastrous consequences. "Not only does this [pastoral practice] not make anyone feel afraid any longer, but it even nourishes defection [of religious practice], and even a sarcasm toward faith."[28]

The last of our three tasks is to recover the core of the eschatological dimension of Christian faith, and to be able to present it in a renewed way to our brothers and sisters. Churches have become silent both about the fulfillment of our faith in a life that is eternal and about the last things.[29] Perhaps they feel guilty for having used these themes as a way of making people follow a certain correct morality. This is the direct result of the fear approach and represents

LIFE BEYOND DEATH

the enormous price of using it. Still, people continue to ask questions concerning life beyond death, and Christian churches do have a message to share with the faithful. The vacuum left by the lack of preaching about life after death is being filled by many other groups in ways that make us ask some serious questions. Today God—at least the God of Christian tradition—no longer seems to be the exclusive point of reference when thinking and speaking about life after or beyond death.

3. An After Death in Heaven or a New Life on Earth?

In the first part of this chapter, I pointed out certain contemporary difficulties with death as the last step in human development. Many people dream of attaining immortality, or a-mortality: that is, of overcoming death. For many people, life after death is no longer situated beyond this earthly life— in heaven—but in a new life on earth.

The Illusion of Immortality

In speaking about new religious tendencies in Western society, Jean Vernette sees the doctrine of reincarnation as an illusion of immortality: a way to confront death both in a society that hides it and in the face of churches that have become mute on the questions of life after death.[30] This illusion of immortality denies the radicalism of death, which the doctrine of reincarnation transforms into a simple passage to a new life here on earth.[31] Death is only one step among many in the cycle of life.[32]

The illusion of immortality is worlds away from the Christian belief in the resurrection of the dead—that is, eternal life. To live forever is not a right of finite and contingent beings but a gift. It is an invitation addressed to humanity, and accepting it means a commitment to oneself, other people, creation and God who is, in Jesus Christ and through the Holy Spirit, the source of eternal life.

An Impersonal Religion

For many people today, life after or beyond death is not limited to paradise or heaven. Neither does what comes after death pertain only to the domain of God as understood in mainline Christianity. Entering into the kingdom of God, or the kingdom of Heaven, is no longer the desire of many people, even of some who still profess to be Christians. Any reference to a personal, transcendent God, or to a transcendent revelation presented by Christianity or by other religions, often appears to lack validity. As Jean Vernette notes, God "is a manifestation of the universal and impersonal Spirit."[33] We are very far away from the idea of the God of the Christian tradition, a God who in Jesus Christ reveals the fullness of life, who loves us and with whom we can establish a personal relationship.

If God is the manifestation of the divine contained in all humanity, as the Energy of the whole universe, and not as a person, then Jesus Christ is conceived more or less as a kind of Master of Wisdom—one master among many others. "Jesus is no longer the Son of God, but one of the multiple incarnations of the cosmic Christ."[34] For many, his incarnation, his divine filiation, his universal mediation, the fulfillment of the revelation in his person disappear from the present scene. In the theory of the reincarnation, Jesus Christ is only one revelation of the Divinity among many others. Here, then, one is far away from the faith that has been received within our Christian communities.[35]

Life beyond death is no longer seen as the perfect fulfillment of a life in communion with God, which began with the death and resurrection of Jesus Christ. Rather, reincarnational life after death is the accomplishment of a process of self-liberation that finishes in a kind of harmony with the All. One can enter into contact with the beyond by accepting advice and acquiring wisdom from those who belong to the other river. "One connects oneself with the beyond as one might connect with one of the channels on her or his radio or television set: a channelling."[36]

If life beyond death is no longer linked with a personal God, and if life is not seen as the accomplishment of our communion with the Holy One, our bodily condition is no longer integrated with and an essential expression of what we are as relational beings. A human being "is no longer a person entering into relation, into dialogue, into a covenant with a personal Being, but is a simple

LIFE BEYOND DEATH

wave of the cosmic ocean, a part—but a conscious one—of the great All."[37]

Simply put, reincarnation and the resurrection of the body are strictly opposed understandings and interpretations of life after or beyond death.

✺

We cannot close our eyes to the current challenges to our understanding of life after or beyond death. We must try to give new answers from our own Christian tradition to contemporary questions about the fulfillment of the present life. As I indicated above, our situation also results from the churches' silence about what lies beyond death. As Marc Leboucher stresses, "as a consequence of receiving unsatisfying answers [from our churches], many people are turning to reincarnation and to the occult sciences."[38] Thus "it is a question of saying again, in new terms, the century-old kerygma."[39]

Human beings are fragile, vulnerable. Now, one should not, indeed, identify fragility and vulnerability with weakness. To be human is to be contingent: it is to be mortal. Death and dying are not stigmas to be hidden and considered shameful. Consequently, we have to learn to reintegrate death into our whole understanding of human development in order to make it the last step in that process. Death and dying are not only the way in which human beings experience the fullness of life. Fullness is understood here as and in terms of a relation to the eternal God who offers everyone a risen life in Jesus Christ. Fullness of life is not just an "after life," but an abiding relation. Christian faith does not direct attention first to the afterlife but to a concern for the present.[40] It is here, in the world, that Christians are called to build a life which reflects the dignity of women and men, and to recreate a solidarity with and within the whole of creation. For Christians the problem is not death and dying but the horizon of the fullness of life within which one lives these realities.

Another challenge that our belief must face in the life after or beyond death is to affirm such life, now that the pastoral practice of fear is no longer effective. The possibility of eternal damnation, or hell, is something that no longer generates the fear that it once did. Neither can we use fear in order to convince people to behave according to Catholic or another religious morality. However, with the abandonment of the pastoral practice of fear, the eternal truths of our faith about the purpose of life also seem to have disappeared from our horizon of concern. For this reason, we are invited to recover the core of the Christian message concerning life after or beyond death in a completely different context. In addition, we have to regain an appreciation of the meaning of life after death as the fulfillment of our life with the God whom Jesus Christ reveals to us. God is not the great All, any more than Jesus can be recognized only as a Master of Wisdom. The God of our Christian tradition, the creator and giver of life, is the One who, in Jesus Christ and in the Holy Spirit, invites us into a personal covenant that is a call and invitation to life everlasting.

In order to present the Christian message about what comes after and lies beyond death in a way that is faithful to the core insight of Christianity, we must first understand the various ways Christian eschatology has been understood as they developed in their historical contexts.

Notes to Chapter 1

1   See P. de Locht, "Death, the Ultimate Form of God's Silence," in *Concilium*, 4 (1992), p. 54; C. Theobald, "Conclusion: 'Original Sin': Still a Disputed Doctrine. Reflections on a Debate," in *Concilium*, 1 (2004), pp. 133–134.

2   See R. Martínez de Pisón, *Sin and Evil* (R. R. Cooper, trans.), Sherbrooke: Médiaspaul, 2002, pp. 167–173.

3   See H. Obayashi (Ed.), *Death and Afterlife: Perspectives of World Religions*, New York: Praeger, 1992.

4   See L. V. Thomas, "L'eschatologie: Permanence et mutation," in L. V. Thomas *et al.*, *Réincarnation, immortality, résurrection*, Brussels: Publications des Facultés universitaires Saint-Louis (Publications des Facultés universitaires Saint-Louis, 45), 1988, p. 20; R. Martínez de Pisón, "L'au-delà: Réponse à nos frustrations ou plénitude de vie?," in *Église et Théologie*, 21/3 (1990), pp. 303–305.

5   See my article "Shame, Death, and Dying," in *Pastoral Psychology*, 51/1 (2002), pp. 27–40. I have incorporated some of the content of this article in my book *Death by Despair: Shame and Suicide*, New York: Peter Lang (American University Studies. Series VII: Theology and Religion, 245), 2006, pp. 7–22. I invite the reader to consult them in order to have a better understanding of the transformation of death into a shameful dimension of life.

6   J. Ratzinger, *Eschatology: Death and Eternal Life* (M. Waldestein, trans.), Washington, DC: Catholic University of America Press (Dogmatic Theology, 9), 1988, p. 70.

7   H. Schwarz, *Eschatology*, Grand Rapid: Ed. W. B. Eerdmans Publishing Co., 2000, p. 4; see also M. de Hennezel, *La mort intime: Ceux qui vont mourir nous apprennent à vivre*, Paris: R. Laffont, 1995, p. 13.

8   Ratzinger, *op. cit.*, pp. 70-71; see also J. Hofmeier, "The Present-Day Experience of Death," in *Concilium*, 4/10 (1974), pp. 19–23.

9   See M. Zundel, "L'expérience de la mort," in *Choisir*, 36 (1962), p. 20; *Id.*, "Le triomphe de la vie," in *Choisir*, 219 (1978), p. 15; E. Kübler-Ross, *Death: The Final Stage of Growth*, Englewood Cliffs: Prentice-Hall, 1975; *Id.*, *On Death and Dying*, New York: Macmillan, 1978; L. Bregman, *Beyond Silence and Denial: Death and Dying Reconsidered*, Louisville: Westminster John Knox Press, 1999; *Id.*, *Death and Dying, Spirituality and Religions: A Study of the Death Awareness Movement*, New York: Peter Lang Publishing, Inc. (American University Studies. Series VII: Theology and Religion, 228), 2003; *Dignity at the End of Life*, in *Journal of Palliative Care*, 20/3 (2004), the whole thematic issue; *Vivre et mourir: Fin de vie et accompagnement*, in *La Revue Réformée*, 234/4 (2005), the whole thematic issue.

10   See R. Martínez de Pisón, "From Fear to Freedom: Toward Spiritual Wholeness," in *Sciences Pastorales/Pastoral Sciences*, 21/1 (2002), pp. 19–39.

11   See P. Gervais, "Péché-pécheur, II: Réflexion théologique et spirituelle," in *Dictionnaire de Spiritualité Ascétique et Mystique: Doctrine et Histoire*, Paris: G. Beauchesne, 1984, vol. 12/1, col. 85; J. S. Piven, "Religion, Pathology, and Death in Psychohistory," in *The Journal of Psychohistory*, 29/2 (2001), pp. 143–145.

12   See J. Delumeau, *La peur en Occident (XIV*ᵉ*–XVIII*ᵉ* siècles): Une cité assiégée*, Paris: Fayard (Pluriel), 1978, pp. 259–303; *Id.*, *Sin and Fear: The Emergence of a Western Guilt Culture, 13th–18th Centuries* (E. Nicholson, trans.), New York: St. Martin's Press, 1990, pp. 40–85.

13   M. Leboucher, *Y a-t-il une vie après la mort?*, Paris: Centurion (C'est-à-dire), 1989, p. 118.

14   Delumeau, *Sin and Fear*, p. 41.

15   Bernard Sesboüé also stresses this aspect of the pastoral practice of fear. For him, the eternal truths about life after death in Christian tradition were used for increasing this pastoral approach in order to bring people to conversion. In this process, the description of the punishments suffered by those in purgatory and in hell played an essential role (see B. Sesboüé, *La résurrection et la vie: Petite cathéchèse sur les choses de la fin*, Paris: Desclée de Brouwer [Petite Encyclopédie du Christianisme], 1990, p. 8).

16   Delumeau, *Sin and Fear*, p. 377.

17   M. Zundel, "Le Dieu vivant," (Homily during a retreat in Bourdigny), August 22, 1937, roneotyped document, p. 46.

18   See Delumeau, *Sin and Fear*, pp. 401–421.

19   P. Gruson, "Lectures de la parabole du jugement (Matthieu 25, 31–46)," in *Catéchèse*, 124 (1991), p. 36.

20   See R. Martínez de Pisón, *The Religion of Life: The Spirituality of Maurice Zundel*, Sherbrooke: Médiaspaul, 1997, pp. 34–37, 70–73.

21   See *Memory*, in *The Way*, 35/1 (1995), pp. 3–54.

22   See R. Martínez de Pisón, "La compasión de Dios: La expriencia de la 'curación interior' y del perdón," in *Communio*, 36/2 (2003), pp. 361–376.

23   M. Zundel, *Wonder and Poverty*, (Retreat preached to the Benedictine Oblate sisters of La Rochette in 1963) (F. Audette, trans.), Sherbrooke: Paulines, 1993, p. 45.

24   *Id.*, *La pierre vivante*, Paris: Ouvrières, 1954, p. 39.

25   See *id.*, "La réforme de l'Église," conference at the "Cenacle" of Geneva, February 13, 1965, roneotyped document, p. 42.

LIFE BEYOND DEATH

26   *Id.*, Unpublished text of 1962, cited in M. Donzé, *L'humble présence: Inédits de Maurice Zundel (vol. 1)*, Geneva: Éd. du Tricorne (Buisson Ardent), 1985, p. 71.

27   *Id.*, *Wonder and Poverty*, p. 162.

28   Sesboüé, *op. cit.*, p. 8; see also my article "De la crítica a la religión al descubrimiento de la espiritualidad," in *Religión y Cultura*, L/228 (2004), pp. 43–50.

29   See Bregman, *Death and Dying, Spirituality and Religions*, pp. 69–92.

30   See J. Vernette, "La réincarnation dans la nouvelle religiosité," in *Lumière et Vie*, 195 (1989), p. 5.

31   See *ibid.*, p. 11.

32   See *ibid.*, p. 11; *Id.*, *Le Nouvel Âge: À l'aube de l'ère du Verseau*, Paris: Téqui, 1990, p. 115.

33   Vernette, *Le Nouvel Âge*, p. 35.

34   *Ibid.*, p. 9.

35   See Sesboüé, *op. cit.*, p. 66; A. Couture, *La réincarnation*, Ottawa: Novalis (L'Horizon du Croyant), 1992; P. Bacq, "Après la mort, résurrection ou réincarnation?," in *La Foi et le Temps*, XXIII (1993), pp. 63-75; J. C. Polkinghorne, *The God of Hope and the End of the World*, New Haven: Yale University Press, 2002, pp. 301-307; Schwarz, *op. cit.*, pp. 301–307.

36   Vernette, *Le Nouvel Âge*, p. 98.

37   *Ibid.*, p. 202.

38   Leboucher, *Y a-t-il une vie après la mort?*, p. 9; see also B. Bastien, "Précurseurs et prophètes," in *Christus*, 153 (1992), p. 28.

39   Vernette, *Le Nouvel Âge*, p. 208.

40   See D. A. Lane, "Anthropology and Eschatology," in *The Irish Theological Quarterly*, 61/1 (1995), pp. 26–29.

2

Historical Developments
of the Eschatological Dimension
# of Christian Faith

Concern for the eschatological dimension of Christian faith has impacted the life of believers in different ways through the centuries. This can best be appreciated when we place the shifting trends within the context of Church history.

The first trend to be noted is the early decline of interest, in spite of some exceptions, in the final end of life.[1] A situation developed in which no connection was made between present life and the Church's final future in a realm beyond death. The concept of the life beyond was something that was to come just at the end. Such eternal truths as death, particular judgment, purgatory, hell, heaven and final (general) judgment were referred to only in order to promote morality through the pastoral practice of fear. This loss of concern for the final end of all things continued until the beginning of the last century. Even today, in our scientific view of the universe, a final fulfillment appears very improbable to many people.

The shift from a communitarian focus—that is, what our fulfillment will be as a community of believers—to an individualistic interest in one's own final has been another important trend. This change of perspective is reflected in a biblical text: "In all you do, remember the end of your life, and then you will never sin" (Sir. 7:36). According to Christian Schütz, interest in one's own death is not what is really involved in the question of eschatology. Rather, eschatology is founded on the certitude that "the end has arrived with Jesus Christ (cf. Heb. 1:2; 1 Pet. 1:20)."[2] There is an eschatological dimension to Christian faith already present in the here and now of life. In fact, says Schütz, "Correctly speaking, 'eschatological' does not refer to events that will happen at the end of the time as such [this was the original meaning of ἔσχατος (*eschatos*, last things)], but it expresses a relationship or a reference [from the present experience and history] to such events."[3] In this way, Christian faith and theology are "eschatological" because they are concerned with the relationship between the present life—or present history—and its future fulfillment.[4] Consequently, we need to recover a sense of the importance of the relationship between our present life or history and the final fulfillment thereof according to God's plan of salvation.

This chapter will deal with the historical development of the understanding of the eschatological dimension of Christian faith. First, I will discuss the early Church's experience of waiting for the end. Then I will stress how this concern was lost during the Middle Ages only to be recovered by the Reformation in the sixteenth century. Finally, I will address the importance of life beyond death for our understanding and appreciation of our present situation, especially in the context of the scientific view of the universe.

1. The Early Church (1st–4th Centuries)

Two important events in the life of early Christian communities illustrate how the eschatological dimension of Christian faith was viewed during the early Church period: the delay of the *parousia* (or the second coming of Christ) and the development of Church structures (with the tendency to centralize authority). Thus,

> Christians now were forced to prepare for a longer stay in this world. Cultic rituals, pastoral epistles and catalogues of virtues and vices bear literary witness to this reorientation. Belief in an imminent parousia remained very much alive, but the fact of organizational growth led to a shift in interest, and the eschatological side of Christian faith suffered its first diminution.[5]

LIFE BEYOND DEATH

The Delay of the Parousia and the Development of Church Structures

Systematizing what Peter Müller-Goldkuhle presents as intrinsic to these two important events in the life of early Christian communities allows us to highlight several points. First, the sacramental life of the Church begins to develop. Through the sacraments, Christians experience what is definitive in the sense that the salvation hoped for is already in the process of being realized.

Furthermore, the delay of the parousia obliges the Church to justify such a delay. The most important thing was no longer the nearness of the parousia but its suddenness, "and it [the delay] stressed the threat of imminent retribution. The delay in the parousia was attributed to the mercy of God, who was offering man one final chance at conversion."[6] Two biblical texts can serve to illustrate this position:

> For yet "in a very little while, the one who is coming will come and will not delay; but my righteous one will live by faith. My soul takes no pleasure in anyone who shrinks back." (Heb. 10:37-38)

> But do not ignore this one fact, beloved, that with the Lord one day is like a thousand years, and a thousand years are like one day. The Lord is not slow about his promise, as some think of slowness, but is patient with you, not wanting any to perish, but all to come to repentance. But the day of the Lord will come like a thief, and then the heavens will pass away with a loud noise, and the elements will be dissolved with fire, and the earth and everything that is done on it will be disclosed. (2 Pet. 3:8-10)

As a consequence, in particular the sacrament of penance began to acquire greater importance, as a way of being prepared for the sudden return of Christ.

Finally, the emphasis on the *here* and *now* of what is definitive will gradually disappear to make room for a final end located completely in the future, at the end of history. As a result, "Everything that could not be explained in terms of the present was projected into the distant future."[7] This situation contributed to a decline in the

Christian community's sense of eschatological waiting. In addition, the conception of time according to the biblical tradition—namely, that of a present open to future fulfillment in God—loses its importance within a Hellenistic world view, where there is a total division between *here* and *beyond*, and between *world* and *God*.

The conversion of the emperor Constantine in the fourth century and the resulting establishment of Christianity as the official religion of the empire also contributed to the decline of a sense of the eschatological within the Christian community. That the Church had acquired this privileged position within the empire was considered a sign that what was expected as definitive had already become present through the visible Church.[8]

From the Kingdom of God to the Hierarchical Church

A second feature affecting the early Church's sense and appreciation of the eschatological was the shift in the way in which the kingdom of God (or kingdom of Heaven) was perceived. Augustine (354–430) influenced this evolution.

As we will see in chapter 6 below, the core of Jesus's message is focused around the theme of the kingdom of God. This is a kingdom about to come, but also already present among us. In this sense, Jesus continues the history of salvation that, from the Old Testament, is centred on the idea of the kingdom of God: "Now after John was arrested, Jesus came to Galilee, proclaiming the good news of God, and saying, 'The time is fulfilled, and the kingdom of God has come near; repent, and believe in the good news'" (Mk. 1:14-15). What is still more interesting is that Jesus not only preaches about the kingdom of God, but that with himself, in his person, the kingdom is already a reality: "if it is by the finger of God that I cast out the demons, then the kingdom of God has come to you" (Lk. 11:20).[9] As Cardinal Ratzinger said,

> In many-faceted parables, Jesus proclaimed the good news of the kingdom of God as a reality which is both present and still to come. . . . [Christianity] no longer proclaimed a pure theology of hope, living from mere expectation of the future, but pointed to a 'now' in which the promise had already become presence.

LIFE BEYOND DEATH

Such a present was, of course, itself hope, for it bears the future within itself.[10]

Nevertheless, the awareness of the actuality of the kingdom and its imminent presence progressively disappeared from the life and concern of early Christians. After the conversion of Constantine, "The establishment of an imperial Church and the christianization of the whole empire realized the definitive form of the kingdom willed by God."[11] This was particularly true with regard to the influence of Augustine and of his *De civitate Dei*, in which the *City of God* represents the celestial and earthly Church. The visible, earthly Church is an image of the celestial one.[12] What appears evident in the work of Augustine is the tension regarding the kingdom, a tension between the reality already here and the distant, future reality:

> Augustine's notion of the kingdom incorporates these two lines of thought. On the one hand, the city of God is the future, definitive shape of Church and State together; it will give heavenly bliss to redeemed individuals. On the other hand, he equates the visible form of the Catholic Church in history with the city of God.[13]

After Augustine, the hierarchical Church will be identified with the kingdom, with the result that the eschatological tension contained in Augustine's thought disappears.

The Individualistic Conception of Salvation

A third characteristic of the early Church's changing understanding of Christian eschatology that will continue in the following centuries, particularly within the Roman Catholic Church, is the influence of the dualistic Greek and Manichaean visions of the world on the development of Christian doctrine and spirituality, resulting in an individualistic conception of salvation. This is particularly true in regard to anthropology. A dualistic idea of human beings as composed of *body* and *soul* developed which stressed the belief in the immortality of the soul, rather than in the resurrection of the body, and which emphasized different states of perfection and the ascension of the soul to its plenitude in heaven. This dualistic conception of human beings was further promoted both by a moralistic view of Christian life based on the idea that we have a soul to be saved, and in a spirituality of contempt for the world.[14]

Millenarianism

The fourth and last characteristic to which we should refer is the beginning of millennialism or millenarianism (chiliasm, in Greek Christian tradition): the belief in a thousand-year reign of Christ before the final accomplishment of everything. This belief was founded, in part, in the text of Revelation 20.[15] However, during the early Church period, and under the influence of imperial Christianity, the millenarianism belief slowly disappeared. Nevertheless, it resurfaces during the Middle Ages and in the Modern Period, particularly under the influence of Joachim of Fiore (ca. 1135–1202).[16]

In summary, at the end of the early Church period, interest in the eschatological dimension of Christian faith had practically disappeared. The visible Church, particularly the hierarchical Church, is considered the manifestation of the kingdom of God. Nevertheless, an interest for eschatology will emerge again at the end of the Middle Ages and during the Protestant Reformation.

2. The Middle Ages (5th–15th Centuries) and the Modern Period (15th–18th Centuries)

Scholasticism, also called scholastic theology, was a new phenomenon in the theological reflection of the Middle Ages employed by the Franciscans and Dominicans.[17] Schools of theology promoted the systematization of theological thought. In this regard, the understanding of the last things, the afterlife and what lies beyond death, appears at the end of the organized presentation of these theological systems. According to Christian Schütz, Peter Lombard (ca. 1100–1160) was the first to include a consideration of explicitly eschatological themes in his *Sententiae (Sentences)*. These "sentences" are basically a summary of citations taken from the Fathers of the Church and other theological experts in the Sacred Scripture.[18]

The treatise on eschatology appears at the end of the discussion of the sacraments and as an effect of their celebration. In this context, and in the face of Greek and Manichean anthropologies, there was an insistence on the identity of the body at the resurrection. This established a relationship between *protology*—the study of the origins of human beings, that is, of creation—and *eschatology*. The resurrection of the body became a symbol of the plenitude of what was already present at creation as it was found in the two creation stories of Genesis (1:1–2:25): the beauty and goodness of everything created.

From an ecclesiastical standpoint, the identification of the visible Church with the kingdom of God has reached its peak. Canon Law influenced the institutionalization of the Church's role: "The elaboration of Canon Law led to new developments in the process of institutionalization. The notion of the Church was cast in juridical terms. The Church was the *societas perfecta* [the perfect society], the Christian body corporate; the doctrine of the two swords, dividing power between Church and State, held sway."[19]

The Pastoral Practice of Fear

The mediaeval belief in the afterlife or life beyond death was accompanied by two other considerations. As already mention in the last chapter, one was the pastoral practice of fear. Besides Jean Delumeau, another French historian, Jacques Le Goff, in his book, *The Birth of Purgatory*, emphasizes this common approach and understanding. With special reference to the emergence of the doctrine of purgatory, Le Goff's book serves as a wonderful resource for learning how fear and reference to the last things were used to promote morality. Those who will not accept the doctrine of the official Church will be punished either temporarily in purgatory or eternally in hell.[20]

The Divorce Between Theology and Popular Piety

The second important dimension of the medieval belief in life beyond death lies in the separation of theology from popular piety. According to Le Goff, theologians became progressively separated from the people. Thus, Le Goff says,

The theologians of the twelfth century—a diverse group among whom we must be sure not to forget the monastic theologians—were abstract thinkers, because science is abstract and theology had become a science. But they were generally alert to what was going on in society around their cathedrals, cloisters, and urban schools, lapped as they were by the rising tide of the new society, and they knew that to think about venial sin or Purgatory was to think about society itself. By contrast, the theologians and canonists of the thirteenth century were products of a corporate movement, mental workers isolated from the manual laborers in the urban workplace. Increasingly, they barricaded themselves behind their academic chairs and their pride as specialists of the spirit.[21]

As a consequence, popular piety developed on its own, and with it the re-emergence of an interest in life beyond death. Various popular movements had their own eschatological conceptions. Therefore,

> The medieval outlook found expression in crusades, miracle stories and mystical visions, in mystery plays, painting and literary works, in the welling tide of membership in the strict monastic orders, in numerous new institutions and charitable works, in the fanciful portraits of wandering preachers, and in the development of the funeral liturgy.[22]

Furthermore, according to Le Goff, the idea of purgatory as an intermediate step between death and resurrection "made even more impressive headway with the populace than it did with the theologians and clergy."[23] This popular piety provided an especially powerful means by which the pastoral practice of fear could be used to subdue ordinary believers. This appears clearly in the transformation of the day of the Lord into the *dies irae*, that is, the day of anger, fury, and rage that is traceable back to the twelfth century of our era.[24]

LIFE BEYOND DEATH

The Official Doctrine of the Church

The magisterium of the Catholic Church took an official doctrinal position regarding the afterlife or life beyond death in the Middle Ages.

> The pronouncement of Benedict XII, in his Bull *Benedictus Deus* (1336), froze the issue [that is, the immediate retribution after death, but without specifying how this occurs] and left it unresolved until our own day. The Bull *Laetentur Coeli* (1439) basically recapitulated the conceptions of an earlier day on this question.[25]

From that time onward, people held the belief in a particular judgment immediately after death.[26] In fact, until now, this has been the position of the Roman Catholic Church: immediately after death, the souls of those who die in the state of grace and without sin are actually contemplating the vision of God; those in purgatory are purging themselves of their venial sins; and mortal sinners are in hell forever. According to Cardinal Ratzinger, "*Benedictus Deus* marks the triumph of Hellenic body-soul dualism—even if the fathers may be judged more leniently."[27] This has created a difficulty in understanding how a soul separated from the body can experience retribution, as we will see in chapter 10 below.

At the end of the Middle Ages, the "official" Christian belief regarding life beyond death can be summarized as follows:

> At death there is a particular judgement, which decides what should happen to an individual soul. Three options are available: heaven for the perfect, hell for the wicked and purgatory for the not-so-perfect and not-so-wicked. The length of one's stay in purgatory is determined by the number of unrepented venial sins and by the unfulfilled expiation for remitted mortal and venial sins. This time can be shortened by the prayers, Masses and almsgiving of the living. At the end of time, at the final reckoning, in a general Last Judgement, the final Doomsday, God publicly divides the good from the bad, and, as the bad go back to hell, the good, including those souls who were still in purgatory, enter into heaven. The punishment of hell and the joys of heaven are

eternal, with absolutely no chance of change. The image of God dividing the good from the bad at the Last Judgement is found illuminated in countless manuscripts and carved in stones over the doors of scores of cathedrals and other churches. The question of one's final fate was difficult to avoid.[28]

The Importance of Mysticism

Finally, the presence of mysticism, which had a great importance in the Middle Ages. From an eschatological point of view, mysticism raised some questions: Do mystical experiences "belong to the realm of faith or to the realm of actual vision? Was it a question of eschatological longing or a real anticipation of beatific vision?"[29] Whatever the answers, the fact is that mysticism played an important role in recovering the eschatological dimension of Christian faith and pushed for a renewal of Christian life. It is in this theological context, then, that we can situate the importance given to the eschatological dimension of Christian faith in the Modern Period (15th–18th centuries).

Modernity: A New Conception of the World

As we will see in the introduction to the next chapter, the first great shift that occurred during the Modern Period of history, particularly under the influence of the Enlightenment in the eighteenth century, involved its epistemological conception of the world. If the Early Period and in the Middle Ages had a theocratic view of the universe, the Modern Period has an anthropocentric view of the world. God is no longer the reference point for understanding the world; human beings are. By reason, not by theology, humans come to a new understanding of the universe and even of revelation. Thus, "Rationalism and enlightenment philosophy developed a view of history based on temporal progress and man's ethical life in the human community. Man was travelling on an ascending path, moving toward ever fuller stages of human perfection."[30]

The world view inherited from the Middle Ages does not serve us well in our understanding of Modernity.[31] The medieval theory of knowledge was founded on Greek philosophy, in which there was a difference between knowledge and experience, that is to say, between reality and phenomenon. For Plato, "true reality . . . is eternal and unchangeable, whereas the phenomenal world is transient and changeable."[32] Our world and our concrete experience do not have any value in themselves. They have value only when referred to reason as its first and more important principle:

> Aristotle agrees with Plato in seeking the ultimate principle of knowledge and existence in reason, and in denying that the objects of experience are a perfect realization of reason, though they do realize it as far as their finite nature will allow. Plato, while he holds that the world is on the whole a rational system, finds in it an element of non-being or finitude that prevents it from being completely rational. This element is described by him in much the same terms as those employed by Aristotle to characterize that to which he gives the name of "matter."[33]

Material things acquire their value only through their relationship with a superior entity; as we contemplate the "ideal world" we can discover the mystery of our life. "Now, this ideal is actually realized in God; and it is by reference to the idea of God that we must explain that divine unrest which will not allow a finite being to be satisfied with anything short of absolute completeness."[34] Only in God, by the divine aspiration that exists in our inmost being, can human beings realize themselves. The visible world is transient and limited.[35]

However, Modernity operates from another epistemological framework: true knowledge is possible only through observation of phenomenon. Galileo Galilei (1564–1642) and René Descartes (1596–1650) were opposed to a science deduced from a first principle, namely, from a Supreme Being. God was no longer a necessity for understanding the world. God disappeared progressively from the human scene. Men and women were the real creators. Only rationalism and materialism remained: God was not demonstrable by reason; the only true reality was the visible world.[36] The traditional science of the Middle Ages was unable to provide an adequate understanding of the modern world.

The Protestant Reformation and the Catholic Counter-Reformation

The magisterium and theologians of the Roman Catholic Church remained attached to Aristotle's vision of the world and opposed the scientific revolution of the Enlightenment. The epistemological conception of Roman Catholic theology had not changed basically. Aristotle's philosophy, christianized by Thomas Aquinas, was invariably the reference point of Roman Catholic Church until the Second Vatican Council (1962–1965). In this context, interest in what lies beyond death, which characterized popular piety during the Middle Ages, progressively faded.

Although there was a rupture between experience and knowledge in the Middle Ages, the Protestant Reformation attempted to reintegrate the two in human life.[37] Reference to the Reformation is particularly useful in helping to recover and understand notions of experience, freedom and the importance of human conscience in our relationship with God:

> In the successors of Eckhart, mysticism assumes a practical and devotional aspect, in which communion with God is regarded as a fact of personal religious experience. . . . This dream was rudely dispelled by the Lutheran Reformation. When Luther [1483–1546] at the Diet of Worms in 1521 refused to retract what he had written, he expressed the principle of the supremacy of the human conscience. This principle cut up by the roots the doctrine that there is a distinction between church and state, clergy and laity, the religious and the secular life. Luther's whole attitude finds its highest interpretation in the doctrine of justification by faith, which meant for him that man needs no external process by which to attain to forgiveness, but is able to see that the inmost nature of God is revealed in the absolute self-surrender of Christ, and therefore that through faith he may share in the righteousness of Christ.[38]

The Roman Catholic Church responded in direct opposition to Reformation ideas with the so-called Counter-Reformation of the Council of Trent (1545–1563), and after. The Catholic Church considered "suspect" the value of experience in the encounter with

LIFE BEYOND DEATH

God. In the long run, the Reformation made a positive contribution to the recovery of a sense of the importance of experience in our partnership with God. Furthermore, it helped to develop a new understanding of divine revelation: revelation depends on one's concept of the world, of tradition, of Church and of human beings.

In summary, the confrontation between the Reformation and the magisterium of the Roman Catholic Church in the sixteenth century was a good example of the clash between two epistemologies that contributed to two different understandings of experience and, finally, of revelation. The medieval religious world conceived of revelation as the whole of divine truths communicated directly by God to the magisterium of the Church before which the believer must be obedient: "To some degree the identification of revelation with truths which were quantitatively added to the truths discovered by natural reason, and which were then handed down by authority and had to be accepted in obedience to external authority, already began in the theology of the Middle Ages."[39] That idea of revelation was no longer valid or relevant within the context of Modernity.

The Reformation brought with it a different concept of revelation that was, in one way or another, already alluded to and made possible through the experience and writings of mystics, which became available to laity during the last part of the Middle Ages and whereby everything external to faith is secondary.[40] The Enlightenment inherited a more personal and subjective way of understanding revelation versus the *ex auditu* (from hearing) of the Roman Catholic approach.[41] Human experience and freedom are the new grounds for understanding divine revelation. Human beings play an active role in the process of revelation as a relationship between human beings and God.

Luther's contribution to the re-evaluation of human experience facilitated an existential relationship with God and a greater focus on Christian experience. This has probably been one of the most important, if not the most important, contributions of the Reformation to Christianity.[42] Within this Christian existential way of experiencing the relationship with God, marked by the re-emergence of spirituality, mysticism and a new understanding of human experience and revelation, the Reformation's basic re-discovery of Christian eschatology is found. Martin Luther "gave historical shape to the battle between Christ and the antichrist, preaching the imminence of the last day and the threat of God's judgment of the world. . . . The more official theology neglected eschatology, the more it was emphasized by other circles."[43] This was also the result of the Reformation emphasis on the Bible and of the development of a new and freer theology in contrast with the more traditional one controlled by the magisterium of the Roman Catholic Church that continued to foster very academic treatises on eschatology.[44]

The Modern world's new epistemology and the Reformation's renewed focus on experience will have a great influence on and provide a strong impulse toward the development of a renewed understanding of Christian eschatology since the nineteenth century.

3. Eschatology's Contemporary Significance in a Scientific View of the Universe (19th–21st Centuries)

There are three aspects to the revitalization of contemporary interest in eschatology. The first one should be situated in continuity with the new vision of the world offered by Modernity and the Reformation's renewal of theological thought. The second is the recovery of eschatological interest within Roman Catholic theology allowing it to open up new paths because of the Reformation and, especially, because of the Second Vatican Council in the last century. Finally, an interest in life beyond death has been systematically challenged in our day by a scientific view of the universe.

The Reformation Renewal of Theological Thought

The Reformation brought about a renewed interest in theology. German theology has played a particularly significant influence in the life of the Church, not only in the churches of the Reformation but also in Roman Catholic thought until the last century. With the development of German theology also came a new interest in eschatology. "Eschatology came sharply into the foreground because of the anthropocentric outlook of the Enlightenment, its

LIFE BEYOND DEATH

emphasis on individual happiness, humanism and moralism, its concept of progress and its rediscovery of the notion of kingdom."[45] This trend was also present among Roman Catholic theologians, but faded during the middle of the nineteenth century because of the imposition of so-called "neo-scholasticism." From a Roman Catholic perspective,

> Neo-scholastic dogmatic treatises on eschatology remained in this rather pitiable state until after World War II. . . . Historical and exegetical criticism of the Bible, encounters with eschatological ideas in Protestant circles, and the challenge posed to older ways of thinking by science, philosophy and exegesis have led to a reappraisal of eschatology in the Catholic world.[46]

Protestant theologians such as Johannes Weiss (1863–1914), Albert Schweitzer (1875–1965) and Karl Barth (1886–1968) will continue to have an important contribution to the renewal of theology, particularly in the concern for eschatology. The new interest in Christian eschatology will be centred around the understanding of the kingdom of God. One major approach—a future-directed one—is characterized by the belief that the kingdom is not yet fully present among us. Promoters of this approach are theologians such as Oscar Cullmann (1902–1999), Wolfhart Pannenberg (b. 1928) and Jürgen Moltmann (b. 1926), among others. Existentialist and transcendentalist approaches are characterized by the insistence in the here and now of the presence of the kingdom of God. We can find the kingdom in our own hearts, that is, in the existential dimension of the believer. Theologians such as Rudolf K. Bultmann (1884–1976), Charles H. Dodd (1884–1973) and John T. Robinson (1919–1983) are representatives of this second tendency.[47]

The Recovery of Eschatological Interest by Catholic Theology

Among Roman Catholic theologians who will have an influence on the importance attributed to eschatological thought and its renewal, especially during the Second Vatican Council, we must mention Michael Schmaus (1897–1993), Karl Rahner (1904–1984), Hans Urs von Balthasar (1905–1988) and Cardinal Joseph Ratzinger (b. 1927). Even if we cannot find a specific treatise on eschatology as such among the Council's documents, the Roman Catholic Church has rediscovered eschatology's importance for Christian faith.[48]

In the Dogmatic Constitution on the Church (*Lumen Gentium*), all of chapter 7 is dedicated to the eschatological nature of the pilgrim Church and its union with the heavenly Church.[49] From a larger and more ecumenical perspective, and not exclusively looking within the community of believers, this eschatological concern can also be found in chapters 1 and 3 of the Pastoral Constitution on the Church in the Modern World (*Gaudium et Spes*).[50] Nevertheless, the Roman Catholic Church, contrary to Protestant theology, still conserves an intermediate state between death and the final resurrection, even declaring a belief in purgatory and that a personal retribution is obtained immediately after death.

The Challenge of a Scientific View of the Universe

The recuperation of a sense of the importance of eschatology to Christian faith is at present being strongly challenged by scientific and materialistic views of the universe. This situation invites us to a dialogue with science.[51] The belief in a fulfillment of our lives in what we refer to as "heaven" is in decline: "Scientific materialism convinced people that the ironclad laws of nature do not allow for heavenly interruption, whether by divine miracles or by divinely decreed end of the world."[52] Thus, hope in an ultimate future, as it will be more developed in the next chapter, is denied by some scientists:

> What began with the big bang [the explosion giving origin to what is believed an eternal cosmic history] will end with the big crunch [the gravity forcing expansion to be halted and reversed], as the universe implodes into a cosmic melting pot. The timescales for these processes are immensely long, spanning many tens of billions of years, but one or another of them is a certain prognostication of the cosmic future. However fruitful the universe may seem today, its end lies in futility.[53]

Science can be an expression of human freedom. Human beings can explain science, but people cannot be fully explained by science. What is manifested in science when one observes its practice by its most authentic witnesses is, beyond the simple power to dominate nature, the requirement of human beings to make themselves creators or the need to recognize that human beings have a vocation to liberty. Science, by its purpose, answers questions regarding the *how* of things—their becoming—but it cannot answer questions regarding the *why* of things. Here, we enter into the domain of belief, and we have to use either our philosophical reflection or theological beliefs in order to answer questions regarding the *why* of things.[54] Furthermore, the Christian belief in life's ultimate fulfillment in the kingdom of Heaven is not founded in human beings but in the God of the promise.

⁊⁊

When I arrived in Canada in 1985, I was surprised by the tendency that I found among so many Canadians to retrace the history of their families' names and backgrounds. However, I soon realized how important it is to come to know our origins. It helps us to understand our present situation and perhaps to foresee what could happen to some of us in the future. We can discover that, within a particular family, there may be a predisposition for certain illnesses or addictions so that we may be on the lookout for them. This is also valid as members of a country. Studying its history, we can recognize some common characteristics that have always been identified with its citizens.

To know the history of our own Christian tradition is essential, too. In this chapter it has been necessary to point out how eschatological concerns had progressively disappeared from the life of believers, except for a few periods in our tradition's history. From living the expected return of Christ and asking for it in the liturgy, as witnessed in the famous exclamation *Maranatha!* "Come, Lord Jesus!" (Rev. 22:20), the emphasis shifted. Once the Church was officially recognized by Constantine in the fourth century and Christianity became the official religion of the empire, the Church came to consider itself as the physical presence of the kingdom of God in which Christians still believed, but had believed that it would come only at the end of time.

We must recognize the importance of the Reformation for the recovery of this essential dimension to Christian faith. Protestant theology spearheaded new reflection on eschatology. Finally, Roman Catholic theology and the magisterium of the Church in the Second Vatican Council reintroduced eschatology into the life of the community and its theological reflection.

Nevertheless, even if interest in the parousia of Jesus Christ slowly faded, and with it the eschatological dimension of Christian faith, this does not mean that Christians lost creativity in imagining ways of living their relationship with God. In fact, the history of the Church shows us that, in spite of all human limits and sins, the Christian community has always been able to maintain until now her fidelity to the God of Jesus Christ.

However, this faith is now being challenged. What is challenged is the heart of Christian life, namely, hope. Does hope have meaning in the Western world? The next chapter will deal with this problematic.

Notes to Chapter 2

1   For the development of this second chapter, I will follow, P. Müller-Goldkuhle, "Post-Biblical Developments in Eschatological Thought," in *Concilium*, 41 (1969), pp. 24–41; C. Pozo, *Teología del más allá* (2nd ed.), Madrid: Editorial Católica (Biblioteca de Autores Cristianos [B.A.C.], 282/Historia Salutis, [20a]), 1980; C. Schütz, "Fundamentos de la escatología," in J. Feiner and M. Löhrer (Eds.), *El cristianismo en el tiempo y la consumación escatológica* (A. Alemany, J. J. Alemany, A. Fierro, J. Larriba, J. Pastor, J. L. Zubizarreta, trans.), Madrid: Cristiandad (Mysterium Salutis: Manual de Teología como Historia de la Salvación, V), 1984, pp. 527–656. Unfortunately, there is no English translation of the book by C. Pozo, nor of the theological collection *Mysterium Salutis* (originally published in German).

2   Schütz, *op. cit.*, p. 535.

3   *Ibid.*, p. 536. In the third and fourth chapters I will address the difference between *eschatology* and *apocalyptic*.

4   See *ibid.*, pp. 537–540.

5   Müller-Goldkuhle, *op. cit.*, p. 24.

6   *Ibid.*, p. 25. John M. McGuckin says the following regarding the delay of the parousia: "Hermas [4th century], following the Pauline doctrine that the End has been extended to allow the church time for repentance and the world time for evangelization, repeats the teaching that the ecclesial mystery, the working-out of God's plan of salvation, is itself the mystery of the eschaton, and not other to it." (J. M. McGuckin, "The Book of Revelation and Orthodox Eschatology: The Theo-drama of Judgment," in C. E. Braaten and R. W. Jenson [Eds.], *The Last Things: Biblical and Theological Perpectives on Eschatology*, Grand Rapids: W. B. Eerdmans Publishing Co., 2002, p. 120)

7   Müller-Goldkuhle, *op. cit.*, p. 26.

8   For a brief, overall view of the history of the Early Church, see F. D. Logan, *A History of the Church in the Middle Ages*, London: Routledge, 2002, pp. 3–12.

9   The tension between the present and the future dimensions of the kingdom of God is already found in the gospels. However, it seems to me that the most important aspect of it is that the kingdom is present and acting in Jesus Christ (see R. A. Greer, *Christian Life and Christian Hope: Raids on the Inarticulate*, New York: The Crossroad Publishing Company, 2001, pp. 16–18, 21). Nonetheless, I agree with Arland J. Hultgren when he says: "In short, the kingdom is not simply something that one experiences inwardly; it is an outer and eternal reality, something greater than the dimensions of our own spiritual potentials in this world. The kingdom in the speech of Jesus exceeds every experience and domain known to anyone, whether temporal, spatial, or spiritual,

even if a person apprehends it in part. It is a reality with which one must reckon. So a prophet speaks of it, indeed an eschatological prophet." (A. J. Hultgren, "Eschatology in the New Testament: The Current Debate," in Braaten and Jenson [Eds.], *The Last Things*, p. 87)

10   Ratzinger, *op. cit.*, pp. 44–45.

11   Müller-Goldkuhle, *op. cit.*, p. 27; see also M. Schmaus, *Justification and the Last Things*, Kansas City: Sheed and Ward (Dogma, 6), 1977, p. 163.

12   See Schütz, *op. cit.*, pp. 556–560.

13   Müller-Goldkuhle, *op. cit.*, p. 27.

14   See Delumeau, *Sin and Fear*, pp. 9–34.

15   The belief in a millennial reign of Christ on earth served as a source of spiritual inspiration for many people (see R. Bauckham and T. Hart, *Hope against Hope: Christian Eschatology at the Turn of the Millennium*, Grand Rapids: W. B. Eerdmans Publishing Co., 1999, p. 133; Schwarz, *op. cit.*, pp. 98–101, 322–337; Müller-Goldkuhle, *op. cit.*, pp. 29–30; J. Le Goff, *The Birth of Purgatory* [A. Goldhammer, trans.], Chicago: The University of Chicago Press, 1984, pp. 82–84). Without putting the two doctrines in the same level, I would like to mention here another dimension of the eschatological faith of the early Church, the belief in an universal salvation (*apokatastasis*), which is related particularly to Origen (ca. 183–ca. 252), and which is rooted in only one explicit biblical text, Acts 3:19–21, as source of its inspiration (see Schwarz, *op. cit.*, pp. 337–352; Le Goff, *op. cit.*, pp. 55–57).

16   Joachim of Fiore was "a Cistercian monk from Calabria, Italy, and the founder of a community of hermits." (Schwarz, *op. cit.*, p. 325; see also pp. 326–329)

17   For a complete view of the history of the Church in the Middle Ages see Logan, *op. cit.*, pp. 13–353.

18   See Schütz, *op. cit.*, pp. 560–561. In fact, "In the hundred years between Peter Lombard and Thomas Aquinas [1225–1274], the basic cast of eschatology was firmly established." (Müller-Goldkuhle, *op. cit.*, p. 34)

19   Müller-Goldkuhle, *op. cit.*, pp. 30–31.

20   See Le Goff, *op. cit.*, p. 169.

21   *Ibid.*, p. 218.

22   Müller-Goldkule, *op. cit.*, pp. 31–32. We have to include in this tendency the great influence of Francis of Assisi (1182–1226): "The person and activity of a Francis of Assisi must be viewed in terms of this popular eschatology rather than in terms of socio-ethical ideals. His poverty betokened the eschatological behavior of the Christian and proved the authenticity of his preaching about the imminent end. It represented full-blown imitation of Christ, who was

ready to appear; Christ's coming was the news that Francis had to proclaim." (*Ibid.*, p. 32) Here, too, we have to situate the enormous influence of the *Divine Comedy* of Dante Alighieri (born in Florence in 1265 and died in Ravenna in 1321) (see Le Goff, *op. cit.*, pp. 334–355; D. Alighieri, *Dante, Theologian: The Divine Comedy* [P. Cummins, trans. and commentary], St. Louis: Ed. B. Herder Book Co., 1953 [c1948]).

23 Le Goff, *op. cit.*, p. 289. F. Donald Logan, in his previously cited book, *A History of the Church in the Middle Ages*, presents an overview of the historical emergence of purgatory and describes its importance for the medieval Church: "It would be nearly impossible to exaggerate the significance of purgatory in the life of the medieval church, especially in the way that life was lived by individual Christians. The antechamber of heaven where the good but not perfect souls suffer their temporary punishment had a fixed place in the beliefs of virtually all Christians in the Western church and deeply affected their religious practices." (Logan, *op. cit.*, p. 287; see also pp. 288–296) In fact, in the face of the risk of being punished for all eternity in hell, the idea of a temporal punishment in purgatory opened a door for hoping in an ultimate eternal salvation in heaven.

24 See Müller-Goldkuhle, *op. cit.*, p. 32. It is interesting to read what Schmaus says regarding the shift between the day of the Lord and the *dies irae:* "In Christian antiquity the emphasis was on the day of judgment as the Day of the Lord which brings salvation, and in anticipation of the coming of Christ hope was the dominant theme. In the early Middle Ages, however, the idea of Christ as the coming Judge who would examine man's life in every detail began to exert a much stronger influence. This was no doubt related to the fact that the focus of the Christian faith had passed to the development of individual life, with a consequent anxiety over spiritual progress. So the trust and confidence which marked the primitive community had diminished into the fear and trembling before the Day of the Lord reflected in the hymn *Dies Irae.*" (Schmaus, *op. cit.*, pp. 200–201) However, this shift was not an invention of the Middles Ages. It founds its roots in the Old Testament in the preaching on the last judgment. The day of the Lord "was thought to be a day of light and the great day of salvation. . . . But the prophets turned these nationalistic eschatological expectations into a pronouncement of calamity and disaster. Especially Amos emphasized the Day of the Lord as a day of darkness and not of light, as a day of gloom with no brightness in it (Amos 5:19–20). It would be a day of the sword, of hunger and pestilence, a day of great slaughter (Isa. 30:25), and great changes would occur in nature, such as earthquakes, darkness, drought, and fire (Mal. 4:1). The judgment that the Lord executes when his great and fearful day comes is one of the main themes of the prophetic proclamation." (Schwarz, *op. cit.*, pp. 43–44)

25 Müller-Goldkuhle, *op. cit.*, p. 35. The official texts of the Constitution *Benedictus Deus* (1336) regarding the beatific vision of God immediately after the death of the just, the immediate damnation to hell for mortal sinners and

the general judgment, as well as the Bull *Laetentur Coeli*, the Decree for the Greeks of the General Council of Florence (July 6, 1439) on the eternal fate of the dead, can be found in *The Christian Faith in the Doctrinal Documents of the Catholic Church* (6th revised and enlarged edition, J. Neuner and J. Dupuis: edited by Jacques Dupuis), New York: Alba House, 1998 (c 1996), nos 2305–2307 (for the Constitution *Benedictus Deus*) and nos 2308–2309 (for the Bull *Laetentur Coeli* of Pope Eugene IV). From now on, *The Christian Faith in the Doctrinal Documents of the Catholic Church* will be cited by the abbreviation *CF*.

26 See Schmaus, *op. cit.*, pp. 234–237.

27 Ratzinger, *op. cit.*, pp. 140–141. The theological unfolding of this official declaration is very important: "Clearly, then, what the Church had to maintain was, on the one hand, the central certainty of a life with Christ that not even death can destroy, and, on the other hand, the incompleteness of that life in the time before the definitive 'resurrection of the flesh.'" (*Ibid.*, p. 147)

28 Logan, *op. cit.*, pp. 293–294.

29 Müller-Goldkuhle, *op. cit.*, p. 36.

30 *Ibid.*, p. 36.

31 See L. Dupré, *Passage to Modernity: An Essay in the Hermeneutics of Nature and Culture*, New Haven and London: Yale University Press, 1993.

32 J. Watson, *The Interpretation of Religious Experience* (The Gifford Lecture; 1910–1912), Glasgow: J. Maclehose, 1924, vol. 1 (Historical), p. 9.

33 *Ibid.*, p. 12.

34 *Ibid.*, p. 17.

35 See *ibid.*, p. 20.

36 See S. Eastham, "How Is Wisdom Communicated? Prologue to Peace Studies," in *Interculture*, XXV/2 (1992), pp. 4–5; R. Martínez de Pisón, "Del conocimiento a la experiencia: El proceso de convertirse en persona y del encuentro con Dios," in *Nova et Vetera*, XVIII/35 (1993), pp. 64–69.

37 For a description of the religious characteristics of the sixteenth century, see B. P. Holt, *Thirsty for God: A Brief History of Christian Spirituality* (2nd ed.), Minneapolis: Fortress Press, 2005, pp. 99–115.

38 Watson, *op. cit.*, pp. 150–151; see also W. von Loewenich, *Martin Luther: The Man and his Work*, Minneapolis: Augsburg Publishing House, 1986.

39 E. Schillebeeckx, *Christ: The Experience of Jesus as the Lord* (J. Bowden, trans.), New York: Crossroad, 1990, c1980, p. 43; see also what Hermann J. Pottmeyer says about the relationship among revelation, tradition and Church: "The close connexion between the *concept of revelation and tradition*, on the one hand, and the *concept of the Church*, on the other hand, is evident. The doctrinal understanding of revelation and tradition as instruction corresponds to a one-

LIFE BEYOND DEATH

sided, ultramontane, hierarchical idea of the church." (H. J. Pottmeyer, "The Traditionalist Temptation of the Contemporary Church," in *America*, 168/5 [1992], p. 104)

40   See Watson, *op. cit.*, pp. 148–149.

41   See Schillebeeckx, *Christ*, p. 44; see also p. 45 concerning the response of the Roman Catholic Church to the Enlightenment's position. Within this context, we have to situate the reaction of the Council of Trent to the Protestant view of the experience of grace and justification. This reaction appears in the General Council of Trent Decree on Justification in January 13, 1547 (see *CF*, nos 1924–1983). On the Roman Catholic side, the Modernist crisis (1890–1910) tried to incorporate the Reformation contribution on experience and revelation into Catholic thought (see J. Creen, "Modernism: The Philosophical Issue," in *Continuum*, 3/2 [1965], pp. 145–151). For Alfred Loisy (1857–1940) and George Tyrrell (1861–1909), human experience plays an important role in understanding faith and revelation (see F. M. O'Connor, "Tyrrell: The Nature of Revelation," in *Continuum*, 3/2 [1965], p. 174; R. R. Ruether, "Loisy: History and Commitment," in *Continuum*, 3/2 [1965], pp. 152–167). However, the official reaction of the magisterium of the Roman Catholic Church, with Pope Pius X and the decree *Lamentabili* (July 3, 1907), the encyclical *Pascendi* (September 8, 1907) and, finally, the *Antimodernist Oath* (September 1, 1910), jeopardized this attempt. Nevertheless, the Second Vatican Council was open to the values of human experience that favored a new understanding of divine revelation, even if, according to Schillebeeckx, "the result of the Dogmatic Constitution on revelation, *Dei Verbum*, promulgated at the Second Vatican Council, is a kind of compromise between the opposition to deism expressed at the First Vatican Council [19th century] and the earlier Christian view of revelation as God's communication of himself in salvation history as the God who is gracious toward mankind." (Schillebeeckx, *Christ*, p. 45)

42   See W. Pannenberg, "Luther's Contribution to Christian Spirituality," in *Dialog: A Journal of Theology*, 40/4 (2001), pp. 284–289.

43   Müller-Goldkuhle, *op. cit.*, p. 40.

44   See Schütz, *op. cit.*, pp. 577–580.

45   Müller-Goldkuhle, *op. cit.*, p. 37.

46   *Ibid.*, p. 39.

47   See Schwarz, *op. cit.*, pp. 107–172; Schütz, *op. cit.*, pp. 587–596; Ratzinger, *op. cit.*, pp. 47–55; Hultgren, *op. cit.*, pp. 70–72; G. L. Murphy, "Hints from Science for Eschatology—and Vice Versa," in Braaten and Jenson (Eds.), *The Last Things*, pp. 147–150.

48   See Pozo, *op. cit.*, pp. 538–578. In these pages, Pozo gives an excellent presentation of the eschatological doctrine of the Second Vatican Council.

49   See n°s 48–51. In the title of Chapter VII of the Dogmatic Constitution on the Church we can find echoes of what I have referred to before regarding Augustine and his concept of the *City of God*. K. Rahner spoke about the relationship between the Church and the *parousia* of Christ. For him, even if we recognize the eschatological dimension of the Church as a community of believers that celebrate already the risen Lord, the Church nevertheless remains "provisional" (see K. Rahner, *Concerning Vatican Council II* [K. H. and B. Kruger, trans.], New York: Crossroad [Theological Investigations, VI], 1982, p. 298; see also pp. 299–312).

50   See n°s 18–21, 39.

51   See Müller-Goldkuhle, *op. cit.*, p. 41; Murphy, *op. cit.*, 150–157; Schwarz, *op. cit.*, pp. 173–209; Polkinghorne, *op. cit.*, pp. 1–49.

52   Schwarz, *op. cit.*, p. 175; see also D. Toolan, *At Home in the Cosmos*, Maryknoll: Orbis Books, 2001, pp. 41–74.

53   Polkinghorne, *op. cit.*, p. 9; see also p. 8; Toolan, *op. cit.*, pp. 173–177.

54   See J. A. Bracken (Ed.), *World without End: Christian Eschatology from a Process Perspective*, Grand Rapids/Cambridge: William B. Eerdmans Publishing Company, 2005.

3

Does Hope Have Meaning in the Western World?

Sometime ago I read "In Front of the Closed Door," an article written by the Spanish socialist Javier Solana.[1] I consider this article to be a parable about the evolution of hope in Western society. The metaphor of the "Closed Door" represents the final moment of four distinct phases in an effort to lead others toward knowledge and progress.

During the first phase, the Middle Ages, the Church opened the door to knowledge and progress. The Church and its theologians dominated society and shaped its epistemology. Governments were theocratic; God was supreme in the universe; Church authority went unchallenged; the laws of right living were imposed and often sanctioned by force. Everything important had already been said by God and was contained in the Bible and correctly interpreted by the magisterium of the Church. Reference to the past was an essential criterion of the Middle Ages.

The second phase rose out of the Enlightenment. The hegemony of the Church declined. Philosophers took over the task of opening the door to knowledge and progress. Reason became the new divinity to be followed. Modernity presented a different epistemology characterized by the primacy of reason and the role of scientific knowledge. The theocratic society of the Middle Ages was replaced by an anthropocentric one. In Modernity, the point of reference was not the past but the future marked by the idea of progress.[2]

The third phase was the scientific revolution with its *credo* of unlimited progress. Science became the new god that would eventually overcome suffering and even death. Church, theologians and philosophers were supplanted by scientists, who became the new holders of the keys to knowledge and progress. This trend characterized Western society during the nineteenth century and well into the twentieth. Hope in a future with God and God's saving action gradually evaporated, leaving only the concern for the present.

Science, however, failed to accomplish what it had promised. Suffering, dying and death were not finally eradicated. Hope entered a fourth phase, leaving Western society standing before a closed door. The disasters of the twentieth century, repeated again at the beginning of the twenty-first, have worked to bring about the decline of serious hope in a positive ultimate future. Apocalyptic and catastrophic prognoses are everywhere. The present times are evil. If an ideal paradise is envisioned at all, it cannot bud forth from what exists now. What most distinguishes the attitude of many westerners is despair—a sense of isolation, loneliness and hopelessness.[3] Despair is a plague of the present times, and suicide, the most tragic fruit of despair, is widespread, especially among adolescents and the elderly.[4]

Openness to the future and hope, as I will show in the first part of this chapter, is essential to human existence. However, the conclusion of the parable is that we are experiencing a decline of hope in the future. As the second part of the present chapter will point out, the future lacks any ultimate meaning. Finally, I will highlight how what is so needful to human existence, that is, a sense of hope, cannot be a human product or a product of human science alone. It must come to us from an Other, as a divine gift. This gift is the great inheritance of the Christian faith, which presents a faithful God to us and promises us a fulfillment—salvation—which is as certain as God's faithfulness.

LIFE BEYOND DEATH

1. The Openness of Humanity and History Toward the Future

During the Middle Ages, society drew its security from the past. Modernity looked toward progress and the future.[5] History today deals not only with the past. It also examines the present in an attempt to learn from both of them and build toward a better future.[6] The future is not just pure speculation. It belongs in a certain manner to the present. We are creatures of time. As such we cannot be confined only to the present or to the past, however much we idealize the past. Without an opening to the future, we risk being suffocated. Human beings, as creatures of freedom and makers of history, are in fact open to the future. They constantly transcend the present moment.[7]

Expectation and Hope

This restlessness with the present, as Edward Schillebeeckx calls it,[8] leads naturally to the classic distinction identified by the Spanish medical doctor and writer, Pedro Laín Entralgo (1908–2001), between expectation and hope.[9] To expect is to look for something in the short term. But this by no means exhausts all the possibilities implicit in hope. Indeed, hope is an integral part of what it means to be human.[10] Hope is nourished when expectations come to pass. But no amount of fulfilled expectation can ever exhaust the possibilities of hope. Hope puts us both into contact with our past and into contact with our future:

> Such hope is usually bolstered by our experience of the past, but it is always determined equally by the inscrutable openness of the future with its attendant terrors. Hope is a matter of both knowledge and will (we know what has happened before, and we know what we desire) but it is characterized above all by the application of imagination and trust to a future which is essentially open and unknown. With its eyes wide open to the threat which the future holds, it nonetheless sees ways of averting this threat. Hope is, in this sense, an activity of imaginative faith.[11]

Different Ways of Being Open to the Future

Three basic attitudes characterize the manner in which human beings have been open to the future over the last two centuries. The first attitude is that of evolutionary humanism. This attitude suggests a humanity and a history in continuous progress, but a progress that in the end is meaningless. According to Raymond J. Nogar,

> Scientific evolution is a highly documented, well-supported fact. It is the ideological projection of some forms of *evolutionism*, in the name of science, which directly confronts the Christian Faith. Because these ideologies are formulated and promoted, not by professional philosophers, but by novelists, dramatists and scientists, theologians are slow to take them seriously. One of the most completely developed forms of atheistic evolutionism today, promoted in the name of science, and directly opposing the Christian revelation, is *evolutionary humanism*.[12]

Julian S. Huxley (1887–1975), an English biologist and writer, presented a systematized understanding of this attitude. For him, human beings and indeed all history are confined to the space-time of this world.[13] The future is open and in continuous development but goes nowhere and means nothing.

The second attitude is represented by Marxist ideology and the socialist utopian hope in a final accomplishment of human beings within the parameters of space-time.[14] Ernst Bloch (1885–1977), a German Marxist philosopher of Jewish ancestry who emigrated to the United States in 1938, best expressed this socialist utopia.[15] Following upon the thought of Feuerbach,[16] Bloch maintained that what Christians consider God is finally nothing more than the projection, in an imaginary being, of what will be the final accomplishment of women and men. This places the socialist utopia, as appropriated in the Marxist-communist regimes, in flat contradiction to the Christian hope in an ultimate future with a transcendent God. This second approach to hope is defined as Total Humanism,[17] or Eschatological Humanism without God.[18]

The inescapable reality of death posed a major problem for this utopian vision of reality. As Marxist ideology and socialist utopia

LIFE BEYOND DEATH

would have it, only those alive when utopia comes to its fulfill-ment will fully profit by their life in the country where a social harmony and final perfection reign. What about those who have died before all this happens? Unfortunately they remain dead, but with the consciousness that they have contributed to a worldly paradise for others.[19]

The third and final attitude regarding the openness of humanity and history to the future is that of the Christian faith.[20] God gives absolute and final meaning to human beings, their history, and their universe. The present is open to an eschatological future. This hope is a pure gift, given by God.[21] The Christian insight also provides an answer to the riddle of death and to the why of the universe. It attests to the resurrection of the dead and the transfiguration of the universe. However, in our day the openness of human beings and history toward the future is widely challenged and even denied.

2. *The Decline of Hope in the Future and in Its Ultimate Meaning*

The decline of hope in the Western world has a number of causes, one being the idea of progress itself, which "in the nineteenth century was connected with science and technology."[22] As suggested above, pessimism regarding the future is endemic. Science and technology have indeed made wonderful contributions to human well-being. Despite that, they have been brought to a halt before more profound existential questions. Death and suffering have not and cannot be dismissed. The Enlightenment has not been able to make good on its claim "that human reason, once freed from the shackles of traditional authority, prejudice and superstition, will take humanity into a new age of freedom and prosperity."[23]

The Limits of Progress

Hans Schwarz gives us a picture of the dream of scientific materialism and its progress once liberated from "prejudice and superstition":

Auguste Comte (1798–1857) captured this sentiment well [that the advancement in scientific knowledge has deeply changed the outlook of most people, Christians and non-Christians alike] in his three-volume *Course of Positive Philosophy* (1835), where he claimed that human intelligence unfolds itself according to a grand fundamental law in three different theoretical stages. The first of these stages is the theological or fictitious phase, the second the metaphysical or abstract phase, and the third the scientific or positive one. Each one is opposed to the others, and the first two have more or less transitional character. While in the first stage the human spirit wants to know the inner nature of being and postulates the existence of supernatural powers, in the second it thinks of abstract powers which are independent entities. Yet the human spirit gradually attains the insight that it is impossible to obtain absolute knowledge, and in a third stage, the positive one, it no longer asks for the origin and purpose of the universe and the inner causes of appearance. At the end of the metaphysical phase of the development of the human spirit, the scientific understanding of nature has won the upper hand. Positive philosophy, which is developing as a truly universal system, can explain the phenomena of nature by realizing that all phenomena are subject to the law of nature and that these laws have irrevocable character. With this insight gleaned by a positive philosophy, as Comte calls it, we have encountered the basic ground rules of scientific materialism.[24]

No one can legitimately disparage the importance of the energy that has produced such benefits to social living as freedom, human rights, education and so forth.[25] But the products of this energy have been deeply brought into question in the last and present centuries because of the tragedies imposed on people by the tools of science. The Holocaust inflicted on the Jews by the Nazis during World War II (1939–1945), the genocides against the Tutsis in Rwanda (in 1994) and the Muslims in Bosnia (in 1995), the terrorist attacks in New York and Washington (September 11, 2001), and the one perpetrated in Madrid (March 11, 2004) are just a few instances of the use to which efficient, modern production has contributed.

An Evolution Ending in Futility

A second cause in the decline of hope is the view that some scientists hold regarding the universe. Contraposed to the big bang, the explosive expansion at the origin of what has been thought to be an eternal cosmic evolution, there is the possibility of a big crunch, the reversion of gravity which will bring the universe to a collapse and ending in futility.[26] In addition, with the development of science and technology, especially "with the new scientific weapons," says Raymund Schwager, "for the first time it became evident that humankind as a whole can destroy itself."[27]

The Ecological Holocaust

A third reason for decline in hope is the threat of an ecological holocaust.[28] This is the consequence of an androcentric world view and patriarchy. The result, according to Claude Lévi-Strauss and Catharina Halkes, is the rape and destruction of the soil, of mother earth.[29] Within this framework there has arisen a critique of the negative role that religions, particularly the Jewish and Christian traditions, have played in the ecological crisis.[30] The main conclusion inferred from the threat of an ecological holocaust is that it is not possible to hope in an ultimate future where only human beings survive. If creation perishes, humanity goes with it.

The End of the Socialist Utopia

The fourth reason for the decline in hope is the downfall of the socialist utopia. This end has been influenced by the collapse of Eastern Bloc communist regimes, particularly after the removal of the Berlin wall.[31] Despite the fact that these regimes eschewed any idea of transcendence, their utopian vision had at least worked to sustain some kind of meaning for the future, some kind of hope.

The Decline of the Christian Conception of God

A fifth and final reason for the decline of hope is the decline of belief in a transcendent God, especially in a God who could allow such immense suffering and violence in the world.[32] An increasing interest in spirituality is undeniably a phenomenon in today's world.

But it is not necessarily an interest in a spirituality that is open to transcendence.[33] Yet, there is a new search for meaning and for a more holistic development in human growth, a desire for living better, for greater personal fulfillment in the present.

As a result of this overall decline in a sense of hope, we are witnessing an excessive concern for the present. This present is detached from its link to the past, and from its projection toward the future:

> More and more rapid change and the pressure to focus on the present as a duration to be used and filled with activity cut us off from continuity with the past. History is not part of a story we ourselves are living, merely a theme-park we visit for amusement. The future, on the other hand, is shrinking to a short-term prolongation of the present, that future which we can extrapolate from the present, the future we have already allocated and planned, the future of long-range diaries, government think-tanks, millennium projects. It is the future already contained in the present, not the sphere of the unpredictable and the unexpected, of an indefinite range of possibilities which might eventuate.[34]

Furthermore, the risk of holding an apocalyptic view of our history is growing today.[35] The inescapably tragic events in recent history, to which I have alluded above, bring with them the desire to escape reality altogether or to consider it as intrinsically evil.[36] Therefore there is a *chiaroscuro* relation between the divine love which is constantly offered to us and the terrible facts that confront us daily which do not in any way reflect this original and liberating love of God. We have created a God who is the projection of our own unsatisfied needs rather than the "Other" who invites us to become open to the divine through the discovery of "others" and to establish a respectful partnership with creation as well.

Not every Christian/religious experience and/or religious expression is a manifestation of the God who leads people to freedom and mutual respect. The increased vigour of religious fundamentalism, intolerance and violence within sects, cults and religious groups is a manifestation of this.[37] However, far from distancing us

LIFE BEYOND DEATH

from the original grace of God, we are invited, as in the parable of the weeds among the wheat (Mt. 13:24-30), not to participate in condemnation and shunning, that is, not to lose trust in the primacy of God's love. To do this, we have to go beyond the gaze that stares at the world's unfortunate situations so that we may contemplate the signs of the presence of goodness within human beings and the beauty of creation.

The Christian faith provides an alternative to the decline of hope in our world.[38] If hope belongs to us as human beings, such hope derives from the creative action of God in us. It is unearned. It is a gift.

3. Christian Hope Is Founded on a Divine Promise

I have already presented in the first chapter above the experience of Israel and the first Christian communities with the liberating God of our biblical tradition. Hope in God's promise and in a future kingdom of justice, freedom, peace and happiness motivated the people of Israel to keep alive their faith in a better future. God's covenant with Noah and with his sons after the flood as well as with their descendants after them (Gen. 9:1-17), which was the same covenant with Abraham (Gen. 15:1–18:1-15) and his descendants after him regarding a future land, inspired the Hebrew people to look toward the future with hope.

Hope as a Divine Gift

The working out of the constantly renewed covenant brought about the liberation of God's people from the slavery of Egypt, as the book of Exodus relates (see chapters 12–24). The covenant pattern is repeated again and again in the Old Testament. The people of Israel needed to be reminded of this before crossing the Jordan to the promised land. They were required to renew their fidelity to God (see Josh. 24). In spite of their shortcomings, God remembers the promise, as Jeremiah prophesied. There will always be a new covenant (Jer. 31:31-34).

Finally, Christians believe that God's covenant with us and with creation came to its fullness in Jesus Christ. In him and through him our present time is a sacred time, a *kairos*, already pregnant with the ultimate future (Heb. 1:1-4; see also Jn. 1:1-18). For Christians the promise is not that which we await at the end of time; it is already with us. But this in no way means that there is no hope for a better present. Christians are called to work for a better world and to give reasons for the hope that is in them, as the apostle Peter says (1 Pet. 3:15b). It is hope that ensures that our expectations will not be confounded.[39]

Hope and Human Responsibility

Faith in God's promise does not absolve us from responsibility for the present. On the contrary, "In enabling us to rethink the present, Christian hope offers resources which counter the Marxist complaint that it must inevitably distract us with false consolation. It need not become a demobilising ideology."[40] For Wolfhart Pannenberg, too, despite the Marxist critique of religion, hope does not relieve human beings of their obligation to work for the transformation of the world.[41]

In summary, the eschatological dimension of Christian faith is founded on the salvific presence of God, even though that presence may be mysterious. We are called to make that presence more visible through our engagement in working for a better world. As Schillebeeckx asserts, "This salvation must be achieved now in our history, in this world, and so this history becomes itself a *prophecy* of the final and transcendent *eschaton*."[42] Present history is sacred history that carries within it the beginnings of the end, even though that end is not yet fully realized.

><

Founded on a divine promise, hope is an intrinsic dimension of being human and it is the heart of Christian faith. Life cannot, therefore, be reduced to any particular expectation in the present. It must always be open to the future.

Christians must confront the present decline of hope. They have not always lived by the faith they profess. Christians have not always presented the Good News as a liberating force. They have not always

LIFE BEYOND DEATH

been a source and inspiration of hope. They too have given in to the malaise of the age, the pessimism in which so many live today. Hope in a future with meaning will come again when Christians begin afresh to revive and relive the faith that is in them through the promise made to them by God. This is the best contribution they can make to the people of our time, believers or not.

Our history is a salvation history. In it we are not condemned to some futile longing. The faith a Christian professes is not for himself or herself alone; it also belongs to the community of believers.[43] To reactivate the faith that is within us, to become convinced once again of the presence in us of our ultimate destiny and our place within that destiny, we need to have recourse to our imagination. Imagination is the milieu by which faith is articulated, and it is essential to keep alive our eschatological hope in a transformed humanity and in a new heaven and new earth.[44]

As we will see in the next chapter, in order to recover hope in the future, and faith in the God of the covenant, we must also re-actualize our interpretation of various assertions regarding the eschatological dimension of Christian faith.

Notes to Chapter 3

1   See F. J. Solana Madariaga, "Ante la puerta cerrada," in *Vida Nueva*, 1258–1259 (supplementary issue December–January, 1980–1981), pp. 33–34. This chapter is a modified version of my article "Does Hope Have Meaning in the Western World?" in *Theoforum*, 36/2 (2005), pp. 175–185.

2   Richard G. Cote summarizes well the basic assumptions of Modernity that will also characterize the third phase—the scientific revolution. These assumptions are the belief in unlimited progress; the exclusive supremacy of reason; the supreme autonomy of the individual; the domination and control of nature; and the importance of success and efficiency (see R. G. Cote, *Lazarus! Come Out! Why Faith Needs Imagination*, Ottawa: Novalis, 2003, pp. 146–147).

3   See J. Goldbrunner, "What is Despair?" in *Concilium*, 9/6 (1970), pp. 70–80; Concilium General Secretariat, "The Dialectic of Hope and Despair," in *Concilium*, 9/6 (1970), pp. 144–158.

4   See H. Ayyash-Abdo, "Adolescent Suicide: An Ecological Approach," in *Psychology in the Schools*, 39/4 (2002), pp. 459–475; Y. Conwell, P. R. Dubertstein and E. D. Caine, "Risk Factors for Suicide in Later Life," in *Biological Psychiatry*, 52/3 (2002), pp. 193–204. I have developed the problematic of suicide in my already mentioned book *Death by Despair*, pp. 23–42.

5   See Bauckham and Hart, *Hope against Hope*, p. 26; E. Schillebeeckx, "The Interpretation of Eschatology," in *Concilium*, 41 (1969), pp. 44–46; J. L. Ruíz de la Peña, *La otra dimensión: Escatología cristiana*, Madrid: EAPSA (Actualidad teológica española), 1975, pp. 10–11.

6   See L. C. Susin, "Introduction: This World Can Be Different," in *Concilium*, 5 (2004), pp. 7–12.

7   See K. Rahner, *Hearers of the Word* (M. Richards, trans.), New York: Herder and Herder, Inc., 1969, pp. 130–149; Bauckham and Hart, *Hope against Hope*, p. 53; A. Case-Winters, "Endings and Ends," in Bracken, *World without End*, pp. 177–196.

8   See E. Schillebeeckx, *God and Man* (E. Fitzgerald and P. Tomlinson, trans.), London: Sheed and Ward (Theological Soundings, 2), 1969, p. 162.

9   See P. Laín Entralgo, *La espera y la esperanza: Historia y teoría del esperar humano* (2nd ed. rev.), Madrid: Revista de Occidente, 1958.

10   See Bauckham and Hart, *Hope against Hope*, p. 52; *Id.*, "The Shape of Time," in D. Fergusson and M. Sarot (Eds.), *The Future as God's Gift: Exploration in Christian Eschatology*, Edinburgh: T. & T. Clark, 2000, pp. 59–62; J. Alfaro, "Christian Hope and the Hopes of Mankind," in *Concilium*, 9/6 (1970), p. 59.

11   Bauckham and Hart, *Hope against Hope*, p. 53. I will highlight the importance of imagination for hope at the end of this chapter.

12   R. J. Nogar, "Evolutionary Humanism and the Faith," in *Concilium*, 6/2 (1966), p. 26.

13   See *ibid.*, p. 28.

14   It is important to recognize the influence that ideology and utopia play in this and in other similar theories. An ideology is the projection of a particular thought as an absolute truth (see K. Rahner, *Concerning Vatican Council II*, pp. 43–58). A utopia refers to "unreality or a dream-world" (Concilium General Secretariat, "Utopia," in *Concilium*, 5/1 [1969], p. 74). In fact, they are related and oftentimes used together: "A utopia is by nature vague and therefore constantly threatened by ideology. By ideology we understand a partial truth which seeks to pass for the whole truth. The strivings of utopia become then identified with its content. The proper nature of an ideology is that it is a conviction which is believed to be evoked by reality but is in fact kept alive by the desire to satisfy individual interests. Utopia can only function as a literary story; as soon as it is taken for the reality it becomes an ideology. . . . Ideology will always tend toward onesidedness. This was clear in the process which prevailed in the Enlightenment: rationalization of the reality is necessary but as soon as it was identified with progress it began to show the one-dimensional character of an ideology." (Concilium General Secretariat, "Utopia," p. 77; see also J. M. Castillo, "Utopia Set Aside," in *Concilium*, 5 [2004], pp. 38–40)

15   See E. Bloch, *The Principle of Hope* (N. Plaice, S. Plaice and P. Knight, trans.), Cambridge, MA: MIT Press (Studies in Contemporary German Social Thought), 1986, 3 vols.

16   See L. Feuerbach, *The Essence of Christianity* (G. Eliot, trans.), New York: Harper (Harper Torchbooks. The Cloister Library, TB11), 1957.

17   See I. Hermann, "Total Humanism: Utopian Pointers between Coexistence and Pluralism," in *Concilium*, 6/2 (1966), pp. 69–77.

18   See J. Moltmann, "Hope Without Faith: An Eschatological Humanism Without God," in *Concilium*, 6/2 (1966), pp. 14–21.

19   See *ibid.*, pp. 17–19; G. Girardi, "Marxism and Death," in *Concilium*, 4/10 (1974), pp. 133–140; J. L. Ruíz de la Peña, *Muerte y marxismo humanista: Aproximación teológica*, Salamanca: Sígueme (Agora), 1978. Concern for the future and its implications was a topic for the dialogue between Marxists and Christians during the 1960s and 1970s. One central theme in this dialogue, left unresolved, was the question of death, and the absolute future without God (see G. Sauter, "The Future: A Question for the Christian-Marxist Dialogue," in *Concilium*, 5/1 [1969], pp. 63–67; Nogar, *op. cit.*, p. 29; D. Fergusson, "Introduction," in Fergusson and Sarot [Eds.], *The Future as God's Gift*, p. 3). Today, given the tragedies of the last, and present, centuries, it seems difficult for many people to find an ultimate meaning of the future without faith in a transcendent God (see Bauckham and Hart, *Hope against Hope*, pp. 1–25). According to Nogar,

"Without a revelation from God, man cannot discover the moral and religious meaning of his destiny, nor raise a finger to extricate himself from the moral pathology into which he has fallen. Belief in the revelation of God and the Redemption of Christ, accessible to the man who is open to the timeless and the divine, is the only release available to the despair of evolutionary [and total] humanism. No plan for the space-time future existence of man is realistic until it solves this fundamental moral and religious issue of absurdity. Huxley's [and Marx's and Bloch's] instinct that the future of man must be thought out and *acted out in the timely* is an authentic one, but the *meaning* of that future can only be found in the timeless, in the gift of the divine." (Nogar, *op. cit.*, p. 29) This is also the position of David Fergusson: "By contrast with varieties of secular hope [evolutionary humanism and Marxism], the Christian faith suggests a fruitful outcome not for those who are privileged to succeed at the end, but for all who have ever lived. The sign of this is the resurrection of Christ. This is described by the New Testament writers in terms which show its integral connection with social hopes for the coming kingdom of God." (D. Fergusson, "Introduction," in Fergusson and Sarot [Eds.], *The Future as God's Gift*, p. 3)

20   See Polkinghorne, *op. cit.*, pp. 94–95; Nogar, *op. cit.*, pp. 29–30; Rahner, *Concerning Vatican Council II*, pp. 43–58; Schillebeeckx, "The Interpretation of Eschatology," p. 53; L. Boros, "Some Thoughts on the Four Last Things," in *Concilium*, 2/4 (1968), pp. 38–43; L. Boff, *La vida más allá de la muerte: El presente, su futuro, su fiesta, su contestación*, Bogotá: Confederación Latinoamericana de Religiosos (Colección Perspectivas-CLAR, 6), 1977, p. 102; Schwarz, *op. cit.*, pp. 203–204.

21   See K. Rahner, *The Theology of the Spiritual Life* (K. H. and B. Kruger, trans.), Baltimore: Helicon Press (Theological Investigations, III), 1967, pp. 141–157; Polkinghorne, *op. cit.*, p. 12; Bauckham and Hart, *Hope against Hope*, p. 43.

22   Bauckham and Hart, *Hope against Hope*, p. 10.

23   *Ibid.*, p. 10.

24   Schwarz, *op. cit.*, p. 174.

25   See Bauckham and Hart, *Hope against Hope*, pp. 10–11.

26   See Polkinghorne, *op. cit.*, pp. 8–9; Schwarz, *op. cit.*, p. 175; Toolan, *op. cit.*, pp. 41–74, 173–177.

27   R. Schwager, "Original Sin as a 'Cultural Matrix' Today (1)," in *Concilium*, 1 (2004), p. 95.

28   See Schwarz, *op. cit.*, pp. 194–209; Toolan, *op. cit.*, pp. 79–125, 159–164; W. H. Becker, "Ecological Sin," in *Theology Today*, XLIX/2 (1992), pp. 152–164; K. J. Hsu, "The Mortality of the Planet," in *Concilium*, 4 (1998), pp. 63–73; D. C. Toole, "Divine Ecology and the Apocalypse: A Theological Description of Natural Disasters," in *Theology Today*, LV/4 (1999), pp. 547–561;

H. Eaton, "Ecology, Religion and Healing," in *Theoforum*, 34/1 (2003), pp. 109–114. It is important to note how the new awareness of the fragility of creation, and the risk of its destruction, as it is manifested by the threat of an ecological holocaust, is due, in a particular way, to feminism. The ecofeminist conception of the world, which is less possessive than the one carried on by patriarchy, obliges us to contemplate life from a different perspective and in a holistic way (see R. R. Ruether, *Gaia and God: An Ecofeminist Theology of Earth Healing*, San Francisco: Ed. HarperSanFrancisco, 1992; S. McFague, *The Body of God: An Ecological Theology*, Minneapolis: Ed. Fortress Press, 1993; *Ead.*, "Imagining God and 'A Different World,'" in *Concilium*, 5 [2004], pp. 42–50; H. Eaton, "Ecofeminism, Cosmology, and Spiritual Renewal," in *Église et Théologie*, 29/1 [1998], pp. 115–128).

29   See C. Lévi-Strauss, *Tristes tropiques*, Paris: Plon (Terre humaine), 1955, p. 103; *Id.*, *L'origine des manières de table*, Paris: Plon (Mythologiques, 3), 1968, p. 422; *Id.*, *L'homme nu*, Dijon: Plon ("Mythologiques," 4), 1971, pp. 614–615; C. Halkes, "The Rape of Mother Earth: Ecology and Patriarchy," in E. S. Fiorenza (Ed.), *The Power of Naming: A Concilium Reader in Feminist Liberation Theology*, Maryknoll/London: Orbis Books/SCM Press (Concilium Series), 1996, pp. 132–141.

30   See Toolan, *op. cit.*, pp. 10–14; Eaton, "Ecology, Religion and Healing," pp. 118–122; *Ead.*, "This Sacred Earth: At the Nexus of Religion, Ecology and Politics," in *Pastoral Sciences/Sciences Pastorales*, 23/1 (2004), pp. 35–54.

31   See Castillo, *op. cit.*, pp. 36–37.

32   See R. Hille, "A Biblical-Theological Response to the Problem of Theodicy in the Context of the Modern Criticism to Religion," in *Evangelical Review of Theology*, 28/1 (2004), pp. 21–37. We have to situate here the Indian Ocean tsunami disaster that affected some areas of South-East Asia countries such as Sri Lanka, India, Indonesia, Thailand, Maldives, and Seychelles December 26, 2004, with all the questions related to the why of this tragedy; particularly all questions related to the relationship between this tragedy and God.

33   See R. Martínez de Pisón, "La dialectique de la foi aujourd'hui: Entre la subjectivité 'sauvage' et le traditionalisme 'intégriste,'" in *Église et Théologie*, 25/3 (1994), pp. 405–423; *Id.*, "La alteridad: El 'lugar teológico' de la experiencia de Dios," in *Religión y Cultura*, XLV/208 (1999), pp. 81–93; *Id.*, "La libertad (transcendencia) de Dios frente al fenómeno religioso contemporáneo," in *Nova et Vetera*, XXIII/47 (1999), pp. 29–46; *Id.*, "De la crítica a la religión al descubrimiento de la espiritualidad," pp. 51–58; M. Kanyoro, "The Sape of God to Come and the Future of Humanity," in *Concilium*, 5 (2004), pp. 53–61; P. Schmidt-Leukel, "A New Spirituality for a Religiously Plural World," in *Concilium*, 5 (2004), pp. 62–68; Bregman, *Death and Dying, Spirituality and Religions*, pp. 33–51.

34   Bauckham and Hart, *Hope against Hope*, pp. 26–27.

35   I consider here as already known the classical distinction that Karl Rahner has made between apocalyptic and eschatology. When we refer to eschatology we speak about the anticipation, from our present life, of what will be definitive: we make reference from the present to the future. However, if we refer from the future to the present, that is called apocalyptic. Thus, apocalyptic underlines a future world already made final by God, without human intervention, contrary to eschatology which accentuates, from present history, the values of human engagement in its transformation (see See K. Rahner, *More Recent Writings* [K. Smyth, trans.], London: Darton, Longman & Todd [Theological Investigations, IV], 1966, p. 337; see also Hultgren, *op. cit.*, pp. 67–69; McGuckin, *op. cit.*, p. 130; C. Gunton, "Dogmatic Theses on Eschatology," in Fergusson and Sarot [Eds.], *The Future as God's Gift*, p. 140; R. Cumming Neville, "Eschatological Visions," in Bracken [Ed.], *World without End*, pp. 28–45). In the next chapter I will develop this difference further.

36   See Schwager, *op. cit.*, pp. 96–97; G. K. Mainberger, "Original Sin as a 'Cultural Matrix' Today (2)," in *Concilium*, 1 (2004), pp. 99–107. Peter Hünermann makes an important remark regarding the risk of using the tragedies of today to deduce "the sinful constitution of human beings." (P. Hünermann, "Experience of 'Original Sin'?" in *Concilium*, 1 [2004], p. 108) This particularly applies to the temptation to consider HIV/AIDS as a punishment from God (see G. West with B. Zengele, "Reading Job 'Positively' in the Context of HIV/AIDS in South Africa," in *Concilium*, 4 [2004], pp. 112–124). This remark is also valid for the tsunami disaster mentioned above.

37   See D. G. Bromley and J. G. Melton (Eds.), *Cults, Religion, and Violence*, Cambridge: UK: Cambridge University Press, 2002; O. McTernan, *Violence in God's Name: Religion in an Age of Conflict*, Maryknoll: Orbis Books, 2003.

38   See P. Clayton, "Eschatology as Metaphysics under the Guise of Hope," in Bracken (Ed.), *World without End*, pp. 130–135.

39   See Ruíz de la Peña, *La otra dimensión*, pp. 16–21; C. Geffré, "The God of Jesus and the Possibilities of History," in *Concilium*, 5 (2004), pp. 69–76.

40   Fergusson, "Introduction," p. 3; see also Bauckham and Hart, *Hope against Hope*, pp. 55–56.

41   See W. Pannenberg, "The Task of Christian Eschatology," in Braaten and Jenson (Eds.), *The Last Things*, p. 2; Schillebeeckx, "The Interpretation of Eschatology," p. 53; J. Hofmeier, "Hope—Instinct, Passion and Understanding," in *Concilium*, 9/6 (1970), pp. 31–41.

42   Schillebeeckx, "The Interpretation of Eschatology," p. 54; see Boros, "Some Thoughts on the Four Last Things," p. 38; O. Cullmann, *Estudios de Teología Bíblica*, Madrid: Studium, 1973, pp. 55–74.

43   See Alfaro, *op. cit.*, pp. 67–69.

LIFE BEYOND DEATH

44   See Bauckham and Hart, *Hope against Hope*, p. 53. A few pages later, these authors insist on the importance of imagination for hope: "Hope transfigures the present precisely by enabling us to transcend it imaginatively and, upon our return, to perceive all too clearly its lacks and needs." (*Ibid.*, p. 56) Richard G. Cote has also highlighted the role that imagination plays in hope—as in faith as such—in his book *Lazarus! Come Out!*, pp. 8–9. This is what he said to the Missionary Oblates of Mary Immaculate in preparation for their 34th General Chapter (held in Rome, Italy, from August 30 to September 28, 2004): "It should come as no surprise that religious imagination is a function—indeed the proper function of Christian hope. What actually makes hope possible is the possibility of taking some initiative, the possibility of 'mission.' Out of imagination arises the anticipation of missionary possibilities and their eventual realization. In this sense one can say that imagination is a function of hope. It enables us to not only envisage 'a new heaven and a new earth' (Rev. 21:1), but also to 'open' and 'project' what we see and to propose it to the world as a real possibility of life." (R. G. Cote, "Theological Hope or Human Optimism?" in *OMI Documentation*, 258 [April, 2004], p. 5)

4

Interpreting Assertions
About the After-Life

Over the last hundred years or so we have discovered the importance of sociological, cultural, economical, political and even ecclesiastical influences on the elaboration of sayings and writings. This suggests that all human activity is conditioned by our differing environments. When a person speaks or writes, he or she relies on certain assumptions, usually in an unconscious way. We integrate these assumptions, contained within our culture, as part of our own development. We are always situated culturally. There is no pure experience. As Robert Lenoble had indicated in the middle of the last century, pure experience is an illusion. It is an illusion that can cause people to have dogmatic and fundamentalist attitudes and to behave in an intolerant way. They come to believe that only they are in possession of the whole truth.[1]

To be situated is intrinsic to being created and particularly to being human. That means that when we are dealing with sayings and writings from the past and/or from other cultural milieus, we must ask what in these sayings or writings is objective and what may have been added by or due to the culture and the language of that time, how the context has conditioned the final product, and so forth. Therefore, we must do a hermeneutical examination of these sayings or writings (hermeneutics is the science of interpretation). As a result, we come to know the importance of the hermeneutical circle, namely, the relationship that exists between the text or event and its context on the one hand, and on the other hand, our present situation—the role of the subject in the interpretation of texts or events.

Furthermore, we have learned the importance of different forms of language, each with its own laws and characteristics. Thus, symbolic language is not the same as conceptual or scientific language, even if all three serve as means of communication. Accordingly, we must know the kind of language in which the texts we read have been written in order to interpret them in a way that is faithful to the essential meaning of such texts and faithful to the intention of the authors.

In addition, it is easy to appreciate how this becomes even more complex when we speak of "realities" that are not objectively verifiable, such as God, the eschatological dimension of Christian faith, or religious experience. Is it possible to speak of God? How can we speak about the last things without any personal experience of such ultimate realities? Independent of what the answers to these questions might be, the fact is that our religious language is always limited and provisional. We find ourselves in the same situation when we speak of eschatology, dealing with what is ultimate, using limited and provisional language.[2] Nevertheless, this way of speaking is extremely important since it shows us that we cannot possess or control Divinity.

The essential question is this: the difficulty of translating an experience of totality, that is to say, Christian eschatology, through a language that is always conditional. How can we speak about the last things to our contemporaries in understandable terms? How can we remain faithful to the heart of the Christian faith contained in an infallible dogma, which is expressed in conceptual and notional categories belonging to another epoch, when we try to express it in a different cultural environment such as ours?

Edward Schillebeeckx makes it clear that theology has a duty to translate biblical and dogmatic assertions into language that is comprehensible for today's world. Concepts used for expressing religious assertions must be connected to the experience within which they originated: "If the concept is isolated from experience, then one is excluded by the fact itself from reality."[3] This is also the position of Jean Ladrière. For him, theological discourse, even recognizing its own specificity, cannot be separated from the faith experience of the community.[4]

Nonetheless, as was indicated in chapter 2, assertions regarding the eschatological dimension of Christian faith, particularly those arising in the Middle Ages, became progressively detached from the life of the community, and most of them remain that way even today. Therefore we have a duty to interpret them in order to keep alive the heart of the Christian message concerning the ultimate meaning of life. This will be the purpose of the present chapter.

First, I will emphasize the importance of hermeneutics with regard to religious language. We will see how there are in fact many different forms of language. We must understand in what language this or that text is expressed in order to ensure that there is a updated continuity of meaning. We will not be using the same language in which most of the biblical texts were written.

Second, I will address the difference between eschatological and apocalyptic language regarding statements concerning what is beyond death. Finally, I will underscore the need to revitalize our Christian imagination in order that we may express the eschatological dimension of Christian faith in a comprehensible and creative way.

1. The Importance of Hermeneutics for Religious Language

Hermeneutics is an essential tool in any effort to understand the Christian message as well as the faith to which it is addressed. The function of hermeneutics is to help us interpret the message in order to actualize it to our own time. There are three interrelated tasks of hermeneutics.

The first task of hermeneutics is to provide solutions to problems created by our efforts to express something in differing times and cultures. When faced with historical events or with texts from the past, we are in fact dealing with events or texts belonging to a different cultural environment than our own. Hermeneutics helps to make us conscious of such differences insofar as it prevents us from translating these events or texts literally from one culture or time to another. In other words, we must take into account their socio-cultural and temporal contexts.

The second task of hermeneutics is to assist us in putting events and texts within a larger frame of reference, namely, to situate the particular events or texts within the context that created the events, the purpose of the author, etc. This is the task of situating the part in relation to the whole. An isolated event or a particular text often cannot be understood apart from other circumstances or other texts. Hermeneutics contributes to finding a greater holistic significance within which the part takes on its true or fuller meaning.

Finally, as applied to religious language and in particular to theology, hermeneutics helps us to connect the original meaning of an event or text to our present. The original meaning of an event or text may be lost because the context in which this event or text is produced is not taken into account. We must analyze the frame of reference within which the event or text came to life. To fail to do this interpretation is to risk translating the event or text in a literal sense and then missing its real meaning. This is the temptation of all fundamentalism and dogmatism. The result is intolerance in the face of diversity.

In summary, in terms of religious language, as James M. Robinson says, the role of hermeneutics is not to contribute to "a new doctrinal development of faith, or to a new dogma that will correct or complete the others,"[5] but to help us to re-actualize the original meaning of the Christian message, or of a dogma, for our own time.

Nature, Culture and History

Humans are incarnated beings, situated within and conditioned by a context. Therefore nature, culture and history are the frames of reference within which we develop ourselves. In this sense, even in its first proclamation, the religious message is already enculturated within a particular community that belongs to a particular time and socio-cultural setting. "Taking into account that Christianity is a historical religion, it is not possible to conceive salvation as a

LIFE BEYOND DEATH

passage into an immutable and intemporal beyond."[6] The language must be adapted to take into account the differences of time and culture. It is for this reason that "the continuity of meaning can only be acquired if the language itself changes in order to be what it was [namely, the proclamation of meaning within a particular context]."[7]

The sayings and deeds of Jesus Christ have always been transmitted as interpretations. Jesus himself belonged to a specific culture and time. But today we are living in a different culture and time than that of Jesus and of the first Christian communities. Hermeneutics helps us to respect the original meaning of the Jesus proclamation and to make it understandable within our own cultural and temporal context. It is true that there is a risk that we may make mistakes, even fall into heresy. But, as Robinson indicates, "avoiding change, even where the meaning [for us] has changed, is also heresy."[8] In short, through hermeneutics we can be faithful to the word of God and proclaim it in our own world.

The Role of Language and Its Different Forms

Once we know what hermeneutics is and understand its importance for religious language, we must consider the role of language itself. We must take into consideration its variety as language that is religious, scientific, conceptual and symbolic. In the middle of the last century, analytical philosophy was against the possible use of any religious, moral or metaphysical language. Its objection was "that statements about what God is doing or about the wrongness of certain kinds of behaviour seem to lack any empirical basis."[9] Consequently, according to these analytical philosophers, we may speak correctly only about what can be verified objectively. In this regard, however, theological assertions, moral judgments, and eschatological proclamations cannot be made subject to any simple empirical test. For analytical philosophers, such claims would be without value. This radical critique has been a very useful challenge in the formulation of religious language in general and for theology in particular. It has forced theologians and Church leaders to revise their understanding of and the way in which they use religious language.

It has also been possible to discover various forms or types of language and their value. Not only empirical language, which is able to give objective information about reality, is acceptable: "There are many uses of language, and consequently there are many languages . . . . The suggestion is that each type of language has its own rules, i.e., its own logic, just as every game has its own rules."[10] Therefore, we cannot simply apply the rules of empirical science to the evaluation of information about life or religion. Neither can we apply religious, moral or metaphysical language to communicate objective, empirical information about reality. Language is not something abstract but is rather a channel of communication.[11] This is very important for a proper understanding and use of religious language.

We receive the Christian message from witnesses, not from external hearers. To follow Paul Ricoeur, the witness is not someone who narrates historical events and nothing more. It is not a question of giving information about God but of bearing witnesses to others concerning God.[12] Through language, the witness exteriorizes, gives form, and expresses her or his religious experience with concepts and categories in order to preserve its meaning and share it with others.

Paul Ricoeur highlights three aspects of the role of witnessing that can be applied also to religious language in general. The first is that one does not bear witness to isolated events. Rather, the witness speaks about the way in which the message carried in the act of witnessing affects or concerns the global meaning of human experience. Second, witnessing is oriented to proclamation: to be a witness for others.[13] Finally, witnessing implies the witness's existential self-engagement. Her or his own life is in itself a testimony, establishing a certain transparency with regard to the proclaimed message.[14] In addition, proclamation and personal engagement do not signify that the events witnessed to did not occur in reality. In other words, to bear witness does not mean to deny the objectivity of the facts.[15]

However, this experiential dimension of religious language is not opposed to conceptualization and systematization. William James (1842–1910), speaking about the varieties of religious experience,

LIFE BEYOND DEATH

stresses the need for its conceptualization, a necessity that is also required for being able to share the experience with others.[16] This has always been the task of theology: to conceptualize the vital meaning contained in religious experience. Theological language is more systematic, speculative and conceptual than the language of religious experience, which is more symbolic and self-engaging.[17] The advantage of theological language is to eliminate the ambiguity contained within any religious experience, an experience made by humans, who are themselves always limited, contingent beings. Through theological language reality is expressed in a clear way. Furthermore, theology is able to systematize its content within a specific frame of reference. Nevertheless, its negative side involves reducing the existential, vital dimension of the religious experience, as against the symbolic language through which the experience is best communicated. Theology risks falling into a very well-elaborated conceptual system that is not rooted in experience. However, even as we recognize the need for conceptualization and the diversity of interpretations, we must take into account, as Gerald O'Collins suggests, that interpretation itself is also always limited.[18]

The most appropriate way of expressing the experience of God, as was the case in the Bible, is through symbolic language. Symbols are open to multiple meanings. Through symbols, human beings are able to transcend physical reality.[19] Furthermore, through a symbol another reality becomes present, as in the case when the body is a symbol of the person.[20] Because of its multiplicity of meanings and its openness to transcendence, symbolic language prevents us from falling into the risk of trying to possess or control the divine. Finally, we cannot translate literally something formulated in a symbolic language into a conceptual language without any interpretation. This is a mistake of many literal, fundamentalist interpretations of the Bible.[21]

The Bible as the Interpretation of a Divine Experience

The Sacred Scripture is already a hermeneutics, that is, it is an interpretation of the experiences of God that people of both the Old and New Testaments had. Thus, the Bible, as Edward Schillebeeckx emphasized, is already a work of interpretation: "Therefore, both the

Old and New Testaments already have an *interpretative* function: they are 'hermeneutics in action'. But for us this collection of writings itself becomes again something that is in need of interpretation. And so hermeneutics becomes the interpretation of an interpretation."[22] Schillebeeckx gives two important reasons why we must continue to do the same interpretative, hermeneutical work that writers of the Bible did in the past. The first reason is that

> we no longer belong to the same culture; we no longer have the same mentality or the same outlook on man and the world, as those that prevailed in the days when the original and the later interpretations of the Christ-event were formulated. The distance in time makes our problem far more difficult.[23]

The second reason is that

> we belong to an age which acknowledges the demands of textual and historical criticism, an age which considers it immoral to surrender oneself unconditionally to something without some rational justification: all people, including those of good will, reject *a priori* a kind of blind faith which has no human and genuine intelligible basis. Even with our unconditional obedience of faith we can no longer avoid the need to make the eschatological dogmas intelligible and in some way understandable.[24]

Schillebeeckx's reasons for the constant need to interpret the sacred Scripture, given the difference of time and the demands of textual and historical criticism, are very important. I would like to illustrate them with five examples taken from the Old Testament. One example comes from the first creation story in the book of Genesis (1:1–2:4a), written during the time when Israel was forced into exile in Babylon (587–539 B.C.). According to the biblical story, God created the world in a "symbolic" week. The author's intention was not to say how long the work of creation took but to set up the basis for respecting the cult of the Sabbath: "And on the seventh day God finished the work that he had done, and he rested on the seventh day from all the work that he had done. So God blessed the seventh day and hallowed it, because on it God rested from all the work that he had done in creation" (Gen. 2:2-3). This

LIFE BEYOND DEATH

intent of the story was apologetic: to encourage a monotheistic faith in God in the face of a polytheist environment. The Sabbath was the theological foundation of the people of Israel who had lost their political independence and were left only with their faith as their distinctive characteristic. We cannot interpret this story literally.

The second biblical example concerns the equality between woman and man. This equality, expressed in a symbolic way, is contained in the second creation story (Gen. 2:4b-25), dating from the time of David or Solomon, about the tenth century before Christ. This story was also written with an apologetic intention: to assure that God was not responsible for evil (Gen. 3). In order to be able to dialogue, human beings need a face-to-face encounter. This is revealed in the man-woman relation in which the symbolism of the rib represents the "ontological equality" of the two created beings:

> So the Lord God caused a deep sleep to fall upon the man, and he slept; then he took one of his ribs and closed up its place with flesh. And the rib that the Lord God had taken from the man he made into a woman and brought her to the man. Then the man said, "This at last is bone of my bones and flesh of my flesh; this one shall be called Woman, for out of Man this one was taken." (Gen. 2:21-23)

Adam recognizes himself as a human being only in the presence of Eve, who is his likeness. As a result, every kind of sexism is excluded. None of the prejudices about female inferiority has any foundation in the creation story.[25] Using symbolic language, the author of the second creation account proclaims what we say, using conceptual language, concerning the essential equality of woman and man.

The third example from the Bible, also expressed in symbolic language, is the garden of Eden or Paradise:

> The Lord God took the man and put him in the garden of Eden to till it and keep it. And the Lord God commanded the man, "You may freely eat of every tree of the garden; but of the tree

of the knowledge of good and evil you shall not eat, for in the day that you eat of it you shall die." (Gen. 2:15-17)

Dependence does not carry a negative connotation. It is meant to remind humans that life is received from God. The tree of the knowledge of good and evil is a symbol that expresses humans' constitutive dependence in relation to the Creator.

The symbolism of the garden of Eden, or Paradise, has great importance for an understanding of human beings. Here it is not a question of a literal, historical or geographical interpretation that tries to locate paradise in a real past.[26] Paradise does not refer to past history but to an existential situation whereby we are engaged with God in the creation of the world. In a culture that is more symbolic than descriptive, we must ask: What is the best way to express God's invitation to communion, to the covenant that from the beginning of creation God wishes to establish with human beings, to women and men invited to become God's image and likeness?

The author of the story could find no better symbolism than that of the garden of Eden or Paradise. This is why the question of its historical reality or geographical location is neither relevant nor of real interest. The truth conveyed by the symbolism is forever valid: the invitation to enter into a communion with God, other people and ourselves by making our world the reflection of divine glory. Paradise depicts within human existence. Reference to it is therefore an invitation arising out of reference to the past that will arrive at its fullness at the end of history.[27] In its full sense, then, the meaning of Paradise does not come from looking backward but from looking toward the present and the future understood as the accomplishment of a divine promise.

The fourth symbolic text comes from the story of the first biblical sin and the role of the woman in it (Gen. 3:1-7). It must be said that the introduction of sin into the world by the woman at the suggestion of the serpent does not have a sexist connotation, or at least not an intentional one, in the text. If, as the author of the second account of creation points out (Gen. 2:22-23), creation reaches its summit in the creation of woman; if sin and evil, which, as the first part of the story indicated (Gen. 2:4b-25) cannot

LIFE BEYOND DEATH

be attributed to God, are generalized in scope, it is then necessary to locate the beginning of evil at the summit of creation, namely, in woman.[28]

Finally, there is a question of the symbolic interpretation of the sin of the origins versus a literal and conceptual one, original sin, as understood in the early period of the Christian Church.[29] Chapter 3 of Genesis introduces us to a sin that breaks the harmony of creation and therefore affects all humanity. It was expressed in a symbolic manner so as to aid in comprehending the reasons for the condition of misery in which the people of the covenant found themselves at the time the second creation narrative was composed. It was not a question of affirming that every human being comes into the world with a personal constitutive stain, but of describing symbolically a sinful situation that precedes humans and characterizes all human relationships.

Nonetheless, in Christian tradition, especially as expressed by Augustine and in the period after him, there arose the notion of an inherited original sin that affects us ontologically and is therefore constitutive of human beings since the sin of the origins. The difference between original sin and the sin of the origins is essential: we have moved from a symbolic interpretation to an ontological reality. This is why the two can no longer continue to be identified, even though we may recognize that both refer to the event of a first sin perpetrated by a human, according to the book of Genesis. In short, a situation that has been expressed symbolically cannot be translated and expressed ontologically without making relevant corrections. By interpreting the sin of the origins ontologically, the Christian tradition has gone farther than what is described in Genesis 3.

It is by doing a correct hermeneutical interpretation of the Bible, and by taking into account the languages in which narratives were expressed, that we can continue to be faithful in our own day to the real meaning these narratives disclose. It is for this reason that we must refer to different theological languages used in speaking of the eschatological dimension of Christian faith.

2. Theological Languages for Life Beyond Death

As I have presented in the last chapter, Christians believe that God fulfilled the covenant through Jesus Christ's incarnation, life, death and resurrection. From this starting point, our present life already bears the signs of the eternity of which Jesus himself, in his resurrection, was the first fruit that, through Christ, we all are invited to share (1 Cor. 15:20-28). Thus, in Christ, as Ladislaus Boros emphasizes, the end is but the beginning of a new life here on earth that will come to its ultimate realization in heaven.[30] On this sacred present is founded the eschatological dimension of Christian faith that is different from an apocalyptic view of salvation.

Apocalyptic and Eschatology

Apocalyptic refers to and stresses the notion of a future world already made final by God without human intervention. In contrast, eschatology refers to and accentuates from the perspective of present history, the values of human engagement in that history's transformation. There is a socio-historical explanation for this difference: "The model of apocalyptic politics arose in those periods of biblical history where the faithful had no opportunity to give public testimony to the religious principles and moral values they believed to be mandated by their ultimate allegiance to the universal reign of God."[31]

Apocalyptic, as a literary genre employing special techniques, was used for about 300 years—from the second century before Christ up to the first century after Christ. The second century before Christ was a time in which Antiochous IV Epiphanes, king of Egypt, persecuted Israel, as the second book of Maccabees attests. However, another book—the book of Daniel which speaks about Israel's Babylonian exile (587–539 B.C.) but which in fact is contemporary with the second book of Maccabees—is illustrative of the apocalyptic literature.[32] The author of the book of Daniel was saying something about the time in which Israel was in exile in Babylon, although he was actually living several centuries later. The author's purpose was to let the Israelites who were persecuted by Antiochous IV Epiphanes know that what they were then experiencing was similar to what the people of Israel had suffered during the exile. Out of Israel's past experience, the author of the book of Daniel created an "ideal" story, a parable with an already known happy ending prepared by God. In this way, the Israelites could keep alive their faith in a divine and liberating intervention.[33] Similarly, the New Testament book of Revelation, written during the first century of the Christian era, also belongs to a period when Rome invaded Palestine and when Jerusalem and its temple were destroyed (in the year 70 C.E.). In Revelation, the author uses apocalyptic language and techniques.

Why then, we might ask, do both the book of Daniel and the book of Revelation use apocalyptic literature to record a happy outcome to their present persecutions, a happy ending presented as something about to occur in the near future and without human intervention, a happy ending already foretold by God and revealed to some privileged prophets?

It is not difficult to understand the use of apocalyptic language in times of persecution. How should it have been possible to say that the present was already salvific when Israel was actually being persecuted in the second century before Christ? How could all this have meaning when, during the first century of Christianity, Christians were being persecuted, as the book of Revelation describes? Their "present moment" was certainly not a salvific experience. Yet for the authors of Daniel and Revelation, it was the best way to encourage believers to remain faithful and to show them a wonderful future already prepared for them as the work of God. Consequently, believers had to resist and simply wait for a while. Hence, this type of literature can be called the literature of resistance.[34] The stories described in these books could be compared to the pamphlets used by the Resistance during the World War II (1939–1945) in order to sustain those resisting the Nazis' invasion of their countries. Apocalyptic literature of course used a language that for us today may seem strange and difficult to understand. Yet it was easy to understand for those to whom the writings were addressed. The authors of these apocalyptic books had to use secret words and numbers in case these writings, again like the pamphlets published by the Resistance, should be discovered by their persecutors.

In summary, the biblical use of apocalyptic language or apocalyptic literature, as it appears in the books of Daniel and Revelation, was a necessity in times of persecution. It is true that both books describe the ultimate end already prepared for them by God. That end was a divine action without human intervention, since the present did not have much to offer: "Apocalyptic politics is a gift from God to the persecuted communities of every age that experience the execution of their leaders and the slaughter of their children, be it in Rome in the last half of the first century or Germany in the early 1940s."[35] Even understanding how historical circumstances can cause believers to doubt that their present might be a sacred *kairos*, that is, a time in which God intervenes, "a blessing in disguise,"[36] Christian faith still enables us to believe that God never abandons us.

Nevertheless, in order to reactivate faith in the presence of what is ultimate among us and of our own engagement with it, we are invited to revitalize the Christian imagination in order to speak about what lies beyond death.

3. Revitalizing Christian Imagination Concerning Eschatology

The revitalization of Christian imagination is an essential need for faith and its eschatological dimension. In fact, the Bible and the assertions of faith in the past have always been nourished by imagination.[37] While it is perhaps true that the way we imagine things today differs from the way in which such things were perceived in the past, we must nonetheless continue to use imaginative interpretations in order to maintain the heart of Christian faith that is pertinent to us and to our world today.

Through imagination we can go beyond the tragedies of our own time and contemplate the emergence of something new and different: the manifestation of the Holy Spirit. Imagination becomes important in times of difficulty and this is especially true in the sojourn in the wilderness that characterizes transitional times such as ours.[38]

LIFE BEYOND DEATH

Imagination and Eschatology

Imagination is also necessary if we wish to revitalize the affirmations we make about life beyond death. As Richard Bauckham and Trevor Hart say, "we aim to restore the category of imagination to its essential role in Christian eschatology, both by exploring the nature of eschatological statements and by reflecting on the major images of the eschatological future that the Bible and the tradition offer us. Christian hope, we suggest, is not imaginary, but it is irreducibly imaginative."[39] In Part Two I will deal with the role of revitalizing Christian eschatological imagination. But first I would like to indicate how this task will affect some of the assertions of our faith.

In dealing with the idea of the judgment of God and of God as judge, we can no longer speak in ways to which we have been accustomed, that is to say, to present God as the "Supreme Judge" of the universe. We need rather to address what the deeply biblical meaning of judge and judgment actually mean when applied to God or to Jesus Christ.

Regarding the so-called punishments the damned will experience in hell, particularly fire, I will explain how these can be interpreted with more imagination. Such graphic symbols have a very different meaning in the Bible than they have for us today, especially when taken literally.

Purgatory, heaven and hell are not physical places to which we go. Even if we believe in a renewed universe, we cannot project literally our concepts of space to the reality that lies beyond death. A similar observation applies to time: How can we conceive of a time of waiting between death and the final resurrection? How can we imagine the time of purification expended in purgatory? Is there any kind of succession in eternity, either in heaven for the blessed or in hell for the damned? Is it possible to conceive of a non-temporal eternity? How do intercessions made in a time continuum relate to the dead in an a-temporal condition?

We have all experienced states of being such as feeling good, bad, and so forth, which can help us as we struggle to speak about purgatory, heaven and hell.[40] At the same time, some events, particularly the bad ones, can seem to drag on for an eternity. Besides, we know what it means to keep alive the memory of the deceased and to pray for and in communion with them.

Finally, we will see how to understand the beatific vision, namely, the vision of God that the just in heaven will enjoy. Certainly we cannot understand it as a physical vision. It would actually be rather boring to sit down and look at God for an eternity with each one of us occupying different seat levels in accordance with our merits. I will suggest that "seeing" in the Bible does not have exactly the same meaning as it does for us today. Rather, to see includes an experience, and seeing God signifies entering into a relationship with God.

Eschatology in Preaching and Liturgy

In the context of the need to revitalize our Christian faith by using the imagination as well as the insights of eschatology, we must consider revitalizing eschatological language in our preaching and in the liturgy of the Church. We also must address the analogical dimension of eschatological language. This will prevent us from falling into the danger of trying to possess or control God.

First, as Carl E. Braaten indicates, "Good preaching and theology call for the imagination to go back and forth between the symbols, concepts, and worldview of the Bible, on the one hand, and the original language of our secular world, on the other."[41] The existential way of speaking about ultimate things must also be manifest in liturgical celebrations. Although living in a technocratic society, contemporary human beings also need to be able to celebrate life.[42] Life does not consist only in doing but also in celebrating, in commemorating. Consequently,

> The Christian has to be a living sign of the presence of God in the world in all his actions and all circumstances of his life, and the Church has to witness to God's saving actions in all its activities, but for both it is the liturgy that both makes this need more pressing and offers the greatest possibilities for its satisfaction.[43]

LIFE BEYOND DEATH

In this perspective, both preaching and liturgy need to be renewed in order to accomplish this existential task of celebrating the ultimate presence of God among us.

Liturgy is not ritualism, "which gives greater weight to gesture and formula than to inner disposition," nor angelism, "which unilaterally stresses the disinterested orientation of the liturgy, with consequent alienation and escapism,"[44] but the way of celebrating the grace of God's salvation among us and our engagement in favour of the transformation of the world. In summary, to a new existential way of speaking about God and about the last things correspond a renewed way of celebrating in the liturgy God's presence and the eschatological dimension of Christian faith. In chapter 2 above I mentioned how in the early Church Christians believed that ultimate things are already present in the sacramental action of the Church through its liturgical celebration. For us this is a reality that belongs to the heart of our faith.

The Role of Analogy

Second, we cannot forget that our religious and in particular our eschatological language is always analogical, since between God and ourselves there cannot be a total correspondence. Furthermore, eschatology considers what is ultimate under the symbol of what is provisional, as is the case in our language. Hence, analogy becomes the best way to refer to the eschatological dimension of Christian faith.[45] Analogy deals with the relationship between two realities (A and B). Through it we recognize both their resemblances (A related to B) and their differences (A as not exactly the same as B). An example would be the use of the image of father or mother in speaking about God. We can say that the idea of God as father or mother (A) is related to the experience that we ourselves have of a human father or mother (B). Nonetheless, God, as father or mother, does not correspond exactly to the idea we have of fatherhood or motherhood (A is not exactly the same as B). *Deus semper maior* (God is always greater).

This analogical correspondence is something that can be applied to all dimensions of religious language and, in particular, to eschatological language.[46] It also shows that our language is always relative, approximative, limited. However, this helps us avoid trying to possess or control God due to our tendency to believe that our assertions concerning God and what lies beyond death are unchangeable. There is always the risk of intolerance and dogmatism. Yet accepting that ambiguity is an essential dimension of faith is what makes it possible for us to look at God's presence in the midst of our own limits and fragility.[47]

We are invited therefore to discover the God who sings in the night of our ambiguity. Accepting this—accepting that our language is always provisional, limited and localized—brings us into a continuing hermeneutical challenge if we are to be faithful to the God who is both self-disclosing, and who always remains mysteriously free in that disclosure. In addition, we must accept the fact that the experience of God is always the human experience of the divine.[48] As such, it is constantly dialectical, since interaction between the already and the not fully yet of faith is ongoing. It challenges us to believe in the presence of the divine in our lives but without absolute certitude and without fully possessing that presence. Our experience of God is also expressed symbolically, because it is mediated by many different realities of life that are always ambiguous.

⅍

Christians are not passive-receptive beings; nor are we slaves of books or norms. Instead, we are invited to enter into a covenant, a relationship with a living God. Thus, Christian faith is not the religion of a book, not even a holy one such as the Bible, but the existential answer to a God who, in Jesus Christ and the Holy Spirit, continues to love us as individuals and as members of a community, the Church. Being always the human experience of the divine, and being humans who share their religious experiences with others, we have to be in a constant process of hermeneutics, of interpreting the experience of God, due to differences in time and socio-cultural environments.

Nevertheless, the experience of the divine is the acceptance, the opening of human beings to a God who comes to us and precedes us in the encounter, one who has constantly been in search of God's

LIFE BEYOND DEATH

own people. For Christians, Jesus Christ, the Word of God made flesh, fulfilled the divine promise of an eternal covenant with all humanity and with the people of the Old Testament. Since God became one of us through Jesus Christ, and since he died and rose, our present time is part of a sacred history, despite the many signs of death around us. This is why we speak about the eschatological dimension of Christian faith. It is why we can say something, from the perspective of our present time, regarding the future accomplishment of everything in God's kingdom.

Finally, as was indicated in the first chapter, faith is always kept alive within a liturgical context. For this reason, we can understand the need to renew our liturgies. Our ancestors in faith also celebrated their encounters with God in their liturgies. In fact, most texts in the Old Testament were born as an expression of the religious experiences Israel had with the God of their forebears. Before putting these encounters with God in writing, such encounters were celebrated liturgically. Theology has always been a reflection on the life of the community. This is also true of the Christian communities in the first centuries. It is amazing to realize that these communities—particularly prior to the fourth century and before the persecution of Christians ended, when they were not able to gather publicly and have provincial and ecumenical Councils—were able to keep their faith in the God of Jesus Christ alive. It becomes even more amazing when we remember that Christians did not begin to have an "official" list or canon of the accepted divinely inspired books of the Bible, even in a provisional way, until the fourth century. Nonetheless, Christians kept the orthodoxy of their faith within the life of their communities and developed it within their liturgical celebrations. Indeed, the most important christological hymns of the New Testament were born in a liturgical context, too.

Consequently, today we are invited to renew our liturgies and our preaching in order that they will be the privileged and sacred times, the divine *kairos*, in which Christian communities will be able to celebrate their encounters with the God of Jesus Christ and bear witness of them to others. Thus, in one way or another, we are also being invited to continue to write the Bible, our Sacred Scripture, in communion with what Judeo-Christian believers of the past actually did. The God of Jesus Christ continues to speak to us in our present time. Christian faith is nourished not only from the perspective of what God wonderfully accomplished in other times but also what God continues to do in our own. Therefore, we should be able to put in writing our own experiences of God, share them with other communities, and proclaim them with all our brothers and sisters. We must recognize the prophets of our own day and write what God has revealed to them in order that they might communicate such revelations to us through their prophetic books. Thus we will have our own book of Job in which to identify the just who are suffering unjustly in our own time. It will allow us to choose the love poems to be used as we write our own Song of Songs and identify our own evangelists, those women and men who have seen, have touched, and have been with the Son of God in a special way and would be able to write their holy gospels for us today.

Divine inspiration is something not only related to the past but is God continuing to reveal his love for us today and inspiring women and men among us. Why should it be that official authorities in Christian churches would not be able one day to recognize these new writings as inspired, too, that is, as canonical and as rules of faith for believers, just as they once did with the canon of the Bible? In fact, from the perspective of the Roman Catholic Church, the last official canon of the Bible, as we have it today, was established by the Council of Trent in the sixteenth century. Accordingly, why is it that the Church of the future would not be able to recognize other writings as divinely inspired, as sacred books, as well?

Nonetheless, and taking into account the decline of hope in the Western world to which I referred in the last chapter, as well as the silence of Christian churches regarding the eschatological dimension of our faith, as I presented in the first chapter, we must revitalize our assertions concerning the ultimate meaning of life, history and creation. We are invited to speak about the last things in more imaginative and creative ways. Part Two will take up this task.

Notes to Chapter 4

1   See R. Lenoble, *Essai sur la notion d'expérience*, Paris: Vrin, 1943, p. 182; see also pp. 144–145.

2   See Schütz, *op. cit.*, pp. 528–533.

3   E. Schillebeeckx, *Revelation and Theology* (N. D. Smith, trans.), London: Sheed and Ward (Theological Soundings, vol. 1, Part 1), 1967, p. 152; see also pp. 153–155.

4   See J. Ladrière, *L'articulation du sens (vol. II): Les langages de la foi*, Paris: Éd. du Cerf (Cogitatio Fidei, 125), 1984, pp. 67–83, 169–170.

5   J. M. Robinson, "L'Herméneutique du Kérygme," in E. Castelli *et al.*, *L'ermeneutica della libertà religiosa*, Padova: CEDAM (Archivio di Filosofia, year 1968, n°s 2–3), 1968, p. 327.

6   *Ibid.*, pp. 327–328.

7   *Ibid.*, p. 328.

8   *Ibid.*, p. 333.

9   J. Macquarrie, "Religious Language and Recent Analytical Philosophy," in *Concilium*, 6/5 (1969), p. 73.

10   *Ibid.*, p. 75.

11   See *ibid.*, p. 77.

12   See P. Ricoeur, *Texto, testimonio y narración* (V. Undurraga, trans., foreword and notes), Santiago (Chile): Andrés Bello, 1983, pp. 21–22.

13   Edward Schillebeeckx says regarding the "narrative structure" of the experience: "Experience is therefore never 'innocent'. For it is communicable. Anyone who has had an experience *ipso facto* becomes himself a *witness*: he has a message. He describes what has happened to him. This narration opens up a new possibility of life for others, it sets something in motion. Thus the authority of experience becomes operative in the telling. The authority of experience has a narrative structure." (Schillebeeckx, *Christ*, pp. 37–38)

14   See Ricoeur, *op. cit.*, p. 24.

15   See *ibid.*, p. 26; L. Dupré, *The Other Dimension: A Search for the Meaning of Religious Attitudes*, Garden City: Doubleday & Company, Inc., 1972, pp. 210–214.

16   See W. James, *The Varieties of Religious Experience: A Study in Human Nature*, Cambridge: Harvard University Press (The Works of William James, [13]), 1985, pp. 338–339.

17   See Ladrière, *op. cit.*, pp. 160–177.

18 See G. O'Collins, "Theology and Experience," in *The Irish Theological Quartely*, 44 (1977), pp. 288–289.

19 See Dupré, *The Other Dimension*, pp. 148–157, 222–242; L. M. Chauvet, *Symbole et sacrement: Une relecture sacramentelle de l'existence chrétienne*, Paris: Éd. du Cerf (Cogitatio Fidei, 144), 1987, pp. 11–162.

20 See K. Rahner, *More Recent Writings*, pp. 221–252.

21 This risk is also called "pure biblicism" by Ratzinger: "In other words, it soon becomes obvious that pure biblicism does not take us very far. One cannot get anywhere without 'hermeneutics,' that is, without a rational rethinking of the biblical data which may itself go beyond these data in its language and its systematic linkage of ideas." (Ratzinger, *op. cit.*, pp. 106–107)

22 Schillebeeckx, "The interpretation of Eschatology," p. 43.

23 *Ibid.*, pp. 43–44.

24 *Ibid.*, p. 44.

25 What Walter Vogels says regarding the feminist critique of this text is illustrative: "The feminist versus patriarchal debate over the reading of the text about who possesses superiority in the relationship of equality is unnecessary. At the beginning, the text speaks about the human being and then only at the end about the man and the woman. It does not consider either of the two to be superior. One can even say that equality is not a concern, for to speak of superiority or even equality belongs to the realm of rights and obligations. The text speaks, rather, of a relation between two beings, of their complementarity and, therefore, of their mutual love." (W. Vogels, *Nos origines: Genèse 1–11*, Ottawa: Novalis [L'horizon du croyant], 1992, p. 89)

26 See J. Delumeau, *History of Paradise: The Garden of Eden in Myth and Tradition* (M. O'Connell, trans.), Urbana: University of Illinois Press, 2000.

27 See L. Moreau, "Le paradis, notre espérance," in *Lumière et Vie*, XLVII/239 (1998), pp. 63–79.

28 See X. Thévenot, *Les péchés: Que peut-on en dire?* (2ⁿᵈ ed.), Mulhouse: Salvator, 1984, p. 39; W. Vogels, "'It is not Good that the 'Mensch' Should Be Alone: I Will Make Him/Her a Helper Fit for Him/Her' (Gn 2:18)," in *Église et Théologie*, 9/1 (1978), pp. 9–39; *Id.*, "'Her Man with Her' (Gn 3:6b)," in *Église et Théologie*, 28/2 (1997), pp. 147–160.

29 See *Original Sin: A Code of Fallibility*, in *Concilium*, 1 (2004), the whole thematic issue.

30 See Boros, "Some Thoughts on the Four Last Things," p. 38.

31 P. H. Hanson, "Prophetic and Apocalyptic Politics," in Braaten and Jenson (Eds.), *The Last Things*, p. 57.

LIFE BEYOND DEATH

32   Rowan A. Greer considers the book of Daniel as the watershed between the prophetic literature, which highlights the importance of hope in the present through the accomplishment of the kingdom of God in the life of believers, and apocalyptic. For him, "what is called apocalyptic developed out of prophecy; and the touchstone that marks the difference is the idea that hope will be fulfilled not in this world but in the age to come. The book of Daniel, which can be securely dated by its references to events in the second century before this era, represents the watershed between prophecy and apocalyptic." (Greer, *op. cit.*, pp. 18–19)

33   I will return to these books, 2 Maccabees and Daniel, in chapter 5, below. These are the first two biblical books that speak about the resurrection of the dead. At the same time, the book of Wisdom of Solomon, more or less contemporary with 2 Maccabees and Daniel, speaks about the immortality of the soul. We can already recognize the influence of the Hellenistic culture in this book, as I will highlight in chapters 5 and 10 below.

34   See C. E. Braaten, "The Recovery of Apocalyptic Imagination," in Braaten and Jenson (Eds.), *The Last Things*, p. 16.

35   Hanson, *op. cit.*, p. 59; see also p. 60.

36   Cote, *Lazarus! Come Out!*, p. 156.

37   See *ibid.*, pp. 7–11.

38   See *ibid.*, pp. 111–170.

39   Bauckham and Hart, *Hope against Hope*, p. xii; see also pp. 84–86.

40   Pope John Paul II, speaking to the pilgrims in Saint Peter's Square (Rome), on Thursday, July 22, 1999, defined heaven and hell not as physical places where one goes, but as "states of being" (see R. Owen, "Heaven a 'state of being,' not a place, Pope says," in *The Ottawa Citizen*, Friday, July 23, 1999, A1, A18).

41   Braaten, "The Recovery of Apocalyptic Imagination," in Braaten and Jenson (Eds.), *The Last Things*, p. 17.

42   See C. Dippel, "Liturgy in the World of the Sciences, Technology and Commerce," in *Concilium*, 2/7 (1971), pp. 100–108.

43   J. Llopis, "The Liturgy Celebrates God's Presence in the World and His Invitation to Man," in *Concilium*, 2/7 (1971), p. 122. This author also highlights the importance of the gratuitousness of God as celebrated in the liturgy: "The liturgy has to show very clearly that the God it celebrates is not one who is there to be 'used' for selfish ends, but one who should be 'enjoyed' in the gratuitousness of love; not the 'useful' God of deism, but the 'useless' God of faith. The liturgy should also be admitted to be 'useless', in that it 'serves' no practical purpose. At the same time, it is absolutely necessary, in that without it

Christians would lose sight of the gratuitous character of God's gift and of the essential freedom of faith." (*Ibid.*, pp. 123–124)

44   *Ibid.*, p. 129.

45   See W. Breuning, "Death and Resurrection in the Christian Message," in *Concilium*, 2/4 (1968), pp. 5–7.

46   It is then in an *analogical* sense that we will be able to understand the meaning of eschatological assertions such as the following: the punishments that will be inflicted on the "damned" in hell; the vision of God by the just in heaven; purgatory as a temporal purificatory intermediate state for those who are not good enough for rejoicing immediately after their death in the presence of God; purgatory, heaven and hell as "states of being" rather than as "physical places" where one goes; and the question of time and eternity.

47   See R. G. Cote, "God Sings in the Night: Ambiguity as an Invitation to Believe," in *Concilium*, 4 (1992), p. 95. In the last section of this article, Cote stresses the experience of ambiguity that the early Church had to confront regarding the delay of the *parousia* to which I have referred in chapter 2 (see *ibid.*, p. 104).

48   I borrowed the expression "the human experience of the divine" from the French title of the book of M. Meslin, *L'expérience humaine du divin: Fondements d'une anthropologie religieuse*, Paris: Éd. du Cerf (Cogitatio Fidei, 150), 1988.

LIFE BEYOND DEATH

PART TWO

Beyond Death in Light of Christian Faith and Church Tradition

In Part One I presented some basic presuppositions, or assumptions, that have influenced the way belief in life after death has been considered in the past, as well as those presuppositions that I think are essential for a better understanding of this belief in our present context. As Christians we belong to a religion with a particular credo. This credo is founded in the biblical heritage constantly interpreted by the Church, a heritage that speaks to us about the ultimate fulfillment of life.

The first thing we must take into account here is that the core of the Christian faith regarding the eschaton is to announce how God offers us life everlasting, that is, eternal salvation. Thus, the divine offer is not either salvation or damnation. From God always comes life, and the divine gift consists in living forever. Only human beings, because they are free, can actually separate themselves from this divine gift. God does not threaten us with the possibility of separation from God for all eternity.

The second important point to be considered here is the need to develop a more imaginative interpretation of the Christian faith as well as traditional Church teaching regarding our ultimate destiny. We have to use our imagination, as our sisters and brothers of the past did, in order to present in a creative manner the essence of the biblical message along with the dogmatic pronouncements of the Church on what lies beyond death. However, to be creative does not mean to be unfaithful to our credo. It involves, rather, interpreting creatively our Christian heritage in such a way that we may continue to present its deepest meaning to the faithful.

Finally, language used in speaking about ultimate realities is always analogical, provisional and limited. Even taking into consideration divine inspiration, biblical language remains the human expression of the divine. This realization should prevent us from falling into the temptation of biblicism, dogmatism and fundamentalism, whose adherents oftentimes consider themselves to be in possession of the whole truth, thereby running the risk of trying to impose their beliefs on others at any cost.

5

Heirs of a Great Promise

The God of our ancestors, the God of Abraham, of Isaac and of Jacob, is experienced as the God of life, as the one who liberates from all oppression. This has always been part of the content of our faith, as has been already highlighted in Part One above. Since it is only from God that life in its fullness comes to us, our choosing to be separated from God amounts to making a choice in favour of death. "To choose life means to choose God, to hold fast to God as a child does to its parents, who are the source and protectors of its life. The path of love is the path of blessing and life."[1] The promise of life in its fullness was the motivation giving hope to the people of Israel. This hope led them into the future.

Nonetheless, whoever lives in hope is confronted, today as yesterday, with the tragedies of existence: a human being, believer or not, ponders suffering and sadness, especially when they are inflicted upon innocent people, the righteous, or infants.[2]

As one is able to see in the Old Testament, the people of Israel believed in retribution, in divine justice: God gives to all persons according to their actions.[3] This retribution was to take place during one's earthly existence where, prior to the still to be developed faith in the resurrection of the dead, one possessed the sole possibility of an encounter with the God of life. However, experience sho⁀s—and this is the dramatic face of existence—the exact opposite on several occasions. The unjust, evil people and oppressors enjoy life while the poor, the believer, the righteous, the widow and the orphan suffer deprivation. This reality forces the believer to raise the following questions: Does God give to all according to their merits? Is this a just God? Is this truly a God of life?

This is the dramatic side of human experience of the past as well of the present. One must await a more explicit faith in the resurrection of the dead in the second century before Christ to be able to come to see the fulfillment of the divine justice, an accomplishment surpassing what was formerly understood in terms of retribution. The resurrection of the dead is a gift of God that reaches beyond the human condition marked by death and by a limited idea of divine justice.

In this chapter I shall address the promise of life and its fulfillment beyond death as reflected in the Old Testament. I will do this by travelling the route of the challenge which confronts the promise: the tragic side of human existence.

1. *Belief in Retribution in the Old Testament*

If life is the greatest and most marvellous gift that we have received, as was emphasized in chapter 1 above, then there is no attribute more appropriate to God than the one of life. That is why, when one speaks of the fulfillment of human life, one speaks of an eternal communion with the divine life.

Having already experienced the presence of God as bringing about liberation, the people of Israel do not feel abandoned. God is the defender of those in peril and the one to whom they cry:

> Happy are those whose help is the God of Jacob, whose hope is in the Lord their God, who made heaven and earth, the sea, and all that is in them; who keeps faith forever; who executes justice for the oppressed; who gives food to the hungry.
>
> The Lord sets the prisoners free; the Lord opens the eyes of the blind. The Lord lifts up those who are bowed down; the Lord loves the righteous. The Lord watches over the strangers; he upholds the orphan and the widow, but the way of the wicked he brings to ruin. (Ps. 146:5-9)

But God is not only the God of life. God is alive and actually transmits life. Living implies a communication with others enabling them to share the life that one lives. There is no prosperity or abun-

LIFE BEYOND DEATH

dance greater than that which comes from communion with God (Deut. 7:7-15; 8:7-10; 28:1-14). Communion with God "surpasses all the material aspects of hope."[4]

For Israel, a long life, its conservation and its enjoyment were great values since they signified communion with God. To live was more than to exist. Life was defined by one's rapport with God: to live meant to be in communion with God. That is why life was always seen as a dynamic reality. From this was born the desire to die in old age and to accomplish a fullness of years, because life is the gift *par excellence* of God (Deut. 5:16; 16:20; 30:19-20; Am. 5:4, 6, 14; Ezek. 18:23, 32). Life was synonymous with happiness, strength, security, well-being and health.

If living was understood as being in communion with God and others, if life was the gift *par excellence*, one can understand why death for the people of Israel was the fracturing of life, an absolute loneliness. However, the tragedy lay not in death itself but in dying young, in being deprived of the promise of God because "the hope of humanity remained dependent on the earthly life. . . . The greatest misfortune was to die prematurely 'without fullness of days.'"[5] And from this misfortune an apparent contradiction emerges: Where is divine justice? To understand the extent of this tragic contradiction, one must reflect on *Sheol* and on the idea of divine justice before undertaking any further examination of retribution considered in its collective dimension.

Sheol

For a long time, Israel perceived death as a door into mystery. After death one was going to end in *Sheol*, "where the shades lead a vaporous life, like a sad sleep (Dan. 12:2), enduring a miserable fate that is close to non-existence (Job 7:8-21)."[6] It was the place of the forgotten, the common destiny of all humanity, the place where life ended: the state with no difference between the righteous and the evil, the underworld, where "only the 'shades' existed (*refaim*: cf. Isa. 14:9: Ps. 88:11; etc.)."[7]

It was thus the place of darkness, the place without return: "As the cloud fades and vanishes, so those who go down to Shē'ōl do not come up" (Job 7:9; see also 10:21; 16:22; 2 Sam. 12:23). It is the place without differences: "I know that you will bring me to death, and to the house appointed for all living" (Job 30:23: see also Ezek. 32:20-32; Isa. 14:9-11). *Sheol* was also the place of the forgotten: "Are your wonders known in the darkness, or your saving help in the land of forgetfulness?" (Ps. 88:12; see also Eccl. 9:10; Job 14:2) where there is no longer rapport with God. "The dead do not praise the Lord, nor do any that go down into silence" (Ps. 115:17; see also 88:5-6). That is why one understands the need to hold on to life:

> For Shē'ōl cannot thank you, death cannot praise you; those who go down to the Pit cannot hope for your faithfulness. The living, the living, they thank you, as I do this day." (Isa. 38:18-19)

> But we [the living] will bless the Lord from this time on and forevermore. Praise the Lord! (Ps. 115:18)

Death was an eternal prison and *Sheol* a land without life. Between God and the dead there was an unbridgeable gap. For Israel, "the good death was one which follows the completion of a full life and leaves behind prosperous descendants while one goes to be interred with one's ancestors. . . . On the other hand, a death lacking these three criteria was a sign of damnation and thus entered within the theological field of sin and its retribution."[8]

Divine Justice

One of the most important aspects of the faith of Israel was its belief in divine justice: God is a just God who gives to all according to their merits (Ex. 34:6-7). There was a kind of almost mathematical relationship between sin and punishment, between righteousness and reward. Therefore, Adam and Eve were chastised for their sin (Gen. 3); Noah was saved because of his innocence (Gen. 7); Abraham's faith was rewarded (Gen. 15); but the corruption of Sodom and Gomorrah merited destruction (Gen. 19). Such retribution was to be considered in terms of earthly rewards and punishments.

However, reality did not always reflect the idea that Israel had about a just God.[9] There were adversities for which there seemed to be no justification: punishments, famines, and military defeats that occurred while Israel faced its enemies (2 Sam. 6:6-7; 1 Sam. 6:19; Gen. 41:25-32; Judg. 6:13).

One might hope to find an explanation to this tragic contradiction in the fact that Israel believed in collective retribution. In what did this form of retribution consist?

Collective Retribution

Before the Babylonian exile, the people of Israel as people seemed more important than the individual, whose value appeared to be conditioned by the community as such. Both rewards and punishments had a collective range. God rewarded the faithful, "yet by no means clearing the guilty, but visiting the iniquity of the parents upon the children and the children's children, to the third and the fourth generation" (Ex. 34:7). This idea of collective retribution was presented by the prophets prior to the exile, by certain prophets after the exile, such as Haggai and Joel, as well as by Deuteronomy, the book of Judges, the books of Kings and the books of Chronicles.

In this concept of retribution, rewards and punishments involved the whole people. There was also a correspondence between sin and punishment: "And it shall be like people, like priest; I will punish them for their ways, and repay them for their deeds" (Hos. 4:9). This correspondence also existed between one's acting well and being rewarded: "If you will only obey the Lord your God, by diligently observing all his commandments that I am commanding you today, the Lord your God will set you high above all the nations of the earth" (Deut. 28:1; see also 5:2-10; 8:18-20; 28; Am. 2:6-9, 13-16; 4:6-12; Hos. 8:3; Isa. 1:5; Mic. 3:10-12; Judg. 2:11-19; 3:7-8; 4:1-2; 6:1-6; 13:1; Joel 2:12-14; 1 Kings 11:1-13).

Despite everything, belief in the retributive justice of God broke down in this period with the growing realization that retribution did not seem to happen. The books of Kings present typical examples of this absence of retribution. Although what happened to Solomon is recognized as an example of the fulfillment of divine justice (1 Kings 11), there are others, righteous and faithful kings like Josiah (ca. 640–609 B.C.), who suffered calamities, and who died at the age of thirty-eight years (2 Kings 23:25, 29-30). There was also an evil king, Manasseh (ca. 687–642 B.C.), who was prosperous and reigned for fifty-five years (2 Kings 21:1-18). But in the cases of Josiah and Manasseh, the author of the books of Chronicles was forced to give a new interpretation in order to justify the traditional idea of retribution (2 Chr. 35:20-25 and 33:1-20). We thus face the obvious contradiction to the idea of divine retribution: there are good, righteous people who suffer and evil people who live long lives and prosper. Hope was up against life's painful realities. Is God therefore unfaithful to God's promise?

2. Hope Confronted with Life's Painful Realities

During the time when Israel believed in the collective dimension of retribution, it was simple to find a justification for divine justice: if we have not sinned, we nevertheless undergo consequences of the sins of our parents and our predecessors. However, with Israel's exile in Babylon we can see a breakdown in this belief. At this point one encounters a revolution in the idea of retribution, which was no longer considered so much as a collective but as an individual reality. Each one will receive, both for good and evil, according to one's personal conduct. A person is no longer responsible for the conduct of others or of their ancestors.

Along with the idea of individual retribution, the overall problem of divine justice gave rise to great anguish. Where before it had been simple to find a justification for the actions of God, one was now hampered by glaring contradictions taking place each passing day.

Individual Retribution

The idea of individual retribution was accentuated in the period of Jeremiah and Ezekiel, around the sixth century before Christ, a period coinciding with Israel's exile in Babylon, but it was a long time before the overall idea of collective retribution really started to

LIFE BEYOND DEATH

weaken. When it did start to falter, it did so especially with regard to the consequences of sins that were committed by others. The second book of Samuel[10] offers a typical example:

> When David saw the angel who was destroying the people, he said to the Lord, "I alone have sinned, and I alone have done wickedly; but these sheep, what have they done? Let your hand, I pray, be against me and against my father's house." (2 Sam. 24:17)

King David found it difficult to accept the infliction of punishment upon innocent people because of his own sin.

Abraham is also presented as having faced difficulty with that idea: How can God chastise the righteous because of the offences of those who are evil? We know the text from Genesis that shows him interceding before God after God told him about the destruction of Sodom and Gomorrah (Gen. 18:16-33). The refrain that appears in the mouth of Abraham is almost always the same:

> "Far be it from you to do such a thing, to slay the righteous with the wicked, so that the righteous fare as the wicked! Far be that from you! Shall not the Judge of all the earth do what is just?" (Gen. 18:25)

Abraham cannot accept that God would act in this way, that is to say, punishing righteous people along with those who are evil.

This breach in the traditional idea of retributive justice grew little by little, finally becoming, with Jeremiah and Ezekiel, a radical criticism of this belief. One must remember that this evolution occurs when there was an insistence on the importance of the individual person, and not solely on the importance of the people and on the community as a whole. Certainly, the exile in Babylon involved Israel's total loss of political influence as a nation, which was of great importance. In addition, there was the growth of the personal dimension of religion and one's relationship with God, which is strongly highlighted by Jeremiah. What became important was the personal relationship to God in the depths of one's very being and not solely the performance of rites. This was the heart of the new covenant (Jer. 31:31-34; see also Ezek. 36:23-28). The idea of personal retribution emerged from this, that is, that God bestows justice on each one according to the individual's conduct: "I the Lord test the mind and search the heart, to give to all according to their ways, according to the fruit of their doings" (Jer. 17:10).

The experience of the Babylonian exile played a decisive role. The feelings of community, of being the chosen people, of solidarity all disappeared. Suffering for the sins of others no longer made sense. Jeremiah and Ezekiel played an important role, for they began to approach the idea of individual retribution:

> In those days they shall no longer say: "The parents have eaten sour grapes, and the children's teeth are set on edge." But all shall die for their own sins; the teeth of everyone who eats sour grapes shall be set on edge. (Jer. 31:29-30)

> What do you mean by repeating this proverb concerning the land of Israel, "The parents have eaten sour grapes, and the children's teeth are set on edge"? As I live, says the Lord God, this proverb shall no more be used by you in Israel. Know that all lives are mine; the life of the parent as well as the life of the child is mine: it is only the person who sins that shall die. (Ezek. 18:2-4)

There was certainly an expectation of an earthly retribution in which each one would share in accordance with one's personal righteousness or evil. No one would carry the consequences of another's faults. The one who does good will live and the one who does evil will be punished, as is shown in a clear fashion in Ezekiel:

> Yet you say, "Why should not the son suffer for the iniquity of the father?" When the son has done what is lawful and right, and has been careful to observe all my statutes, he shall surely live. The person who sins shall die. A child shall not suffer for the iniquity of a parent, nor a parent suffer for the iniquity of a child; the righteousness of the righteous shall be his own, and the wickedness of the wicked shall be his own. (Ezek. 18:19-20)

Thus, questioning divine justice becomes inevitable and distress reaches its high point in light of the suffering of the innocent and

LIFE BEYOND DEATH

the persecution of the righteous. Once it becomes impossible to recognize divine justice in the midst of such distress, the question then arises: But where is God whose eyes are closed to the suffering of the innocent?

Conflict and Stress Resulting from the Absence of Personal Retribution

Although the people of Israel retained a firm belief in personal retribution, they still continued to measure God's justice within what seemed to be an almost mathematical structure. Yet they found that daily experience radically contradicted this model. All kinds of reasons were sought to justify the divine conduct. For example, faults may be unknown, or perhaps there will be a response from God in a short while. However, sooner or later, one was driven to the inevitable: God does not always appear to act justly. The best example is found in the book of Job. Here it would seem that life itself has no meaning. And so the conclusion at which Qoheleth (Ecclesiastes) arrives: it is necessary to know, during this life, how to gain the greatest profit.

a) "Yet a little while" (Ps. 37:10)

The prophet Jeremiah brought an end to the idea of retribution as it was known in his time, namely, retribution considered in terms of a kind of mathematical equation. He suffered because of his prophetic mission: "O Lord, you have enticed me, and I was enticed; you have overpowered me, and you have prevailed. I have become a laughingstock all day long; everyone mocks me" (Jer. 20:7; see also 20:8-18). God, in whom the prophet has placed his hope, seems not to be a just God:

> You will be in the right, O Lord, when I lay charges against you; but let me put my case to you. Why does the way of the guilty prosper? Why do all who are treacherous thrive? You plant them, and they take root; they grow and bring forth fruit; you are near in their mouths yet far from their hearts. But you, O Lord, know me; You see me and test me—my heart is with you. Pull them

out like sheep for the slaughter, and set them apart for the day of slaughter. (Jer. 12:1-3)

His suffering finds no justification. The evildoer lives very well: Why have you abandoned me, Lord? Jeremiah cries to a God who has apparently become mute. "Why is my pain unceasing, my wound incurable, refusing to be healed? Truly, you are to me like a deceitful brook, like waters that fall" (Jer. 15:18). The suffering of the innocent, the persecution of the righteous, which Jeremiah experiences in his own flesh, do not seem to find an explanation. God appears to be hiding: Is this a just God?

The experience of the prophet Jeremiah is echoed in other texts of the Old Testament, especially in the Psalms. The sight of evil people prospering scandalizes believers who are faithful to God and who maintain the idea of divine justice:

O Lord, how long shall the wicked, how long shall the wicked exult? They pour out their arrogant words; all the evildoers boast. They crush your people, O Lord, and afflict your heritage. They kill the widow and the stranger, they murder the orphan, and they say, "The Lord does not see; the God of Jacob does not perceive." (Ps. 94:3-7; see also Ps. 10; Mal. 3:13-15)

In view of this evidence, an agonizing question arises: Is it possible that the God of the promise has turned against the faithful who keep the covenant? Such a painful prospect may find an answer in the exhortation to be patient and to wait a little longer in order to be able to see the reign of divine justice. God will ultimately demonstrate his justice without any doubt:

Be still before the Lord, and wait patiently for him; do not fret over those who prosper in their way, over those who carry out evil devices. Refrain from anger, and forsake wrath. Do not fret—it leads only to evil. For the wicked shall be cut off, but those who wait for the Lord shall inherit the land. Yet a little while, and the wicked will be nor more; though you look diligently for their place, they will not be there. But the meek shall inherit the land, and delight themselves in abundant prosperity.

LIFE BEYOND DEATH

(Ps. 37:7-11; see also Prov. 2:21-22; 3:33; 10:27-32; 11:3-8; 29; Mal. 3:14-21; Hab. 1:13; 2:1-4)

However, this short wait produces nothing and God remains silent before the anguish of the oppressed. Each day's experience mocks any faith in divine justice. Anguish has arrived at its peak, as Job witnesses; in this situation, "how can one maintain hope?"[11]

b) The Suffering of the Innocent: Job

The book of Job[12] presents the problem of retribution in a most dramatic fashion. The author underlines the unbearable character of the suffering of the innocent, and it is in the light of this reality that Job revolts against God himself, whom he considers responsible for his misfortune: "He has kindled his wrath against me, and counts me as his adversary" (Job 19:11; see also 13:24; 30:21).

The central part of the book, Job 3–42:6, poses the question: Why must the righteous suffer while the evildoers continue to enjoy peace and prosperity? The problem is not expressed in an abstract, intellectual but in an existential way as part of a dialogue between Job and God about Job's experience. From this point of view, the question of the historicity of the book is completely secondary.

Job is a man of great virtue, a righteous man faithful to God, who suffers all sorts of misfortunes and adversities (Job 1–2).[13] The writer deals with the issue of *theodicy*, that is, the justification of God's conduct. If God is not responsible for unjust suffering, then it is necessary to find a response to the burning question of how to explain such suffering. The book unrolls as a drama in which three different groups of characters take part, namely, Job's friends, Job and God.[14]

Eliphaz of Theman, Bildad of Shuah, and Zophar of Naamath (Job 2:11), who make up the group of friends, represent the traditional thesis on retribution: suffering is the result of Job's evil actions even if he is not conscious of them.[15] Eliphaz says to him: "'Think now, who that was innocent ever perished? Or where were the upright cut off? As I have seen, those who plow iniquity and sow trouble reap the same. By the breath of God they perish, and by the blast of his anger they are consumed'" (Job 4:7-9; see also chapter

15). However, faced with the inadequacy of the first three friends' thesis, another friend, Elihu (Job 32–37), believes that he can go further: Suffering has a purifying, disciplinary value:

> "…, then he [God] opens their ears, and terrifies them with warnings, that he may turn them aside from their deeds, and keep them from pride, to spare their souls from the Pit, their lives from traversing the River. They are also chastened with pain upon their beds, and with continual strife in their bones, so that their lives loathe bread, and their appetites dainty food. Their flesh is so wasted away that it cannot be seen; and their bones, once invisible, now stick out. Their souls draw near the Pit, and their lives to those who bring death. Then, if there should be for one of them an angel, a mediator, one of a thousand, one who declares a person upright, and he is gracious to that person, and says, 'Deliver him from going down into the Pit; I have found a ransom; let his flesh become fresh with youth; let him return to the days of his youthful vigor.'" (Job 33:16-25)[16]

Job remains convinced of his innocence. This is why he regularly responds to his friends' interventions in an ever more violent manner until even God is called into question: "'When disaster brings sudden death, he mocks at the calamity of the innocent. The earth is given into the hand of the wicked; he covers the eyes of its judges—if it is not he, who then is it?'" (Job 9:23-24) In chapter 21, Job gives a description of the happiness of the wicked that fills him with horror (see especially Job 21:9-15), thus contradicting the thesis of retribution. He is persuaded of his own innocence and believes that he has been afflicted by God without cause. For this reason, he would like to be able to put God on trial even though that should prove to be impossible, "'For he is not a mortal, as I am, that I might answer him, that we should come to trial together'" (Job 9:32 see also chapter 31). Thus,

> Job's new theology [contrary to the retributionist theology] is that God is a monster, motivated by cruelty and spite, who has not only attacked the innocent Job, but is also guilty of negligence and injustice on a universal scale. Job has no doubt that there is a

LIFE BEYOND DEATH

god, for it is he who is wrongfully assaulting him; but he denies the goodness of that god.[17]

The universal dimension of suffering is emphasized in Job's discourses. Job is the representative of a humanity that undergoes every kind of affliction (Job 7:1, 6-7; 9:25-26; 14:1-12; 21:26; 25:6), the origin of which is attributed to God. Job thus revolts against God and questions God's strange behaviour:

> Why is light given to one in misery, and life to the bitter in soul, who long for death, but it does not come, and dig for it more than for hidden treasures; who rejoice exceedingly, and are glad when they find the grave? Why is light given to one who cannot see the way, whom God has fenced in? For my sighing comes like my bread, and my groanings are poured out like water. Truly the thing that I fear comes upon me, and what I dread befalls me. I am not at ease, nor am I quiet; I have no rest; but trouble comes. (Job 3:20-26; see also 7:17-21; 19:1-22)

Job continues to be certain of his own justice and innocence. In the end, he obtains what he wants: he makes God intervene (Job 38–41), the third actor in the drama.[18]

God intervenes without feeling obliged to do so. "Yahweh's speeches are famous for their refusal to address Job's questions. Their failure to respond to his problem is implicitly a refusal of the validity of his complaint."[19] Furthermore, not without a certain irony does he answer to the one who has interrogated him: "'Who is this that darkens counsel by words without knowledge? Gird up your loins like a man, I will question you, and you shall declare to me'" (Job 38:2-3). God shows Job his smallness before the grandeur of creation and the splendour of the divine majesty (Job 38:3–39:30). Little by little, Job recognizes the force of the divine intervention. Then revolt and fury give way to feelings of guilt:

> Then, Job answered the Lord: "See, I am of small account; what shall I answer you? I lay my hand on my mouth. I have spoken once, and I will not answer; twice, but will proceed no further." (Job 40:3-5)

The poem ends with a moving confession that is equivalent to a conversion. Job has encountered a God very different from the one presented by the thesis of retribution:

> Then Job answered the Lord: "I know that you can do all things, and that no purpose of yours can be thwarted. 'Who is this that hides counsel without knowledge?' Therefore I have uttered what I did not understand, things too wonderful for me, which I did not know. 'Hear, and I will speak; I will question you, and you declare to me.' I had heard of you by the hearing of the ear, but now my eye sees you; therefore I despise myself, and repent in dust and ashes." (Job 42:1-6)

The epilogue (Job 42:7-17), which links back to the prologue (Job 1–2), gives the impression of contradicting what has been affirmed in the poetic part of the book, that is to say, non-retribution for the righteous.

It seems to me that the importance of the book of Job does not lie in the theoretical responses that try to discover at what point divine justice seems indeed to be arbitrary. Rather, it helps us by making it possible for us progressively to discover God's grace and by aiding us to encounter a God who is different from the one presupposed and represented by a thesis of retribution that applies an almost mathematical idea of retributive justice to God.[20] Following Gustavo Gutiérrez, we can say that the key to interpreting the book of Job is found in this question:

> Can human beings have a disinterested faith in God—that is, can they believe in God without looking for rewards and fearing punishments? Even more specifically: Are human beings capable, in the midst of unjust suffering, of continuing to assert their faith in God and speak of God without expecting a return?[21]

This is the point at which the book of Job parts from the traditional thesis on retribution. In Job there is a break in the idea that we have about God. God regains God's own freedom.[22] We cannot understand God without letting ourselves be invaded by God. We cannot project onto God our sometimes very limited ideas and visions about justice. At bottom, God cannot be seized as an object.

LIFE BEYOND DEATH

Job's spiritual journey leads to meeting a different God. From this follows his conversion. Job's journey goes from the exterior to the interior. It leads him from the concept of a distant God to a God who can be met with the greatest unconditional giving and openness, without God feeling obliged to do so when and as we wish.[23]

Job takes a spiritual journey that leads to progressive detachment. Even if he perceives himself as being righteous, he must first detach himself from external things such as wealth and health. The detachment becomes more difficult when Job feels that he has to free himself from his very limited human idea of God as an administrator of justice. Yet, for Job, the most difficult detachment is from his own desire to justify himself. The marvellous thing is that, when Job renounces his certainty about his own righteousness, God appears to Job without in any way being obliged to do so, completely by grace. This is when Job confesses: "'I had heard of you by the hearing of the ear, but now my eye sees you'" (Job 42:5). If God gives something to Job, it is not because God feels obliged to do so, as the thesis of retribution would have it, but out of pure grace. Gustavo Gutiérrez says: "Job now understands that the world of justice must be located within the broad but demanding horizon of freedom that is formed by the gratuitousness of God's love."[24]

God does not give Job a theoretical answer. God becomes present in Job's life in a completely different way, and Job is capable of grasping this presence and letting himself be converted by it.[25]

c) Life Is a Deception: Qoheleth

If the author of the book of Job resents all the tragedy and contradictions that seem to revolve around of the problem of retribution, the author of Ecclesiastes (Qoheleth)[26] has already passed through this crisis and arrived at a practical conclusion filled with disillusionment: "There is no justice here below. However, he is not diverted from the faith; but he notes that all is vanity here below, from the perspective of death."[27] Life is a continuous deception: "Vanity of vanities, says the Teacher [Qoheleth], vanity of vanities! All is vanity. What do people gain from all the toil at which they toil under the sun?" (Eccl. 1:2-3; see also 1:4-11; 2:10-11)

One cannot speak of retribution toward the righteous and the evildoer. That is irrefutable: "What is crooked cannot be made straight, and what is lacking cannot be counted" (Eccl. 1:15; see also 8:1-14; 9:2-3, 11-16). *Sheol* is always the destination of everyone, and that is why "a living dog is better than a dead lion" (Eccl. 9:4; see also 3:18-21).

Qoheleth has arrived at a certain practical optimism: "There is nothing better for mortals than to eat and drink, and find enjoyment in their toil. This also, I saw, is from the hand of God" (Eccl. 2:24; see also 3:12; 5:17-19). As for life, it is best to seek the greatest profit:

> Go, eat your bread with enjoyment, and drink your wine with a merry heart; for God has long ago approved what you do. Let your garments always be white; do not let oil be lacking on your head. Enjoy life with the wife whom you love, all the days of your vain life that are given you under the sun. Whatever your hand finds to do, do with your might; for there is no work or thought or knowledge or wisdom in Shē'ōl, to which you are going. (Eccl. 9:7-10)

The wisdom of Qoheleth is that of a person strengthened by the difficulties of life, but who has endured as much good as evil. He could only endure the setbacks of his existence; otherwise he would have risked becoming totally embittered. All the same, he gives a lesson of relative calm in a situation where one is incapable of changing things.

3. Beginning of Faith in the Resurrection of the Dead

The problem of retribution could only find a solution when some in Israel came to believe in the resurrection of the dead. However, arriving at this solution took some time. A slow deepening of hope in God was needed. The people were unable to renounce their belief in God's faithfulness; that was a theological certainty.[28] One should never forget that "the Hellenistic wisdom and the apocalyptic literature had largely contributed to the definitive formulation of this faith which, in the New Testament, appears so

LIFE BEYOND DEATH

deeply rooted."[29] The wish to remain with God forever was finally realized in a faith in the resurrection of the dead which was much more than a simple answer to the problem of divine justice.

The Hope of Always Remaining Close to God (Ps. 16; 49; 73)

Israel was not able to forget that it had been formed by God, who had created humanity to become God's image and likeness (Gen. 1:26-27). The desire to live in communion with God was stronger than the experience of death. This desire is expressed in a particularly magnificent fashion in three Psalms: 16; 49 and 73.[30] The desire to live with God exceeds all constraints, difficulties and limits.

The author of Psalm 73 is confronted by the problem of retribution but, unlike Qoheleth, surmounts the crisis through faith in God's love in union with God:

> When my soul was embittered, when I was pricked in heart, I was stupid and ignorant; I was like a brute beast toward you. Nevertheless I am continually with you; you hold my right hand. You guide me with your counsel, and afterward you will receive me with honor. Whom have I in heaven but you? And there is nothing on earth that I desire other than you. My flesh and my heart may fail, but God is the strength of my heart and my portion forever. (Ps. 73:21-26)

God held out God's right hand (Ps. 73:23) and showed saving action and closeness. From this closeness came true liberation, a life-giving achievement. The faithful were able to take refuge in God: "But for me it is good to be near God; I have made the lord God my refuge, to tell of all your works" (Ps. 73:28). There is total faith in God who will not deliver the faithful to *Sheol* forever but will bring them close to God for all eternity.

The Resurrection of the Dead (Daniel, 2 Maccabees and Wisdom of Solomon)

The desire of communion forever with God is satisfied through faith in the resurrection of the dead. If God is a God of life, God is stronger than death. This faith arose at a time when Israel was the victim of an extreme cruelty. Therefore, this belief did not flow from an abstract reflection on the condition of the dead but rather was founded on the experience of suffering and persecution that was at the heart of the last centuries of the history of the people of the Bible, as is expressed by Rebic:

> The faith in the resurrection of the dead is a response to numerous events with which the Jews were confronted at the end of the Old Testament era (in particular the persecution of Antiochous IV Epiphanes [second century before Christ]). The biblical tradition meditated these events relying in the Yahwist school, progressing in such a way to the full certitude in the resurrection of the dead.[31]

If there is no retribution, why die as a martyr because of faith? Therein was born the conviction of faith in the resurrection: "The creating God, capable of forming life inside a woman, is also the God of re-creation, capable of definitely re-giving life."[32] This is the manner in which a mother speaks to her children, encouraging them to persevere in the faith, before martyrdom:

> The mother was especially admirable and worthy of honorable memory. Although she saw her seven sons perish within a single day, she bore it with good courage because of her hope in the Lord. She encouraged each of them in the language of their ancestors. Filled with a noble spirit, she reinforced her woman's reasoning with a man's courage, and said to them. "I do not know how you came into being in my womb. It was not I who gave you life and breath, nor I who set in order the elements within each of you. Therefore the Creator of the world, who shaped the beginning of humankind and devised the origin of all things, will in his mercy give life and breath back to you again, since you now forget yourselves for the sake of his laws." (2 Macc. 7:20-23; see also the entire chapter 7 and 12:38-46)

The experience of a saving and liberating God, which was the point of departure for theological reflection on creation, is also "the

LIFE BEYOND DEATH

fundamental principle of the development of the biblical faith in the resurrection."[33]

The author of the book of Daniel arrives at the same conclusion in presenting the resurrection of the dead as a definitive accomplishment of retribution, of divine justice:

> Many of those who sleep in the dust of the earth shall awake, some to everlasting life, and some to shame and everlasting contempt. Those who are wise shall shine like the brightness of the sky, and those who lead many to righteousness, like the stars forever and ever. (Dan. 12:2-3)

Sheol, the place common to all the dead, will be considered as a stage of transition awaiting the resurrection of the dead, before it finally becomes identified with hell.[34]

In another cultural context but during the same period, the book of Wisdom of Solomon, reflecting the Hellenistic culture, proclaims the same faith but in a different language when it speaks of the immortality of the soul (Wis. 3–5).

Life does not end with the experience of death; rather, it awaits a definite fulfillment in the resurrection of the dead. The gift of God awaits its fullness. God's justice surpasses all that human anticipation could accomplish.

⸕

The people of the Old Testament, marked by a tragic sense of life, took a long time to arrive at belief in the resurrection of the dead. They had to make the journey from the knowledge of a God who had become very distant and conceptual to the experience of the inner, free and gracious God that Job found.[35] Gustavo Gutiérrez has highlighted this very well in summarizing how Job's encounter with God can be compared to our own experience:

> God assails the pretended knowledge of Job and even more than that of his friends, who regard everything as foreseen and think they know for certain when and how God has punished sinners. What God is criticizing here is every theology that presumes to

pigeonhole the divine action in history and gives the illusory impression of knowing it in advance. The outlook God is rejecting is obviously the one that Job's theologian friends defend and, despite himself, Job shares at bottom. God will bring him to see that nothing, not even the world of justice, can shackle God; this is the very heart of the answer.[36]

God retains freedom even if human beings are always trying to appropriate it for themselves. For us, the mystery of divine freedom is unfathomable, but by that very fact it becomes a source of hope for all.[37] No horizon is ever closed. This conviction of faith is anchored in the God of life and not in humans' mathematically conceived and calculated idea of retribution. It is a certitude founded on pure grace and not on any obligation whatsoever on the part of God to enter into our all too human views of retributive justice. It is the experience of surrender to the love of God. As Gutiérrez says: "God's love, like all true love, operates in a world not of cause and effect but of freedom and gratuitousness."[38] Job experiences life and the free gift of love from God who is present in suffering. This is an experience for all times, yesterday and today.

The suffering of the righteous, the poor, and the abandoned is a cry of pain and revolt that we continue to address to God in whom we have placed our hope. Our God does not explain suffering, but is its first victim.[39] God in Jesus Christ reveals to us the only valid attitude to human suffering: compassion.[40]

This promise of life goes beyond the fragility of our existence scarred by the experience of death, and it will receive a new depth in Jesus Christ. In him, victory over death is not attached solely to the idea of divine justice and retribution. It is linked even more to the promise of eternal life as a gift surpassing all that we might deserve. The next chapter is dedicated to a reflection on the fulfillment of this life in Jesus Christ.

LIFE BEYOND DEATH

Notes to Chapter 5

1   G. Gutiérrez, *The God of Life* (M. J. O'Connell, trans.), Maryknoll: Orbis Books, 1991, p. 6.

2   In chapter 3 above, and particularly in its note 32, I referred to the problem of *theodicy*, that is, the justification of God in the face of all human tragedies and suffering.

3   For the study of retribution in the Old Testament, I follow, in particular, Ruíz de la Peña, *La otra dimensión*, pp. 63–101 and J. Alonso Díaz, "El 'más allá': Doctrina del Antiguo Testamento," in *Biblia y Fe*, 19 (1993), pp. 22–50.

4   P. Grelot, "Le cheminement de l'espérance," in *Catéchèse*, 124 (1991), p. 24; see also R. Muñoz, *Dieu: "J'ai vu la misère de mon peuple"* (S. de Unamuno, trans.) Paris: Éd. du Cerf (Libération. Économie, société, théologie), 1990, pp. 164–170; L. Boff, *Trinité et société* (F. Malley, trans.), Paris: Éd. du Cerf (Collection Libération, 5), 1990, pp. 146–151.

5   Sesboüé, *op. cit.*, p. 28.

6   *Ibid.*, pp. 27–28.

7   A. Rebic, "Foi en la résurrection dans l'Ancien Testament," in *Communio*, XV/1 (1990), pp. 17–18.

8   I. Chareire, "Croire à la résurrection des morts," in *Lumière et Vie*, 195 (1989), p. 63.

9   See Sesboüé, *op. cit.*, pp. 29–31.

10   The two books of Samuel were composed between the eighth and the sixth centuries before Christ.

11   Grelot, *op. cit.*, p. 25.

12   The author of the book of Job is unknown. He was a person tormented by the problem of retribution and he presents all of its ecumenical aspects. We can see that the author had quite broad experience and a highly developed sense of the beauty of nature. The exegetes divide the book into two parts: one part is in prose (chapters 1–2; 42:7-17) and the other is poetry (chapters 3:1–42:6). On the period of the composition of this book (around the fifth or fourth century before Christ), see J. Lévèque, *Job: Le livre et son message*, Paris: Éd. du Cerf (Cahier Évangile, 53), 1985, p. 6; G. Gutiérrez, *On Job: God-Talk and the Suffering of the Innocent* (M. J. O'Connel, trans.), Maryknoll: Orbis Books, 1987, p. 1, note 1; W. Vogels, "Job a parlé correctement: Une approche structurale du livre de Job," in *Nouvel Revue Théologique*, 102 (1980), pp. 835–852; *Id.*, *Job: L'homme qui a bien parlé de Dieu*, Paris: Éd. du Cerf (Lire la Bible, 104), 1995; J. P. Prévost, *Dire ou maudire sa souffrance? Les enjeux du livre de Job*, Montreal: Paulines (Déclic, 13), 1994; E. Tamez, "Job: 'Even when I cry out "Violence!" I am not answered,'"

in *Concilium*, 5 (1997), pp. 55–62; F. Mies, "Le livre de Job: De l'excès du mal à l'altérité du mal?" in *Nouvelle Revue Théologique*, 121/2 (1999), pp. 177–196.

13   See A. Kamp, "With or Without a Cause: Images of God and Man in Job 1–3," in *Concilium*, 4 (2004), pp. 9–17.

14   See D. J. A. Clines, "Job's God," in *Concilium*, 4 (2004), pp. 39–51.

15   See P. Van Hecke, "'But I, I would converse with the Almighty' (Job 13.3): Job and his Friends on God," in *Concilium*, 4 (2004), pp. 18–26.

16   "For Elihu," says Clines, "God is the Great Communicator or Educator. When there is suffering, one is not to ask, What has this person done to deserve such punishment?, but What lesson is to be learned?, What has God to say through this affliction? Affliction is intended not for punishment but for deliverance: 'He delivers the afflicted by their affliction, and opens their ears by their distress' ([Job] 36.15). Sometimes God uses dreams to warn people against committing sins they may be contemplating ([Job] 33.15–18); at other times he sends suffering for discipline, which lead, if rightly discerned, to deliverance for the sufferer ([Job] 33.19–28). . . . God's educational intentions are for the improvement of humanity, and the inculcation of a proper attitude towards him as their deity." (Clines, *op. cit.*, p. 43; see also p. 44) The purifying and disciplinary value of suffering is something that has been transmitted up to the present time in a kind of Christian spirituality which valorizes the offering of our suffering to God. Unfortunately, as a consequence, many of our brothers and sisters have been imbued with this concept of suffering and have been induced to undergo all sorts of ordeals, even the most unjust (see Martínez de Pisón, *Sin and Evil*, pp. 131–136; Bregman, *Death and Dying, Spirituality and Religions*, pp. 81–83; P. Wells, "La souffrance physique a-t-elle un sens?" in *La Revue Réformée*, 234/4 [2005], pp. 32–47).

17   Clines, *op. cit.*, p. 44.

18   See N. C. Habel, "The Verdict on/of God at the End of Job," in *Concilium*, 4 (2004), pp. 27–38.

19   Clines, *op. cit.*, p. 47.

20   See S. Ticciati, "Does Job Fear God for Naught?" in *Modern Theology*, 21/3 (2005), pp. 353–366.

21   Gutiérrez, *On Job*, p. 1.

22   See S. Wendel, "'We cannot fathom the Almighty.' Defining the Relationship between Transcendence and Immanence in the Light of 'Job's God,'" in *Concilium*, 4 (2004), pp. 52–66.

23   See E. Tamez, "From Father to the Needy to Brother of Jackals and Companion of Ostriches: A Meditation on Job," in *Concilium*, 4 (2004), pp. 103–111.

24   Gutiérrez, *On Job*, p. 16.

25   See H. Hëring, "Who is Responsible?," in *Concilium*, 4 (2004), pp. 67–82. Susannah Ticciati highlights the originality of the book of Job and the counter-cultural dimension that it represents for us in the importance given by its author to the process of conversion—as obedience to God, rather than to the result of it: "This is profoundly counter-cultural in a society which puts so much emphasis on the acquisition of knowledge as opposed to the learning of wisdom; on the finding of answers as opposed to a grappling with questions; on the achieving of goals rather than an enjoyment of the part leading to them; on the acquisition of commodities of all kinds (from stocks and shares to academic qualifications, from life-style accessories to 'transferable skills'); in sum, on anything that can be assessed, quantified and 'packaged'. This is precisely the problem with most 'theodicy' [the justification of God in the face of the problem of evil] approaches to the book of Job. For those who expect to come away from the book with an answer to the problem of evil, reading it can only bring disappointment. The process that is portrayed within the text requires of the reader a corresponding hermeneutic: that one enter into interaction with the text in a continual wrestling with it that never presumes to be able to 'sum it up' and replace it with a set of concepts. Rather than offering us new answers in this way, it leads us on a journey of transformation, disrupting even the way we construe the questions." (Ticciati, *op. cit.*, pp. 365–366; see also M. K. Martin and R. Martínez de Pisón, "From Knowledge to Wisdom: A New Challenge to the Educational Milieu with Implications for Religious Education," in *Religious Education*, 100/2 [2005], pp. 157–173)

26   Ecclesiastes (Qoheleth) was written around the third century before Christ when Palestine was under the influence of Alexandria and, therefore, infiltrated by Hellenistic culture (see W. Vogels, "Performance vaine et performance saine chez Qohélet," in *Nouvelle Revue Théologique*, 113 [1991], pp. 363–385; J. Ellul, *La raison d'être: Méditation sur l'Ecclésiaste*, Paris: Éd. du Seuil, 1987; J. J. Lavoie, *Qohélet: Une critique moderne de la Bible*, Montreal: Médispaul [Parole d'actualité, 2], 1995).

27   Grelot, *op. cit.*, p. 26.

28   See Chareire, *op. cit.*, p. 64.

29   Rebic, *op. cit.*, p. 14.

30   See Sesboüé, *op. cit.*, p. 37; Rebic, *op. cit.*, pp. 19–20.

31   Rebic, *op. cit.*, pp. 14–15.

32   Sesboüé, *op. cit.*, p. 34.

33   Rebic, *op. cit.*, p. 17.

34   See Sesboüé, *op. cit.*, p. 33.

35   Even in Jesus' time the traditional idea of retribution was shared by many, as the Gospel of John expresses in regard to the man blind from birth: "As

he walked along, he saw a man blind from birth. His disciples asked him, 'Rabbi, who sinned, this man or his parents, that he was born blind?' Jesus answered, 'Neither this man nor his parents sinned; he was born blind so that God's works might be revealed in him'" (Jn. 9:1-3).

36   Gutiérrez, *On Job*, p. 72; see also pp. 51–92.

37   See my article "La libertad (transcendencia) de Dios frente al fenómeno religioso contemporáneo," in *Nova et Vetera* XXIII/47 (1999), pp. 29–46.

38   Gutiérrez, *On Job*, p. 87.

39   See R. Martínez de Pisón, "Le Dieu qui est 'victime': Le problème du mal dans la pensée de Maurice Zundel," in *Science et Esprit*, XLIII/1 (1991), pp. 55–68.

40   See *id.*, *Sin and Evil*, pp. 158–165, 189–208.

6

A Promise Fulfilled in Jesus Christ

Jesus is the human face of God; in him a new covenant has been realized between God and humankind. He is also the one who gives the gift *par excellence* of life. His mission is to bring us to the fullness of that life: "The thief comes only to steal and kill and destroy. I came that they may have life, and have it abundantly"(Jn. 10:10). Jesus not only gives us life, he is life. In him is found access to God: "Jesus said to [Thomas], 'I am the way, and the truth, and the life. No one comes to the Father except through me. If you know me, you will know my Father also. From now on you do know him and have seen him'" (Jn. 14:6-7).

For Christians, by his incarnation, his life and his message, his death and his resurrection, Jesus Christ becomes the point of reference enabling us to understand the meaning of life and its achievement. In Jesus the kingdom of God is among us: the ultimate is already present in the world. This prevents us from losing interest in the present; through sharing our past we come together and share a certain solidarity with our brothers and sisters.

This promise of new life for each of us is still to be fulfilled. When complete, it will bring us a newness that can never be fully understood. Yet this newness is a gift from God, a fruit of the Spirit underlying all our actions and giving meaning both to humanity itself and to the transformation of the world. The journey we shall undertake in this chapter involves exploring this promise and its implications.

1. The Death and Resurrection of Jesus

The dialogue which God began with humanity in the Old Testament reached its complete fulfillment in Jesus Christ. One is able to read this in the Letter to the Hebrews:

> Long ago God spoke to our ancestors in many and various ways by the prophets, but in these last days he has spoken to us by a Son, whom he appointed heir of all things, through whom he also created the worlds. He is the reflection of God's glory and the exact imprint of God's very being, and he sustains all things by his powerful word. When he had made purification for sins, he sat down at the right hand of the Majesty on high, having become as much superior to angels as the name he has inherited is more excellent than theirs. (Heb. 1:1-4)

The Son is the ultimate word of God and all that precedes him is simply a preparation and a road leading to him. Furthermore, by faith in Jesus Christ we become sons and daughters of God:

> Now before faith came, we were imprisoned and guarded under the law until faith would be revealed. Therefore the law was our disciplinarian until Christ came, so that we might be justified by faith. But now that faith has come, we are no longer subject to a disciplinarian, for in Christ Jesus you are all children of God through faith. (Gal. 3:23-26)

Christians know who God is and who they are through Jesus Christ:

> In Christ's incarnation, death and resurrection (three immanent stages of one and the same mystery) God has accomplished and revealed his definitive act of salvation; the destiny of mankind and of the world to share with him in God's eternal life has been irrevocably established in Christ.[1]

The promise of life was given concrete expression already in the Old Testament under the name of the kingdom of God. The kingdom of God, as the fulfillment of life, stands in relationship with the good news, with pardon, peace, the abolition of sin and

LIFE BEYOND DEATH

death, and with the re-establishment of friendship between God and humankind, as reflected in Deutero-Isaiah (Isa. 40–55) and in certain Psalms (see, for example, Ps. 145:10-13).

In Jesus, the kingdom is made present among us. The Scriptures are fulfilled in him (Mt. 1:22; 2:15; 4:14; 8:17; 12:17; 13:35; 21:4) and he has declared that he came to fulfill the law and the prophets (Mt. 5:17; see also Lk. 4:16-21). The kingdom of God constitutes the essential element of Jesus' message, and its proclamation is the principal purpose of his public ministry. Jesus did not only preach the coming of the kingdom but also that it became present in himself. That is the essential message of the gospels (Lk. 11:20).[2] There is "a sense of urgency of the present moment. It does not take as its subject speculations about the where and when of space-time. At its heart stands the person of Jesus himself."[3]

Jesus announced the kingdom of God not only by his words, but also by signs, by marvellous acts of the merciful power of God: the miracles. This is indicated in his response to the questions of those sent to him by John the Baptist. Jesus replies by alluding to the prophet Isaiah (35:5-6):

> When John heard in prison what the Messiah was doing, he sent word by his disciples and said to him, "Are you the one who is to come, or are we to wait for another?" Jesus answered them, "Go and tell John what you hear and see: the blind receive their sight, the lame walk, the lepers are cleansed, the deaf hear, the dead are raised, and the poor have good new brought to them. And blessed is anyone who takes no offense at me." (Mt. 11:2-6)

The miracles do not take on the splendour hoped for by the prophets but, rather, acquire the familiar dimension desired by Jesus. I agree with Rowan A. Greer when he says that the presence of the kingdom of God cannot be exclusively identified in the ministry of Jesus with his performance of miracles:

> They are, indeed, ahead of time and can be regarded as inklings of the future Kingdom. But they are not normative here and now. The present Kingdom, then, is not triumphalist but is hidden and often found in poverty and suffering. Jesus' parables

draw this contrast between the humble, hidden present and the glorious, open future.[4]

The miracles are inseparable from the attitude of Jesus Christ: one who acts with authority (Mk. 1:21). The authority of Jesus is not linked with physical force or constraint; it is presented as liberty of action, as integrity in acting. His authority does not have any bond with the recognized authorities of his time.

With this symbol of the kingdom, God's salvation is presented as a reality. To accept salvation is to enter the kingdom; to refuse it is to see oneself excluded from the kingdom, to be plunged into great solitude. In principle, no one is excluded from participation in the kingdom of God or from its benefits. Such participation is God's gift to all with the grace of forgiveness (Mt. 20:1-16; Lk. 15:11-32). The only conditions for entry into the kingdom are conversion (Lk. 13:1-14) and faith (Mk. 1:15).[5] In addition, the presence of the kingdom is particularly manifested in the community of believers:

> More importantly, we find the presence of the Kingdom in Jesus and his band of followers. In other words it is in community that we find the Kingdom present. Those incorporated into this new community find a deliverance from their alienation in this world. This seems to me why there is such an emphasis in the New Testament on the poor, the sinful, and the outcast. People who had no real place to belong in their world for one reason or another find in the community of the Kingdom a belonging they had never known. The promise of the Kingdom, therefore, is a present reality as well as a hope oriented toward the future.[6]

Consequently, the kingdom of God will only attain its fullness in the future. The person and the work of Jesus presented the kingdom as the fulfillment of divine promises, but this kingdom can only attain its complete accomplishment later. In Jesus' preaching, the juxtaposition of the present and future kingdom leads up to his inaugural proclamation: divine sovereignty has penetrated the world and its victory is assured (see the Parable of the Sower: Mk. 4:1-9; the Parable of the Mustard Seed: Mk. 4:30-32). The continuity between an obscure though real beginning and a splendid ending is analogous to the process of seeding and harvesting. The fulfillment of the coming of the kingdom is brought about by a special action of divine power.[7]

Finally, as it is said in the Second Vatican Council in number 22 of the Pastoral Constitution on the Church in the Modern World (*Gaudium et Spes*), in Jesus Christ, human beings also find fulfillment:

> The truth is that only in the mystery of the incarnate Word does the mystery of man take on light. For Adam, the first man, was a figure of Him who was to come, namely, Christ the Lord. Christ, the final Adam, by the revelation of the mystery of the Father and His love, fully reveals man to man himself and makes his supreme calling clear. It is not surprising, then, that in Him all the aforementioned truths find their root and attain their crown.

> He who is "the image of the invisible God" (Col. 1:15), is Himself the perfect man. To the sons of Adam He restores the divine likeness which had been disfigured from the first sin onward. Since human nature as He assumed it was not annulled, by that very fact it has been raised up to a divine dignity in our respect too. For by His incarnation the Son of God has united Himself in some fashion with every man. He worked with human hands, He thought with a human mind, acted by human choice, and loved with a human heart. Born of the Virgin Mary, He has truly been made one of us, like us in all things except sin.

> As an innocent lamb He merited life for us by the free shedding of His own blood. In Him God reconciled us to Himself and among ourselves. From bondage to the devil and sin, He delivered us, so that each one of us can say with the Apostle: The Son of God "loved me and gave himself up for me" (Gal. 2:20). By suffering for us He not only provided us with an example for our imitation. He blazed a trail, and if we follow it, life and death are made holy and take on a new meaning.

> The Christian man, conformed to the likeness of that Son who is the firstborn of many brothers, receives "the first-fruits of the

Spirit" (Rom. 8:23) by which he becomes capable of discharging the new law of love. Through this Spirits, who is "the pledge of our inheritance" (Eph. 1:14), the whole man is renewed from within, even to the achievement of "the redemption of the body" (Rom. 8:23): "If the Spirit of him who raised Jesus from the dead dwells in you, then he who raised Jesus Christ from the dead will also bring to life your mortal bodies because of his Spirit who dwells in you" (Rom. 8:11).

Pressing upon the Christian, to be sure, are the need and the duty to battle against evil through manifold tribulations and even to suffer death. But, linked with the paschal mystery and patterned on the dying Christ, he will hasten forward to resurrection in the strength which comes from hope.

All this holds true not only for Christians, but for all men of good will in whose hearts grace works in an unseen way. For, since Christ died for all men, and since the ultimate vocation of man is in fact one, and divine, we ought to believe that the Holy Spirit in a manner known only to God offers to every man the possibility of being associated with this paschal mystery.

Such is the mystery of man, and it is a great one, as seen by believers in the light of Christian revelation. Through Christ and in Christ, the riddles of sorrow and death grow meaningful. Apart from His gospel, they overwhelm us. Christ has risen, destroying death by His death. He has lavished life upon us so that, as sons in the Son, we can cry out in the Spirit: Abba, Father!

The incarnation of Jesus Christ reveals the vocation of the human person and the deep meaning of that person's humanity. The fulfillment of God's promise in Jesus Christ brings us the most profound and complete revelation of our value: the call to be God's children through God's son Jesus Christ.

Jesus Reveals that, for God, Human Beings Are Equals to God

The God Jesus Christ reveals is a God present in life, a God who appears through a human transparence, a God indissolubly united

LIFE BEYOND DEATH

with the fact that one is both human and in the process of becoming free. On the cross, says Zundel, at the summit of redemption, having given himself fully for us, "Jesus has truly written, at the core of history, this prodigious equation: for God, *a human being = God.*"[8] This is the value of human beings before God. There is now no place for constraint, for defacement, but rather only for freedom because of the reciprocity of the gift, namely, of the love between God and humans taken individually or collectively.

Far from leading to a consideration of God as a restriction on the human person and that person's liberty, this view of Jesus Christ helps us to see that it is uniquely in becoming entirely oneself that the human person is able to encounter God who is always revealed through the transparence of the human person:

> Therefore, the God of whom I wish to speak is, always, Him to whom the Presence attests at the precise moment where my *human* existence warms as an outburst of love toward the infinite Gift who nourishes me as a gift. At the same moment, I exist in encountering God and I give myself to Him in becoming in act a person, a source of light, a real presence.[9]

In the relationship between God and a human being, God is far from being a rival who suppresses and restrains the human person and imposes God's own will. Rather, God and the human person find themselves on a mutual search, participating in the same experience of which Jesus Christ is the perfect realization. The death and the resurrection of the Son of God are the first fruits of a new life already at work in and around us.

Jesus' Death and His Resurrection: First Fruits of a New Life

Jesus' death, as the direct consequence of his condemnation as a false prophet, is not just another event tacked on to other things that normally happen. It might have been only that, had not several witnesses affirmed: the Crucified is living! From that moment, the confession of the Christian faith proclaims, according to the words received by Paul himself, that

Christ died for our sins in accordance with the scriptures, and that he was buried, and that he was raised on the third day in accordance with the scriptures, and that he appeared to Cephas, then to the twelve. Then he appeared to more than five hundred brothers and sisters at one time, most of whom are still alive, though some have died. Then he appeared to James, then to all the apostles. Last of all, as to one untimely born, he appeared also to me. (1 Cor. 15:3b-8)

From this experience, the apostles recognize more than a man in the life of Jesus and in his passion. They recognize in him the Christ, the Messiah in whom are accomplished God's promises to Israel. He who was condemned is living (Rom. 1:3-5; Phil. 2:6-11; Acts 2:22-40; 3: 12-26; 4:8-12; 5:29-32; 10:34-43; 13:15-41). God's promises are fulfilled in Jesus of Nazareth who became Lord and Christ by his exaltation to the right hand of God. "For the world as a whole, Jesus' resurrection [comprised also as exaltation and glorification] signifies a turning point, the beginning of something totally new that possesses ultimate validity. A new era has begun in which man is enabled to reach his full human potential."[10]

The resurrection of Jesus is God's victory over all the negativity of history and is also the full manifestation of God's love. With the resurrection of Jesus, God attests to the veracity of the work of Jesus Christ. Jesus' prayer on the cross was heard: the righteous, the innocent, the persecuted, the widows and orphans do not remain prisoners of death. Paul expressed this saving character of Jesus' resurrection when he used the term of *first fruits:* "But in fact Christ has been raised from the dead, the first fruits of those who have died. . . . But each in his own order: Christ the first fruits, then at his coming those who belong to Christ" (1 Cor. 15:20, 23). Death has come through a human being (1 Cor. 15:21), but in Christ all are risen, that is to say, they are led to a new life: "for as all die in Adam, so all will be made alive in Christ" (1 Cor. 15:22). The first fruits, in Paul's use of the term, are not gifts which humans offer to God, but the gift of God to humans. In saying that we "have the first fruits of the Spirit" (Rom. 8:23), Paul wishes to say that we will have everything, namely, that we are destined to a future

LIFE BEYOND DEATH

glory (Rom. 8:18-25). In the resurrection of Jesus Christ we have the first fruits of the resurrection of the dead, the beginning of a new life, of the ultimate life. In him we have been freed from the power of sin, from the law and from death. This freedom became a reality in life through the power of the Spirit of Christ.

A Liberation Present in History Through the Spirit of Christ

In the same way that the Holy Spirit was present in the life of Jesus of Nazareth from his conception (Lk. 1:35; Mt. 1:20) and accompanied him throughout his public life (baptism: Mk. 1:9-11; Mt. 3:13-17; Lk. 3:21-22; Jn. 1:32-34; beginning of public ministry: Lk. 4:18; Acts 4:27; 10:38), so with the resurrection of Jesus the Holy Spirit became the gift of Jesus *par excellence*. The gift of the Spirit is a consequence of the resurrection of Jesus (Jn. 20:22; Acts 2:1-4; 4:21; 10:40).

If in the Old Testament the Spirit was the gift of God announced for the end of time (Isa. 44:3; Ezek. 36:26-32; 37:14; 39:29; Joel 3:1-5), the fact that the Spirit is now given after Jesus' resurrection affirms that final salvation is already present (Acts 2:15-21). The end is already among us, even if its fulfillment has not yet come about. From Jesus Christ, and through him, an invitation comes to all of humanity to participate in a glorious life. This participation is made real in our lives by the Spirit of the risen Jesus:

> This destiny is interiorized in man during his earthly existence by the gift of the Holy Spirit, who calls him to share in God's life; the presence within man of the glorified Christ through his Spirit is his guarantee and foretaste of the resurrection to come (Rom. 5:5; 8:11, 14-17; 2 Cor. 1:22; 5:5): already man receives 'eternal life' from Christ (Jn. 3:36; 6:40; 10:10, 28; 1 Jn. 3:15).[11]

Leonardo Boff says, in citing a text of Irenaeus of Lyons (ca. 140–ca. 202), that the Son and the Spirit are the "two hands" through which God touches us and moulds us to God's image and likeness: "They were sent into the world to erect their tent among us, to assume our personal situation in view of our salvation and of our entering into the triune community."[12] The Son and the

Spirit opened the way to and made real the offer of final salvation from God.

2. A New Life In and Among Us

If the kingdom of God is already within and among us, human life becomes a parable of that which lies beyond death, a transparent reflection of the divine. Beginning with the death and the resurrection of Jesus and through the gift of the Spirit that comes from God and from the Son, all human life, in its individual and collective dimensions and through our action, creation, indeed, our expanded body, is called to become a transparent revelation of the ultimate, of a final something already at work in a hidden but real fashion in human history.

The question of what lies beyond death brings us back to our life here and now. Here, in our daily life, we are called to construct a life worthy of the human person, to foster solidarity among ourselves, to recreate our universe, so that it may become for us a sign of the presence of God. Briefly, we are called to overcome all the signs of death which at times sweep over us. Therefore, for Zundel, the essential question is not what will occur after death, but what we are accomplishing here in our life: "Is it reckless to conclude from these reflections that questioning what will happen after death is not the real problem, and that the true problem, for us, is what happens before death: what we decide to do to overcome death?"[13] The kingdom of God should blossom within our history and with our collaboration. We are called to make heaven a reality among ourselves, in our lives, for it is here that human dignity is violated, here that Jesus Christ continues to suffer his passion in the suffering of his brothers and sisters.

The call to become fully human does not consist in detachment from life. The beyond is realized in the here and now, and that is why our calling is to establish life as a transparent manifestation of God. If God gives to us through the signs of life, it is also by them that we give ourselves to God. As a result, we are called to live a spirituality entirely different from the one that might invite us to flee from the world. The divine calling to become fully alive can-

LIFE BEYOND DEATH

not be attained apart from and in relation to all of creation. Men and women have to rediscover creation's original and fundamental beauty and goodness beyond any dualistic and Manichaean world view that separates body from spirit, earth from heaven, and that assumes we are here to suffer. That is not the kind of life God invites us to share. Christian spirituality must be the manifestation of the deepest human desires and possibilities. "There is no longer any duality between time and eternity, nor between the visible and the invisible. All that is one, one in the unique Presence which is the Life of our Life."[14] Christians believe that the discovery of God is a liberating encounter[15] which helps them toward full personhood by enabling them to attain true interiority and transcendence. Only when women and men become fully themselves does God's revelation reach its summit.[16]

The human person becomes a transparent manifestation or reflection of the divine because, in the humanity of Jesus Christ, God is made present among us. The God whom Jesus Christ reveals to us, as we have seen above, is a God present in life and who is united to humanity for its liberation. Therein is found our grandeur, shown by our capacity to enter into a personal relationship with God through Jesus Christ. Our present life is, in consequence, destined to become a sacrament of what lies beyond it.

The Second Vatican Council, in number 39 of the Pastoral Constitution on the Church in the Modern World (*Gaudium et Spes*), reminds us of the presence of the kingdom already inaugurated within human activity. All that we believe to be good, beautiful, great and marvellous in life is called to endure until and in its final fulfillment:

> For after we have obeyed the Lord, and in His Spirit nurtured on earth the values of human dignity, brotherhood and freedom, and indeed all the good fruits of our nature and enterprise, we will find them again, but freed of stain, burnished and transfigured. This will be so when Christ hands over to the Father a kingdom eternal and universal: "a kingdom of truth and life, of holiness and grace, of justice, love and peace." [Preface of the Feast of Christ the King] On this earth that kingdom is already

present in mystery. When the Lord returns, it will be brought into full flower.

That which lies beyond death does not distract us or move us away from our present life. Rather, it roots us in the very life we are in. Eternal life is the final fulfillment and perfection of our present life, with all that it brings to us anew.

We Are Called to Become Creators

If that which is considered as lying beyond death is inserted into our present life by the death and resurrection of Jesus Christ and by the gift of his Spirit of Life, we are called to find a real fulfillment here and now, to be happy, in brief, to make real the calling to become the image and likeness of God (Gen. 1:26-27). Nevertheless, far from being a totally completed reality, a human being is always in the process of becoming. His or her completed reality is not given with nature, but has to be gained while becoming a person. He or she is to attain this highest potential, which is to become truly free, through the liberation of himself or herself in light of divine self-revelation. In addition, a human being is not locked up absolutely by any determinism. The spiritual dimension of the person, the refusal to be or become a robot, demonstrates the capacity to go beyond all the constraints and determinisms received at birth. A human being, becoming ever more fully a person, brings to the world a demand for liberty. This demand is inseparable from the overall process of becoming ever more fully human. Thus the human person becomes, while being free, open to the presence of others.

The kingdom of God coincides with the fulfillment of the human person and with the realization of that person's calling to become a creator of his or her own world, rather than a despiser of that world. In a beautiful text, Maurice Zundel says, while speaking of the kingdom, that

> the reign of God coincides with the reign of the person. The reign of God is, just as he teaches us, as Jesus shows us on his knees at the Washing of the feet, the reign of God, it is a human being who opens himself, a human being who consents, a human be-

ing who discovers within himself this marvelous space where he dialogues with a Presence until now unknown, who is going to place himself at the heart of a human being's intimacy revealing to him the extent and the power of his freedom.[17]

The call to freedom is a vocation intrinsically linked to our human development, to our personal growth in maturity. Freedom is rooted in the human capacity to become fully alive. This is why one of the greatest of human adventures is the acquisition of and growth in personal freedom. Human beings are not born free, but bring to the world a demand for freedom which is the result of a progressive liberation from all the external and internal constraints and fears:

> A person's freedom is not a *given*, does not find humanity in the cradle. The great error of the Declaration of the Rights of the Human Person, that was the prelude to the French revolution, is precisely the affirmation that human beings are born free. All that they bring to the world is a *possibility* and a *demand* for freedom. That is an attainment that calls for an entire life. This very acquisition constitutes all of our purpose, our only purpose: the duty of freedom.[18]

Freedom is the result of the recreation of oneself, the result of a liberating process that goes from outside to inside, and from inside to transcendence. If freedom is usually understood as a liberation from external constraints and submissiveness, as the capacity to do what we like, of not being obliged to do anything at all, we should not forget that despite the widespread nature of this primary attitude, there is another deeper dimension of freedom. This deeper dimension consists in not being a slave to oneself, in the liberation from all internal constraints and fears that keep us at the biological, animal level. Liberty is an internal dimension of the person, and not only an external concession. Yet, the liberation of oneself becomes possible only in the process of giving oneself to others and to the transcendent. Liberty, in terms of the possibility of not suffering anything, consists of giving of oneself to the other rather than to oneself. By giving oneself, the person ceases to be folded in on her- or himself and constrained by her or his determinisms. Freedom is something we receive, not from outside but within, at that interior level of the person where the person is identified with the gift of self to others.

The Gospel supports rather than restricts the quest for freedom. Consequently, it is urgent for all Christians to be able to demonstrate with their lives that the Gospel does not impose any limits on the most profound desires of human beings. On the contrary, it is precisely there, in the Gospel, that the inexhaustible source of liberation resides:

> The whole human grandeur is within ourselves. What is important for humanity is that each one may be the creator of an inner worth, the only true common good. All the richness of man is in man, provided man yields himself to the Presence inhabiting him. Our Lord himself knelt before this human grandeur. We can say that Jesus brings us back to man—for loving God must be a matter of course—and the last judgement will bear upon the material needs of the neighbour: "I was hungry and you gave me to eat. . ." The Gospel is thus centered on man because man is the Kingdom of God.[19]

The Gospel, far from imposing limits on the desire to be truly free, offers instead an inexhaustible source of liberation. Freedom and transcendence are not opposed; they exist in an intrinsic relationship. The experience of human freedom is not an impediment but, rather, an excellent way to experience the God of Jesus Christ. God is not a God who is external to human beings, opposed to their desire for liberation, but a liberating Presence. As a result, the experience of God implies an encounter with the self. God needs us in order to be able to manifest the divine presence, but there is a preliminary condition: we must free ourselves of all limits and become a person in order to become the transparent manifestation of God:

> God's self-manifestation, says Zundel, occurs in transparence, through a human experience, and this experience is perfect to the degree that the being is stripped. The great person is the

LIFE BEYOND DEATH

one who is not hooked to the self, but who gravitates around a Presence within and goes beyond oneself to others. The stripping that constitutes the greatness of God fulfils that of the human person. It is effectively impossible to discover God elsewhere than in the human phenomenon; it is through human experience that God is revealed.[20]

The freedom that constitutes the true and highest dimension of our existence, of our human experience, is equally an essential dimension of the God revealed by Jesus Christ. Thus, the newness that the revelation of Jesus Christ brings affects, first, the very perception of God: from a God who is perceived as an absolute monarch we pass to the manifestation of a Triune God, of a God who is pure Love, a Love that is pure gift to another. This is where we find the decisive turning point in the revelation of Jesus who speaks of the God who establishes a relationship not of dependence but of love and liberty with human beings.

Therefore, far from considering God as a constraint to human beings and their freedom, we need to realize that it is only by becoming fully oneself that one can have an experience of God. The divine presence always discloses itself through the transparency of human experience of freedom. As a result, if God and freedom are seen not in opposition but in solidarity with one another, if becoming an autonomous human being, responsible and free, is an extraordinary way of experiencing the liberating God of Jesus Christ, then human beings are themselves the hope of God. They are called to manifest God's presence through their own personal transformation in order that life becomes the transparent manifestation of God's love. Thus, God is neither a constraint nor a limit in our lives. On the contrary, the divine desire is that human beings, called to become God's image and likeness as well as to re-create the universe in accordance with this new call (Gen. 1:26-27), may attain their full splendour. In consequence, human beings are called to become God's cradle.

The first article of Zundel's creed can be the affirmation of a faith in humanity: "It is not so important to believe in God, but it is much more important to believe in humanity. Because in the name of God everything can be said. Jesus Christ, himself, was sentenced in the name of God!"[21] Therefore if men and women do not believe in themselves, if they are extraneous to themselves, God shall always be a distant divinity without any real importance in their lives. We are invited to believe in a God who is in solidarity with men and women: "Only when we can say from the core of our heart: *'I believe in the human person!'* will we be able to say authentically: *'I believe in God,'* since it is impossible to encounter God without making the discovery of the human person."[22] This is the centre of Jesus Christ's revelation: the inseparable solidarity between God and human greatness.[23]

Christian Hope:
Its Communitarian and Historical Dimensions

The communitarian and historical dimensions of the kingdom of God already present among us are essential characteristics of Christian hope. The person is a being who is open, not only to God but also to others and to the world. A human being is not a narcissist who contemplates himself or herself. The "other" is not an enemy whom I ought to repulse but rather one before whom I am able to recognize myself as human, as was the case with Adam, who recognized himself as human by the presence of another human being, Eve: "Then the man said, 'This at last is bone of my bones and flesh of my flesh'" (Gen. 2:23). Therefore,

> Human existence is more than just personal. As a member of the human community, each man is called to take part in the transformation of the world and in the creation of history. His existence is bound up with mankind's advance towards its future; thus the question of mankind's future affects the meaning of each individual's existence: humanity's future is mine as well. Modern man is increasingly more aware of his social projection into the future.[24]

Jesus Christ is the Saviour and the Lord (Acts 4:12; 10:36; Jn. 4:42; 12:32); he is the sole mediator of creation:

LIFE BEYOND DEATH

He is the image of the invisible God, the firstborn of all creation; for in him all things in heaven and on earth were created, things visible and invisible, whether thrones or dominions or rulers or powers—all things have been created through him and for him. He himself is before all things, and in him all things hold together. He is the head of the body, the church; he is the beginning, the firstborn from the dead, so that he might come to have first place in everything. For in him all the fullness of God was pleased to dwell, and through him God was pleased to reconcile to himself all things, whether on earth or in heaven, by making peace through the blood of his cross. (Col. 1:15-20; see also Jn. 1:1-4; 1 Cor. 8:6)

The revelation of God which Jesus manifested also has socio-historical implications. The personal liberation that opens us to God also implies an opening to others through whom we experience the divine Presence. The socio-historical implications deriving from the revelation of God are founded in the dignity of the person as manifest in Jesus Christ and in those with whom he is identified, particularly those most in need (Mt. 25:31-46). This dignity of the person is the common good which all society should protect. It is also the end purpose of right and of law: to protect and promote human dignity freed from external and internal limitations.

If humanization should accompany all dimensions of human activity, we are not allowed to forget that this dimension also embraces the relations of the person with the universe which itself is called, thanks to the mediation of a human being, to become a sign, a sacrament of the presence of God. There is not, therefore, a heaven without the earth: "Then the human race as well as the entire world, which is intimately related to man and achieves its purpose through him, will be perfectly re-established in Christ (cf. Eph. 1:10; Col. 1:20; 2 Pet. 3:10-13)."[25]

"No Heaven Without Earth"

From the first centuries on, Christianity was subjected to influence from the Greek world view which, especially in Platonism, presented a dualistic vision of the world with a tendency to deprecate material things. This had negative consequences for the biblical vision of creation and of human activity. The biblical vision was dimmed, if not forgotten and replaced, by a certain contempt of the world that was characteristic of much of early Christianity. Nature, time and evolution appeared to be devalued. Thus, one forgets the fact that creation was the very good work of God (Gen. 1:31).

Nevertheless, if there is one essential truth deriving from the Christian tradition, it is the privileged role of the person in creation (Gen. 1:26-28). Adam, according to Genesis 2:19-20, was to name things; he was responsible for the destiny of creation. Although the world was created for the benefit of humankind, this fact should not obscure the reality of human responsibility for the destruction of his own milieu. The abuse of liberty contains negative consequences, such as a loss of respect for nature. The human failure to assume appropriate responsibility toward nature has had very negative consequences, as no one can doubt. The ecological crisis of the modern world confronts us with a disastrous relationship between the person and creation.[26] This crisis challenges us in our own time to build a new covenant with creation.

It appears to me that at the basis of this new covenant of the person with creation there needs to lie a rediscovery of the cosmic dimension of human life. It is important to realize that the universe is our body, a body which we are not able to discard. The world is not a jail from which we must flee, as it was for many in the Greek world. We were created in solidarity with all other creatures of the cosmos. We are creatures of Planet Earth, our home, and it is very important not to forget that.[27] If the universe is our body, we have a duty toward it: to integrate it into our own human development, to act so that the universe, through us, becomes personalized. The invitation to live as the image and likeness of God includes important consequences for nature. We share our home, the Earth, with many other creatures with whom we are in solidarity. We must discover therefore our common "belonging" to the earth. This also means that we are responsible for the future of creation.[28]

God is the key to a world that does not yet fully exist. Yet, without the positive action of men and women toward creation,

LIFE BEYOND DEATH

this world will forever remain *in fieri*, that is, undeveloped. The final arrival of the kingdom of God awaits the liberation of human beings. This liberation is also required in order for creation to achieve its final accomplishment. Human work is one of the most beautiful expressions pointing to our responsibility for human liberation and care for creation. Work is not only a means of subsistence but is also an expression of the creative character of the human person. Human beings are invited to establish a new covenant with their natural milieu. That is why technology, an expression of human creativity, should always be used in a manner that respects the environment. Scientific progress cannot be separated from human development.

Only the development that recognizes the person holistically and integrates our encounter both with others and with creation itself can be said to be truly human. This situation allows us to become aware of the need to establish a new rapport, more global and less reductionist, between science and faith and, at the same time, of the need to attain the "naturalization" of the person, that is to say, his intrinsic link with nature.

Discovering that a human being is also a product of nature is part of our calling to become creatures of our world. That this essential dimension has been forgotten seems obvious: we need merely glance at our environment! Nevertheless, the biblical message of creation does not permit us to justify wastefulness. We are responsible for the face which the universe assumes.

Creation moves toward a completion founded in the self-realization of humanity. A romantic return to nature, divinizing it, forgets that nature is a creation of God. The human being, the only creature formed to become the image and likeness of God, is specifically called to make of nature an image of the image—to imprint the God's sovereignty upon creation, not to be its destroyer:

> For the creation waits with eager longing for the revealing of the children of God; for creation was subjected to futility, not of its own will but by the will of the one who subjected it, in hope that the creation itself will be set free from its bondage to decay and will obtain the freedom of the glory of the children of God.

We know that the whole creation has been groaning in labor pains until now; and not only the creation, but we ourselves, who have the first fruits of the Spirit, groan inwardly while we wait for adoption, the redemption of our bodies. (Rom. 8:19-23)

As is true for human beings, creation here does not appear as a reality already completed, behind us, but as a calling before us, as a challenge yet to be met, one arising from a proper solidarity existing between two partners: God and the person. Of course, the fulfillment of this calling is a gift of grace.

That which lies beyond death is therefore a fullness of life where we celebrate the ultimate victory over death and the transformation of the universe. It is a fullness already coming into being and actually being lived on earth even as this new life itself is calling us to a fullness yet to come.

3. On the Way to Fulfillment

We cannot over-emphasize an important point, namely, that the fulfillment of our faith regarding the final ends takes the form of a future already operating in the present, as was indicated in chapters 3 and 4. With this affirmation as an important point of departure, we are forced to admit that it is henceforth impossible to treat the Christian future as a reality disconnected from human history which is being written daily in the humble realities of our world.

The question of what lies beyond death draws us toward the circumstances of present-day life. Life makes me think of a musical work. The musician who is composing a symphony is not yet in a position at the stage of composition to know all the beauty and grandeur of his or her work. It is only at the end of the last movement that he or she sees the achievement, the fullness, the accomplished work. It is an accomplishment which surpasses all that he or she is able to know or imagine at the time of composing. The symphony achieved goes beyond all expectation; the achievement has brought about something new and unexpected. Nevertheless, one cannot say that the end, while it surpassed all expectations, has no connection to the process followed by the composer: the joys, the anticipation, the work, the setbacks, the tears, the sorrows, all that he or she had experienced play a role in the composition of the symphony and contribute to its completion.

Finally, Christians know that they are not solitary Titans or Don Quixotes who fight against giants. Within themselves and through their actions they are able to recognize the presence of the Spirit of God and of the Son, the action of grace. They believe that the fulfillment of life is also a gift of the Spirit, the action of grace which leads all effort to the total completion of those efforts.

Fulfillment and the Gift of the Holy Spirit

I have already indicated that a human being is not a solitary Titan. A human being recognizes the presence of God in the present as well as in the past. Grace accompanies and moves the history of humanity toward a transcendent future which is, at the same time, the fulfillment of our present, of our immanence. The full-achievement is not only the accomplishment of the person, but a gift of grace which makes us live the present in hope: "Thus it is God himself (Absolute Future, Future as Absolute Grace) who in giving himself to man brings mankind and its history towards their fulfilment."[29]

The Second Vatican Council, in number 45 of the Pastoral Constitution on the Church in the Modern World (*Gaudium et Spes*), reminds us of what is at the centre of Christian hope:

> The Lord is the goal of human history, the focal point of the longings of history and of civilization, the center of the human race, the joy of every heart, and the answer to all its yearnings. He it is whom the Father raised from the dead, lifted on high, and stationed at His right hand, making Him Judge of the living and the dead. Enlivened and united in His Spirit, we journey toward the consummation of human history, one which fully accords with the counsel of God's love: "To re-establish all things in Christ, both those in the heavens and those on the earth" (Eph. 1:10).

Grace, the gift of God to the person, the presence of the Spirit of Christ who leads history to its fulfillment, does not annul human action. On the contrary, it makes possible its fulfillment.

※

Eternal life is already present among us. "In the enduring love of God, man ('resurrected' man) is the union and summit of all nature, the highest expression of all cosmic relationships, of the world's total meaning."[30] The kingdom, or the sovereignty of God, also represents this final stage of a restoration or complete renovation of all things. That is why this kingdom incorporates in itself the overcoming of two limit situations, that is to say, death and the fullness of history. The resurrection of the dead and the promise of a renewed universe where the transformed human community will live constitute the achievement of our hope:

> Therefore, the promised restoration which we are awaiting has already begun in Christ, is carried forward in the mission of the Holy Spirit, and through Him continues in the Church. There we learn through faith the meaning, too, of our temporal life, as we perform, with hope of good things to come, the task committed to us in this world by the Father, and work out our salvation (cf. Phil. 2:12).[31]

This destiny of the person is interiorized during its earthly existence through the gift of the Holy Spirit who calls us to a life of communion with God. The presence of Christ, glorified by the Holy Spirit, is for each person a guarantee and an anticipation of the future resurrection. From this point on the person possesses the eternal life of Christ.

How can faith present the different dimensions of this achievement of the fullness of life which responds to our hope? The following chapters will endeavour to respond to this question.

LIFE BEYOND DEATH

Notes to Chapter 6

1 Alfaro, *op. cit.*, pp. 65–66.

2 See Greer, *op. cit.*, pp. 16–21.

3 Ratzinger, *op. cit.*, p. 30; see also pp. 24–45.

4 Greer, *op. cit.*, p. 23; see also pp. 24–26.

5 "The demand of the Kingdom," says Greer, "requires people to practice what they preach, but it also deepens and completes the old Law. Matthew's Sermon on the Mount [Mt. 5–7] is his way of explaining the new Law and the new righteousness and of articulating the demand of the Kingdom." (*Ibid.*, p. 26)

6 *Ibid.*, p. 26; see also Müller-Goldkuhle, *op. cit.*, pp. 26–27; Bauckham and Hart, *op. cit.*, pp. 159–173; Polkinghorne, *op. cit.*, pp. 80–82.

7 Greer described the tension between the present of the kingdom and its future accomplishment in the following terms: "The Kingdom of God, then, in Jesus' proclamation and teaching, at least as they are represented in the Synoptic Gospels, is both 'then' and 'now.' It lies in the future beyond the confines of this world order. And in this mode it represents a vision of what will be. All evils will disappear. There will no longer be war or violence, hunger and thirst, cold and nakedness. Weeping and sorrow will be no more. Death's reign will end. Moreover, the Kingdom yet to come will see a transformation of all the values held dear in this world. Power and wealth will count for nothing. Even the wisdom we think we have now will be transformed to the true wisdom of God. Jesus seems to have preached this vision primarily as a promise. To be sure, the threat of exclusion from the vision may still be part of the picture; but that is not where the emphasis lies. And we can also recognize that entering into this vision will mean hardship, anguish, and suffering. The end of the world will not be easy or pleasant. And waiting in this world for the vision to come will be attended by difficulty and persecution. . . . But the waiting and the hardship will find their reward in the fulfillment of the vision in the age to come." (Greer, *op. cit.*, p. 26)

8 M. Zundel, *The Inner Person: Finding God Within* (Retreat preached at the Vatican in 1972) (B. Zagolin, trans.), Sherbrooke: Médiaspaul, 1996, pp. 145–146.

9 *Id.*, "Le monde en sursis," in *Entretiens à Saint Séverin*, February, 1950, roneotyped document, p. 11.

10 A. Grabner-Haider, "The Biblical Understanding of 'Resurrection' and 'Glorification,'" in *Concilium*, 41 (1969), p. 72; see also pp. 69–76; Breuning, *op. cit.*, pp. 5–13.

11 Alfaro, *op. cit.*, p. 66.

12   Boff, *Trinité et société*, p. 37.

13   Zundel, "L'expérience de la mort," p. 23; see also pp. 18, 20–21.

14   *Id.*, *Wonder and Poverty*, p. 162.

15   See W. Barry, *Spiritual Direction and Encounter with God: A Theological Enquiry*, Wheaton: BridgePoint Book, 1992, pp. 27–28.

16   See Martínez de Pisón, "From Fear to Freedom," pp. 25–28.

17   M. Zundel, "Je crois en Dieu, parce que je crois en l'homme," in *Id.*, *Ton visage, ma lumière: 90 sermons inédits de Maurice Zundel (vol. 2)*, Paris: Desclée, 1989, pp. 48–49.

18   *Id.*, "Le respect des passions," in *La Vie Spirituelle*, 82 (1950), p. 599.

19   *Id.*, *Wonder and Poverty*, pp. 22–23.

20   *Id.*, "La clé du Royaume," in *Choisir*, 200–201 (1976), p. 6.

21   *Id.*, Unpublished text of 1954, quoted in M. Donzé, *L'humble présence: Inédits de Maurice Zundel (vol. 1)*, Geneva: Éd. Tricone (Buisson Ardent), 1985, pp. 15–16.

22   *Id.*, *Ton visage, ma lumière*, p. 49.

23   See Martínez de Pisón, "From Fear to Freedom," pp. 28–34.

24   Alfaro, *op. cit.*, p. 63. I have developed the importance of the future in chapter 3 above.

25   Second Vatican Council, Dogmatic Constitution on the Church (*Lumen Gentium*), n° 48.

26   I have noted in chapter 3 that the so-called ecological holocaust is also responsible for the overall decline of hope in an ultimate future.

27   See McFague, *The Body of God*, pp. 99–129.

28   See *ibid.*, pp. 1–25.

29   Alfaro, *op. cit.*, pp. 68–69.

30   Boros, "Some Thoughts on the Four Last Things," p. 42.

31   Second Vatican Council, Dogmatic Constitution on the Church (*Lumen Gentium*), n° 48.

7

Living with God Forever

The kingdom of God in its fullness represents the ultimate victory over sin and death, the acquisition of a happy and harmonious existence that is shared with others human beings and with creation. It is the fulfillment of our life in its relationship to God, namely, with what we have come to describe as heaven, paradise, or vision of God (beatific vision). Then, we will become in its totality the image and the likeness of God in Jesus Christ and the adopted children of God.

Essentially, heaven is the total achievement of the promise of God, already present in our life through the death and resurrection of Jesus Christ. This achievement will integrate in its complete flowering the resurrection of the dead, life everlasting, and the new creation, where humanity will live transformed into a beatific communion with God—what has been called the vision of God. We do not speak here of a chronological process but of multiple dimensions of one and the same reality.

The resurrection of the dead, eternal life and the transformation of all of creation are gifts *par excellence* from God. Thus, eternal life does not belong to the essence of being human which, as such, is mortal; resurrection and eternal life constitute an invitation that God offers us in Jesus Christ in order to participate in his divinity and to become God's adopted sons and daughters. It seems to me, therefore, that the resurrection is not simply a preamble to a final judgment. To make the resurrection of the body a condition for presenting one to the "tribunal" of God is not only to devalue the resurrection but also to ignore the profound theological meaning of the final judgment as the ultimate triumph of God over all the negative aspects of existence. The resurrection of the body is already the ultimate victory over death; one does not receive a revivified body but a glorified body, transfigured, transformed. To better understand the resurrection it is necessary to see it as a synonym for life in its fullness. In rising, we become participants of what is ultimate, eternal glory. We will then be a new humanity in a transformed creation.

This chapter presents this ultimate achievement of life as a gift of God: the resurrection, eternal life and the transformation of humanity within a renewed universe.

1. Resurrection of the Dead

The resurrection of the dead represents the greatest accomplishment of the kingdom of God. This reality, achieved through the death and resurrection of Jesus Christ, is already acting in us: this is the central message of the Gospel.

For Paul, the resurrection and the glorification of Jesus Christ are at the heart of Christian faith. Through his resurrection from the dead, Jesus Christ has become in fullness the Son of God and the Saviour: "Therefore God also highly exalted him and gave him the name that is above every name, so that at the name of Jesus every knee should bend, in heaven and on earth and under the earth, and every tongue should confess that Jesus Christ is Lord, to the glory of God the Father" (Phil. 2:9-11). Thus, the belief in Jesus Christ's death and resurrection is a condition for obtaining salvation from God, "because if you confess with your lips that Jesus is Lord and believe in your heart that God raised him from the dead, you will be saved" (Rom. 10:9).

The resurrection and the glorification of Jesus Christ provide the promise and the guarantee of our own resurrection. God, by the Spirit who lives in us, will create in us a new life (Rom. 8:11), and we will then be conformed to the glorious body of Jesus Christ (Phil. 3: 20-21). This is not only a promise but through our baptism the resurrection of Jesus Christ becomes an on-going reality in our life.

LIFE BEYOND DEATH

What Christ began ought to be continued in our history: he was the first to participate in the glory of God, and we are all invited to participate in it with him (Rom. 5:1-2; Jn. 17:22). Those who are ready to suffer with Christ, to share his existence with others, receive the hope of entering with him into the glory of God because, as Paul says, "I consider that the sufferings of this present time are not worth comparing with the glory about to be revealed to us" (Rom. 8:18).[1]

The new life, already a reality in our present existence, also represents the victory over sin leading to death:

> When this perishable body puts on imperishability, and this mortal body puts on immortality, then the saying that is written will be fulfilled: "Death has been swallowed up in victory." "Where, O death, is your victory? Where, O death, is your sting?" The sting of death is sin, and the power of sin is the law. But thanks be to God, who gives us the victory through our Lord Jesus Christ. (1 Cor. 15:54-57)

For Paul, if death is presented as an enemy of life, victory over death through the resurrection of Jesus Christ assures the establishment of life in its fullness. God is not a God of death but a God of life.

The resurrection of the dead is a dogma of faith defined by the magisterium of the Church in the Symbol of Constantinople (381) of the First General Council of Constantinople,[2] in the Pseudo Athanasian Symbol *Quicumque* (dating from around the fourth century),[3] and the Symbol of Lateran (1215) of the Fourth Lateran Council.[4]

The Gift of God Through the Resurrection of Jesus Christ

The resurrection of the dead is the gift of life in its fullness that God gives us through the resurrection of Jesus Christ. "With the resurrection of Jesus we arrive at the heart of the Christian message regarding the human being and his salvation."[5] The resurrection of Jesus is the most certain guarantee of our own resurrection: "[I]n fact Christ has been raised from the dead, the first fruits of those who have died" (1 Cor. 15:20).

Through Christ's resurrection, the reign of God triumphs over all creation; Christ has the splendour and the glory of God in its fullness (1 Cor. 2:8; 2 Cor. 4:4). What Christ has started must be carried on in the history of humanity. The first to attain the glory of God, he invites us all to participate in the same glory (Rom. 5:1-2). By the resurrection of the Lord, life in its fullness and glory is offered to all humans.

Even though Christ is risen, the possibility of creation coming to its true being still remains open. It is not just anyone's death that expands the resurrection; it is that Jesus gave his life for all human beings. The resurrection leads to a new life in those who accept an existence like his own. Christ continues to live bodily in those who risk living a freedom, an obedience and a love following that of Christ. In this way, we have a hope that people will develop fully their possibilities as creatures. This hope leads beyond the time of our passage on earth and is a call to live and not to perish. Such an experience permits us to find the road to our own fulfillment, a road which leads to God. Human existence will then consist in harmony and in self-growth. It will become the love of God made manifest in the existence of Jesus and awaiting its fullness. It gives rise to our own hope that all human life may generate the seed of plenitude in the mystery of God.

The resurrection and eternal life are not, therefore, uniquely things of the future. Since the resurrection and the glorification of Christ, the future in God is already given to us by anticipation. The bodily resurrection, as it will be highlighted in chapter 10 below, is already in development here and now, since the Spirit of God that has been given to us is acting within human beings, calling out for this new reality. This Spirit was given to those for whom God's love has become a reality:

With Christ's resurrection and glorification the anticipation of the future has begun. . . . In the same way, the glorification of the body is also anticipated, though the climax of God's glorification lies in the future (Rom. 5:2; 8:18). In Romans 8:30, and

LIFE BEYOND DEATH

nowhere else in his Letters, Paul tells us that God has already glorified those whom he has justified.[6]

To say that the ultimate began with Christ does not signify that a human being no longer has a responsibility for his or her own development and the transformation of the universe. On the contrary, we are called to become creatures of this new life already present among us: "Therefore, my beloved, be steadfast, immovable, always excelling in the work of the Lord, because you know that in the Lord your labor is not in vain" (1 Cor. 15:58). Accordingly, faith does not alienate Christians from the world in which they live but correctly places them in a life-situation from which they can bring about a new creation in the world. After the resurrection of Christ, everything positive in human history takes on a permanent value.

As God has not abandoned Jesus Christ to the power of death, neither will God abandon humankind to this power. What came to humanity through Christ had profoundly marked the community of his disciples. Jesus is the resurrection and the life (Jn. 11:25); those who follow his word will live (Jn. 5:25). Now to live, not to lose one's self, to have eternal life, all this refers to the resurrection on the last day (Jn. 6:39-40, 44). This resurrection to eternal life is in effect participation in the life of Jesus Christ: "'Those who eat my flesh and drink my blood have eternal life, and I will raise them up on the last day'" (Jn. 6:54).

We Are Already Risen in Christ by Baptism

Facing the refusal of the Greeks to accept the resurrection of the body, Paul presents the resurrection as a central theme of his good news of salvation. If Christ is not resurrected from the dead, our faith is in vain:

> Now if Christ is proclaimed as raised from the dead, how can some of you say there is no resurrection of the dead? If there is no resurrection of the dead, then Christ has not been raised, then our proclamation has been in vain and your faith has been in vain. We are even found to be misrepresenting God, because we testified of God that he raised Christ—whom he did not raise

if it is true that the dead are not raised. For if the dead are not raised, then Christ has not been raised. If Christ has not been raised, your faith is futile and you are still in your sins. Then those also who have died in Christ have perished. If for this life only we have hoped in Christ, we are of all people most to be pitied. (1 Cor. 15:12-19)

The most ancient text in this regard is that of 1 Thess. 4:13-18, where Paul speaks of the destiny of the dead at the hour of the return of the Lord. They will be joined with Christ, because he is risen from the dead:

> But we do not want you to be uninformed, brothers and sisters, about those who have died, so that you may not grieve as others do who have no hope. For since we believe that Jesus died and rose again, even so, through Jesus, God will bring with him those who have died. For this we declare to you by the word of the Lord, that we who are alive, who are left until the coming of the Lord, will by no means precede those who have died. For the Lord himself, with a cry of command, with the archangel's call and with the sound of God's trumpet, will descend from heaven, and the dead in Christ will rise first. Then we who are alive, who are left, will be caught up in the clouds together with them to meet the Lord in the air; and so we will be with the Lord forever. Therefore encourage one another with these words.

The central position on the resurrection in Pauline theology is, however, given in 1 Cor. 15 and in 2 Cor. 5:1-5.

The resurrection of Jesus Christ already has consequences for those who believe in him. For Paul, the key elements of the resurrection are actually found in baptism and in the return of Christ (*parousia*) at the end of time. Baptism is already a real beginning of the resurrection of Jesus Christ in us (Col. 2:12). Baptism moves us from our earthly lives into the dynamic of the death and resurrection of Jesus Christ:

> What then are we to say? Should we continue in sin in order that grace may abound? By no means! How can we who died to sin go on living in it? Do you not know that all of us who have

LIFE BEYOND DEATH

been baptized into Christ Jesus were baptized into his death? Therefore we have been buried with him by baptism into death, so that, just as Christ was raised from the dead by the glory of the Father, so we too might walk in newness of life.

For if we have been united with him in a death like his, we will certainly be united with him in a resurrection like his. We know that our old self was crucified with him so that the body of sin might be destroyed, and we might no longer be enslaved to sin. For whoever has died is freed from sin. But if we have died with Christ, we believe that we will also live with him. We know that Christ, being raised from the dead, will never die again; death no longer has dominion over him. The death he died, he died to sin, once for all; but the life he lives, he lives to God. So you also must consider yourselves dead to sin and alive to God in Christ Jesus.

Therefore, do not let sin exercise dominion in your mortal bodies, to make you obey their passions. No longer present your members to sin as instruments of wickedness, but present yourselves to God as those who have been brought from death to life, and present your members to God as instruments of righteousness. For sin will have no dominion over you, since you are not under law but under grace. (Rom. 6:1-14)

Since baptism, Christian existence is a process of assimilation to the life of Christ which the Holy Spirit realizes in us: "If the Spirit of him who raised Jesus from the dead dwells in you, he who raised Christ from the dead will give life to your mortal bodies also through his Spirit that dwells in you" (Rom. 8:11). The parallel between the resurrection of Christ and ours appears many times in Paul (see, for example, 1 Cor. 6:14; 2 Cor. 4:14; Col. 1:18).

But with what body will the dead be resurrected? It is a question to which Paul must respond, for his listeners are rather skeptical about the destiny assigned to the dead.

"I Believe in the Resurrection of the Body"

To speak of resurrection and of glorification (or of eternal life) is to admit that these two realities are to be taken into account. In this regard, it is important to consider the biblical perception of the person, in both the Old Testament and in the New, rather than to accept the dualistic definition of Hellenism.

Paul is one of the authors who speaks most of the person as an *united totality*. A human being does not have a body: *it is a body*. Human existence is embodied, either to accomplish good or to do evil. For Paul, a human being is, in body and in the body parts, a field of battle between the power of the resurrection of God and the power of death through sin. A human being has the double possibility of being closed off from others and isolated from communal activities, or to being open to others and accomplishing a community life with love. The body—that is, the entire person—must decide for God or against God, to live with brothers and sisters or without them. It is as a bodily being that we live out our history:

> The body of a human being is a bearer of a history, composed of many figures beginning with their infancy, moving to adolescence, to adulthood, and to old age. All the events of our history: the sicknesses and wounds of life, and also the love and the friendship, all are inscribed in our corporal being. Our body and flesh are not only a structure, but are history. To believe in the resurrection of the body is to believe that the living God is able to assume again not only our bodily structure as a human being, but also our human history which carries the mark of time and which is transported by our body.[7]

Paul continually emphasized the bodily dimension of the resurrection in the face of a powerful culture which despised physical creation. For him, even though there is a disproportion between our actual body and our risen body (1 Cor. 15:42-44), the same fundamental reality would exist although transformed and glorified. In the same way that there exists a mysterious continuity between the planting and the harvest, there is also a continuity between our body in its present state and the glorified body, lifted up by

LIFE BEYOND DEATH

God. Even though we do not understand how this is going to take place, we believe that "he who has the power of creation also has the power of re-creation."[8] Christ will transform our body into a glorious body like his own (Phil. 3: 21; Rom. 8: 23; Eph. 2:5-7, 10; 4:22-24; Col. 3:4).

For Paul, as I will underline further on in the last chapter below speaking about the difference between immortality of the soul and the resurrection of the body, the body has a communitarian connotation before its individual dimension, that is, it is through the body that we enter in relationship with others and with creation. As we are members of the body of Christ through baptism, and because through his death and his resurrection the body of Jesus is already risen, the risen body of Christ awaits its fullness until the moment individuals are able to come to the resurrection as members of that same body (1 Thess. 4:15-17; 1 Cor. 15: 20-28; Rom. 7:4; Eph. 1:20-23). Christ is the saviour of the body (Eph. 4:1-16).

In the middle of the first centuries of Christianity, the Church established a kind of parallel between our actual body and the risen body. But we must surmount the materiality of this affirmation in order to reach the reality which is enclosed there: the faith in the corporal dimension of the person, a created being; the affirmation of the goodness of the creation of God in the face of a culture that devalues matter.[9]

Faith in the resurrection of the body—in the resurrection of the flesh—became part of the belief in the God of life. It represents the triumph over all that is negative in existence. This resurrection has no similarity with a kind of revival of the body; it is a transformation, a birth to a new life, as if the centre of the person (that which constitutes human identity) remains identical. Just as we are unable to conceive ourselves outside of our corporeality, we cannot conceive an ultimate non-incarnated existence.

The resurrection of the body also represents a confirmation of the value of all created reality: "Faith in the resurrection of the flesh is in fact faith in the resurrection of the world."[10] Beginning with the death and the resurrection of Jesus Christ, "what we hope for beyond death is not to survive, but to be reborn with Christ to a profoundly new life."[11]

If it is through our body that we enter into a relationship with other human beings, with the rest of creation and with God, then it is also through our glorified body that we continue to be in relationship in the ultimate state of salvation. "It is through the body that we live, it is because of him that we will die, it is in him that we will rise. All of that, in and through the Spirit."[12] Thus it is a question of a personalized body,

> a body which made history, which listened and which spoke in the world of events. A body which has its own name, because God called it, and it responded to that call. A body which has its personal name, because it took its place in the world of social exchange, preceded by the word and speaking at his turn. The resurrection does not depersonalize: it fulfills the personal identity.[13]

It is impossible to conceive of a final covenant between divinity and humanity, as it was manifested in Jesus Christ, without the bodily dimension: "And so it is true that, for Christians, life is the resurrection, and that the resurrection is the body."[14]

The resurrection, therefore, represents the fulfillment of creation, the accomplishment of the divine invitation to become God's image and likeness (Gen. 1:26-27). This is how the fullness of eternal life will be manifested.

2. Heaven as Life Everlasting

As we have already seen above, since the Old Testament, life is an existence filled with the blessings of God. One can only enjoy its fullness by attaching oneself to the life of God in a relationship of intimate and constant friendship, as Moses oftentimes experienced (Ex. 33:12-23). On the threshold of the New Testament, the pious Israelite is convinced that the Lord will reward him or her (Wis. 5:15), that he or she will be raised to eternal life (Dan. 12:2; 2 Macc. 7:9, 14).

LIFE BEYOND DEATH

The kingdom of God carries with it the idea of surpassing the simple individualism of the blessing, and will awaken an understanding of eternal life as the triumphant presence of God which fills the entire creation with his majesty.

For Christians, eternal life is a relation and personal participation with Christ and, through him, with God (1 Jn. 1:3; 2:23-24). And so the terms kingdom of God, paradise, heaven, beatific vision, eternal life, can be defined as being-with-Christ in a form of ultimate existence. It is the total reconciliation of human beings with themselves and with the universe, and of the cosmos with itself.[15] The fulfillment of beatitude is the heart of the Christian message:

> And I heard a loud voice from the throne saying, "See, the home of God is among mortals. He will dwell with them as their God; they will be his peoples, and God himself will be with them; he will wipe every tear from their eyes. Death will be no more; mourning and crying and pain will be no more, for the first things have passed away." (Rev. 21:3-4; see also verse 23)

Then the calling of humanity to become the image and likeness of God will be accomplished (Gen. 1:26-27).

It is not correct to oppose eternal life—heaven—to this world. Rather, one should see it as the fulfillment of this world, where we will be freed from everything that limits us, from all that wounds us, and from all that divides us. Such a faith does not alienate us from our present, but it enables us to transform it. As Cardinal Ratzinger said,

> Heaven, therefore, must first and foremost be determined christologically. It is not an extra-historical place into which one goes. Heaven's existence depends upon the fact that Jesus Christ, as God, is man, and makes space for human existence in the existence of God himself. One is in heaven when, and to the degree, that one is in Christ. It is by being with Christ that we find the true location of our existence as human beings in God.[16]

Eternal life, as the fulfillment of our faith, includes the vision of God, the ultimate communion with God through Jesus Christ;

but this communion with God implies also a perfect communion among ourselves, the fulfillment of a transformed humanity in a new heaven and new earth.

The Vision of God

Seeing God, in the Old Testament, designates an existential experience. It is the experience that Job had at the end of his spiritual journey, as noted in chapter 5 above, where Job is led to reject a too limited idea of God and was able to see God, that is to say, to encounter God in an existential way: "I had heard of you by the hearing of the ear, but now my eye sees you" (Job 42:5).

The New Testament will use also the expression to see God to speak of the existential content of the transfigured life: "Blessed are the pure in heart, for they will see God"(Mt. 5:8; see also 1 Jn. 3:2). As in the Old Testament, the vision of God is perceived on the horizon of the expectation of the kingdom of God: the expectation of participating in this divine life, of living in his presence. It is, therefore, a personal participation with Christ and, through him, with God (1 Jn. 1:3; 2:23-24). Briefly, it is an existential communion which is brought about through the participation of life in Christ. This participation comes from God where its fullness is only found and communicated in the Son (Col. 2:9; Jn. 1:14, 16-17).

Before the Second Vatican Council, in the last century, the vision of God was conceived in a theocentric way rather than in a christocentric one, by interpreting the vision in an intellectual rather than existential manner.[17] Nevertheless, the Second Vatican Council's Dogmatic Constitution on the Church (*Lumen Gentium*), in numbers 48-51, works with the biblical sense of the vision of God in a manner which is more existential. There is no other way of attaining the vision of God except by the vision (participation) of God in the man Jesus: "Philip said to him, 'Lord, show us the Father, and we will be satisfied.' Jesus said to him, 'Have I been with you all this time, Philip, and you still do not know me? Whoever has seen me has seen the father'" (Jn. 14:8-9).[18] In summary, as Schoonenberg highlights, speaking about the vision of God, "It is therefore an interpersonal communion with God [through Jesus Christ] which must be expressed just as strongly in terms of love.

LIFE BEYOND DEATH

And so, this vision and this communion in love cannot exclude the creation and certainly not our fellow human being."[19]

Personal communion with Christ is personal communion with the Son. Yet the Son has a fundamental and exclusive relationship with God and the Spirit. Therefore, our personal and immediate relationship with him brings us, at the same time and through him, to an immediate relationship with God and the Spirit who, in their turn, are in a relationship with the Son.

This eternal life will preserve and bring to perfection the social and earthly character of the person. To be in communion with God through the Son and the Spirit implies also living in communion with a transfigured humanity.

Transfigured Humanity

If the resurrection is the manifestation of the fullness of life, the people of God are the recipients of this fullness. All those who are open to the action of God share in the resurrection of Jesus Christ. Only when the last of the predestined are configured to the image of Christ, who is the Lord of God's people (Rom. 8:29), will they reach their final form. The people of God, entered into glory through the resurrection of Christ, will then be shown as the people of Christ, acquired through the death and the resurrection of the Lord.

As the ultimate symbol of eternal life, a transfigured humanity has already begun to experience this fullness, although its effective and total consummation will take place only through the resurrection of the dead and the transformation of humanity.

The death and resurrection of Jesus Christ are also the foundation of the new humanity, even though while the earthly world lasts there will be a kind of veil over the community of human beings united with Christ, just as over the community of life founded on Christ.

In our history and in its full flowering, the Holy Spirit perfects the transformation initiated by Christ. The heavenly community is, therefore, a community where the Holy Spirit is not only present but active.

A symbol that accurately portrays a transfigured humanity is the image of the heavenly city, the new Jerusalem:

> Then I saw a new heaven and a new earth; for the first heaven and the first earth had passed away, and the sea was no more. And I saw the holy city, the new Jerusalem, coming down out of heaven from God, prepared as a bride adorned for her husband. And I heard a loud voice from the throne saying, "See, the home of God is among mortals. He will dwell with them as their God; they will be his peoples, and God himself will be with them; he will wipe every tear from their eyes. Death will be no more; mourning and crying and pain will be no more, for the first things have passed away." And the one who was seated on the throne said, "See, I am making all things new." Also he said, "Write this, for these words are trustworthy and true." Then he said to me, "It is done! I am the Alpha and the Omega, the beginning and the end. To the thirsty I will give water as a gift from the spring of the water of life. Those who conquer will inherit these things, and I will be their God and they will be my children. But as for the cowardly, the faithless, the polluted, the murderers, the fornicators, the sorcerers, the idolaters, and all liars, their place will be in the lake that burns with fire and sulfur, which is the second death." (Rev. 21:1-8; see also verses 9-27; Eph. 2:19; Heb. 12:22-24)

In the heavenly city, we are the full image and likeness of God in Jesus Christ.

Becoming the Image and the Likeness of God in Jesus Christ

The human being, drawn from the earth, created in solidarity with the rest of creation, is invited to respond to the call, written in the depth of one's being, to become the image and likeness of God (Gen. 1: 26-27). In all creation, only human beings are called to resemble God. That is to say that only they are capable of transcending the present, of opening themselves to what is beyond their own destiny, briefly, to become free from all external and internal constraints. That is the essential vocation of the person.

LIFE BEYOND DEATH

Recall the prohibition given to the Old Testament people against making images of God: "You shall not make for yourself an idol, whether in the form of anything that is in heaven above, or that is on the earth beneath, or that is in the water under the earth" (Ex. 20:4). This is rooted in the calling that humans received from God: only humans are able to become the living image of God. Nonetheless, we know that the image *par excellence* and the perfect resemblance to God is Jesus Christ (Col. 1:15; Heb. 1: 23). The mystery of the person finds in Jesus Christ, the image of God, its final realization (Rom. 8:29; 2 Cor. 3:18). That is the ultimate calling of the person:

> The human being, incorporated in Christ by baptism, becomes the image of God. As such, he has a responsibility to make this image into a full likeness of God and to find, under the inspiration and fire of the Spirit, a personal, yet unique manner of his being one in Christ.[20]

Thus it is that a human being becomes another God, sharing in the community of the Trinity; having finally arrived at the fulfillment of ultimate connection with God who was not only creator but who wished to become a partner, an ally, a father, a mother, a brother and a friend.

Now the fullness of humanity is shown also in the fullness of all of creation. This relationship is established in the social dimension of human beings as well as in their action in the world. The life of the person is a life in the world and with the world. This unity has numerous and profound relationships.

3. "See, I am making all things new" (Rev. 21:5)

Christ is the source of the transformation of the world. Acting within the world, Christ acts through the Holy Spirit, to bring the world to its fullness. Through him creation will be freed from corruption. Just as creation was incorporated in the sinful history of the human being, it will now be incorporated in the salvation history of the person (Col. 1:13-17; Rom. 8:19-23). "It is the universe in its totality which is called to enter into the eternity of God, to become the Kingdom of God, 'a new heaven and a new earth.'"[21]

The Second Vatican Council, in number 39 of the Pastoral Constitution on the Church in the Modern World (*Gaudium et Spes*), has proclaimed the faith received from the apostles in a new earth and a new heaven. That is an essential dimension of faith which was overlooked with the passing of centuries because of an exaggerated insistence on the contempt of the world, an emphasis that caused many ravages and gave the impression that we have only a soul which needs to be saved. However, as the Church said:

> We do not know the time for the consummation of the earth and of humanity. Nor do we know how all things will be transformed. As deformed by sin, the shape of this world will pass away. But we are taught that God is preparing a new dwelling place and a new earth where justice will abide, and whose blessedness will answer and surpass all the longings for peace which spring up in the human heart.
>
> Then, with death overcome, the sons of God will be raised up in Christ. What was sown in weakness and corruption will be clothed with incorruptibility. While charity and its fruits endure, all that creation which God made on man's account will be unchained from the bondage of vanity.
>
> Even though Christ is the foundation of this transformation, human beings should not passively contemplate the building of this new creation. They are the active agents of this re-creation, even though its fullness is at the same time a grace.

Creation is a history of two where we are engaged as partners with God. Thus, creation does not only refer to a forgotten past, but it is also, in our present, called to be new creation, which will become the image of the image. Yet while arriving at its fulfillment as the image and likeness of God in Jesus Christ, the person is not able to lose his or her dimension as a creature. The new being needs a new earth. Transfigured humanity, the renewed people, will dwell in a transformed earth. The earth, thus transformed, will have its

LIFE BEYOND DEATH

own consistency, its power and its beauty; it will be configured to the image of the glorious body of Christ.

Creation: A History of Two

God did not create robots, but men and women called to become free and to be co-creators of a world which does not yet exist and which cannot exist without us because it "is a human being, with his freedom, who is the performer of his history."[22]

The person does not dwell in a universe already made, completed, and fulfilled. Creation is a continuing process which awaits the liberation of the children of God and, through it, to become free of all its limits (Rom. 8:19-22). Human beings are, therefore, partners with God in the creation of their universe, "of a universe which, essentially, is not yet finished, of a universe which has not yet attained its true dimensions, of a universe until now still embryonic."[23]

Creation is neither the fruit of a magic gesture by God nor a fabrication: it is the gift of God's love. This gift, as such, forever demands reciprocity. However, in this reciprocity a gift is offered that can also be refused. This is why freedom is the axis of this universe centred on the spirit:

> The divine creation implies, for us, the supreme actualization of our freedom, since it is constituted, finally, as a history of two, by a pure relationship of love, which excludes a subservient domination as much as a despotic possession: in the fuzzy reciprocity where our poverty is exchanged with the divine Poverty, to which the universe, through us, is suspended: like a home fashioned by love and for love.[24]

We are responsible for the face which the universe will take. That is why a human being is called to be aware of his vocation as creator. The universe is always before us: "the true God will only be known at the moment when this true creation will be accomplished,"[25] that is to say, when human beings will have acquired their freedom. Thus, according to Zundel, "creation begins today in the measure that we accept the golden ring of the eternal betrothal!"[26]

The New Creation

If creation is a history of two, if it is always before the person as a possibility, then the new creation is always to be realized. It invites us to look ahead and will be the fruit of the solidarity between the person and God.

The announcement of a new creation exists already in the Old Testament. The experience of a saving God, both in the Old Testament and in the New, was the point of departure for all biblical reflection. The people of Israel reflected on creation in beginning the experience of liberation. God is not a rival, an enemy who crushes and who should be discarded. For Israel, to have a relationship with the Other, to be dependent on God, is to receive life in all its fullness. As indicated in chapter 1 above, this liberating experience (from the oppression of Egypt) constitutes the centre of the creed of Israel (Deut. 26: 5-9; 6:20-23; Josh. 24). This is also the reason why, when Israel underwent the exile to Babylon, around the sixth century before Christ, Deutero-Isaiah replaced the theme of creation with the new creation, the final salvation. For Deutero-Isaiah, one did not understand creation by looking to the past but in looking ahead, with eyes fixed on the ultimate salvation promised by God (Isa. 40:3; 41:17-21; 43:18-29; 45:20, 24; 65:17-25). The people awaited a new creation which God promised to them in a future coming.

In the same way that Israel reflects on the salvation-creation rapport as part of the concrete experience of history, an experience of liberation, the first Christians reflected on the rapport of a salvation-new creation through the death and the resurrection of Jesus Christ. There will be a new heaven and a new earth which awaits us according to his promise, where justice will dwell (2 Pet. 3:13; see also Rom. 8:19-23; Rev. 21). In summary,

> Resurrection hope is radical faith in the God who remains faithful to his material and mortal creation, valuing it too much to let it perish. Christian resurrection hope is radical faith in the God

who became incarnate in material and mortal human nature, setting the seal of his own presence on its eternal value for him. Christian resurrection hope is radical faith in the God who raised Jesus from death, thereby pledging himself to raise also those who believe in Jesus.[27]

The redemption of the universe does not consist solely in the resurrection of the dead; it awaits the universe which will be freed from all it presently contains of vanity, slavery and corruption "and will obtain the freedom of the glory of the children of God" (Rom. 8:21). If the human was drawn from the earth, if nature is his expanded body, then the total accomplishment of his life can only be realized in solidarity between the new humanity and the transformed world.

A Renewed People in a Transformed Universe

I have presented an understanding of solidarity between heaven and earth, in other words, that there is not a heaven without earth. Our life as human beings cannot be accomplished without solidarity with nature, our common source.

In the accomplishment of our faith, we cannot forget the fact that we were created in rapport with others, in communion with the universe. We are not disincarnate spirits; "all that pertains to our identity as men and women," says Sesboüé, "is an identity modelled by our own earthly history and this therefore must continue to be so in a transfigured way."[28]

The foundation of our heritage, here and now, is to construct a solid humanity, to establish a less destructive and more respectful relationship with all of nature, in keeping with our reality as created beings and recalling that the transformed creation is called to endure.

Creation, as it is written in the book of Genesis, is the excellent work of God: "God saw everything that he had made, and indeed, it was very good" (Gen. 1:31). The flowering of the Christian faith is not the product of a dis-incarnated spirit, freed from an evil creation from which we will need to be detached, little by little, throughout our life. Christian faith presents heaven as the total accomplishment of human life and an incarnate communion: the communion of human beings among themselves, in the communion with the trinitarian life through Jesus Christ, and, lest we forget, in communion with the transformed earth. That is why Christian faith is different from certain trends which exist in the modern world, such as the doctrine of reincarnation. In the same way, Christian faith impedes the symbiosis with various traditional visions leading us to believe that we have only a soul to save, and that, in consequence, we should scorn the world itself. We understand now that the Christian idea of creation is opposed to dualism of the platonic type. We are not in fact invited to separate ourselves from life and from the earth but to incorporate them so that we are in transformation leading to full communion with the divine life.

Spirituality and mysticism lead us to contemplate while already here on earth the Jesus who is risen, who, through his Spirit, continues to act in the events of our history and in our world which is mysteriously but really a world being transformed into a holy land.

⸎

When God invites us to life, it can only be to a life in fullness. God created us to become totally free humans, created for a complete success.

The resurrection is God's response to our awaiting, although it may be yet unknown, for an achievement which is not owed to us, but which is a magnificent gift that God made to us through Jesus Christ and the Holy Spirit.

The resurrection of the body, the total fulfillment of life, heaven in short, will be the completion of God's saving action, the fruit of God's victory over all the negative aspects of existence, the victory over death.

The resurrection is not a kind of neutral preamble, acting to bring us before the judgment of God. It is already the saving action of God actuated by the death and resurrection of Jesus Christ.

However, if we have been invited to understand the resurrection in a slightly different fashion from that displayed in another

LIFE BEYOND DEATH

ecclesiastical context, this will also lead us to discover the saving dimension of the last judgment which, it seems to me, has little to do with the judicial meaning that it had taken on in the Middle Ages and seems to retain even today. *I believe in a final judgment; but what kind of judgment?* I will attempt, in the following chapter, to answer this question.

Notes to Chapter 7

1   See Grabner-Haider, *op. cit.*, pp. 69–73.

2   See *CF*, n° 12. The Symbol of Constantinople is also known as *Nicene Creed*. In fact, the Symbol of Constantinople is an amplified version of the Symbol of Nicaea of 325 (see *CF*, n° 7).

3   See *ibid.*, n°s 16–17.

4   See *ibid.*, n° 20; see also Schmaus, *op. cit.*, pp. 187–199.

5   Sesboüé, *op. cit.*, p. 43.

6   Grabner-Haider, *op. cit.*, pp. 78–79.

7   C. Dagens, "Notre corps promis à la résurrection," in *Communio*, XV/1 (1990), pp. 8–9. In the Bible, the *body* designates a *human being* in her or his totality, as Daniel Marguerat remarks: "When the Bible speaks of the body, it is referring to the whole person. On this point the New Testament inherits from the Old: the body is not perceived as it is by the Greeks, as the spirit's material envelope, a shell to be scorned or idolized. For believers in Israel as for the first Christians, a human being does not *have* a body, but *is* a body. The body is the way of being present to others and to God. By my body, I am. Without a body, I do not exist. The body is the place of the 'me,' and through the body the person stakes out a presence in the world. That is why Jewish tradition, and following it the New Testament, will not imagine a bodiless resurrection; new life necessarily means new body. Israel has thus bequeathed to Christianity an awareness of the corporeal nature of human existence, concretized in Hebrew by requisitioning the corporeal vocabulary to express feelings. Similarly, for New Testament authors the heart is the seat of deliberation and not of feelings. The feelings are located at the level of the intestines, while the spirit is the place of dialogue with God. Long relegated to the category of primitive beliefs, this awareness of the body as at once the theatre of existence and the memory of a personal past, would bring no smiles today except from the ignorant." (D. Marguerat, *Le Dieu des premiers chrétiens* [2nd ed.], Geneva: Labor et Fides [Essais Bibliques, 16], 1993, p. 38)

8   Sesboüé, *op. cit.*, p. 59; see also pp. 53–62, 165–167.

9   See Ratzinger, *op. cit.*, pp. 112–119, 172–181.

10   F. Varillon, *Joie de croire, joie de vivre: Conférences sur les points majeurs de la foi chrétienne*, Paris: Centurion, 1990, p. 176.

11   P. Scolas, "Je crois a la résurrection de la chair," in *La Foi et le Temps*, 19 (1989), p. 482.

12   H. Bourgeois, *Je crois à la résurrection du corps*, Paris: Desclée, 1981, p. 27.

13   *Ibid.*, p. 288.

14   *Ibid.*, p. 324; see M. R. Miles, "Sex and the City (of God): Is Sex Forfeited of Fulfilled in Augustine's Resurrection of the Body?" in *Journal of the American Academy of Religion*, 73/2 (2005), pp. 307–327.

15   See A. E. McGrath, *A Brief History of Heaven*, Malden: Blackwell Publishing (Blackwell Brief Histories of Religion), 2003.

16   Ratzinger, *op. cit.*, p. 234; see also pp. 233–238; Schoonenberg, *op. cit.*, pp. 97–112.

17   See, for example, the Bull *Benedictus Deus* (1336) of Pope Benedict XII, in *CF*, n°s 2305–2307; and the General Council of Florence's Decree for the Greeks (1439), in *CF*, n°s 2308–2309.

18   See Sesboüé, *op. cit.*, pp. 121–126.

19   Schoonenberg, *op. cit.*, p. 108; see also Bauckham and Hart, *Hope against Hope*, pp. 168–173.

20   O. Clément, *Question sur l'homme*, Quebec: Anne Sigier, 1986, p. 50.

21   Dagens, *op. cit.*, p. 10; see also Schwarz, *op. cit.*, pp. 365–407.

22   Dagens, *op. cit.*, p. 11.

23   M. Zundel, *Je est un Autre*, Quebec: Anne Sigier, 1986, p. 46.

24   *Id.*, *La liberté de la foi*, Paris: Plon, 1960, pp. 85–86.

25   *Id.*, "Naître de nouveau pour accomplir l'univers," in *Id.*, *Ton visage, ma lumière*, p. 69.

26   *Id.*, "Le mal: La création, oeuvre d'amour à deux," (Retreat given to the Cistercian Abbey of Timadeuc [Morbihan], in April 5, 1973), roneotyped document, p. 52.

27   Bauckham and Hart, *Hope against Hope*, p. 124; see also pp. 122–127.

28   Sesboüé, *op. cit.*, p. 129.

8

The Final Judgment as Liberation

In the creed we proclaim that Jesus Christ "shall come again to judge the living and the dead."[1] In the faith of the Christian community, we believe in the return of Christ in glory in the *parousia*, which is linked to the last judgment.[2] However, among the articles of our creed, nothing is more poorly interpreted than the idea of the last judgment.

The return of Christ in glory will be the final manifestation of the Lord, who will establish the kingdom of God in its fullness. It will therefore be the ultimate epiphany of Jesus as Christ, as Son of God, as Saviour and Liberator. It will be the attainment of the ultimate victory of the Lord Jesus Christ, the complete accomplishment of the new life already initiated in his incarnation, life, death and resurrection. In joy one is to await the bridegroom, in order to enter with him into the ultimate wedding-feast in the kingdom of God. Here there will no longer be tears or sorrows, but only communion with God through Jesus Christ and in the Holy Spirit, in solidarity with our brothers and sisters, and in harmony with a new heaven and a new earth. It is for this reason that the first Christian communities awaited with anticipation the day of the Lord.

The early Church not only believed in the imminent return of the Lord, but Christians also celebrated his return as an event truly present in liturgical celebrations, and in a special way in the Eucharist. Thus, they were able to strongly proclaim *Maranatha:* "Come, Lord Jesus!" (Rev. 22:20).

The *parousia* and the last judgment are aspects of the same event: the ultimate triumph over all the elements of death, that is to say, the victory over death, the fulfillment of history, and the transformation of the universe. The last judgment was awaited with the same joy as the return of Christ. However, the day of victory was soon perceived as a "day of anger." A juridical mentality and a pastoral practice influenced by fear gradually transformed the return of Christ and the last judgment into a frightful event.

We are invited to recover the saving dimension, as expressed in the Bible, of the return of Christ and the last judgment understood as a day of victory and liberation, a joyful event. The reinterpretation and re-actualization of the biblical meaning of the last judgment has great consequences for pastoral activity. We need to replace the difficult problem of judgment understood as a "rendering of accounts" in a juridical sense. I will try to interpret the judgment in a manner corresponding to its saving dimension as shown in the Bible.

It is certain nonetheless that the judgment of God is a liberating action before which one ought to place oneself during one's earthly existence. In this sense one is able to speak of a "self-judgment": of one who opens or closes oneself during one's journey toward this salvation that is being offered so graciously. We will treat all of this in the present chapter.

1. *The Return of Christ*

Christian faith implies hope in the second coming of Christ in glory. When Christ was lifted to the heavens on the Mount of Olives, the disciples who were watching heard this message: "They [the two men in white robes] said, 'Men of Galilee, why do you stand looking up toward heaven? This Jesus, who has been taken up from you into heaven, will come in the same way as you saw him go into heaven'" (Acts 1:11).

The expression most frequently used in the New Testament to designate the *parousia*, or the second coming of Christ, is the day of the Lord: "For you yourselves know very well that the day of the Lord will come like a thief in the night" (1 Thess. 5:2). This is an expression borrowed from the Old Testament that designates a great event. In this manner, the return of Christ was linked with the eschatological expectations of the Old Testament and, at the same time, with Christian hope centred now on Christ, as seen in the

LIFE BEYOND DEATH

Gospel of Mark (where the text of Daniel 7:13-14 is used): "Then they will see 'the Son of Man coming in clouds' with great power and glory" (Mk. 13:26).

Believing this promise, the Church continued to proclaim its faith in the second coming of Christ, a faith which should become a force giving rise to hope on our voyage in this world. This is indicated in number 48 of the Dogmatic Constitution on the Church (*Lumen Gentium*), in the Second Vatican Council:

> We reckon therefore that "the sufferings of the present time are not worthy to be compared with the glory to come that will be revealed in us" (Rom. 8:18; cf. 2 Tim. 2:11-12). Strong in faith we look for "the blessed hope and glorious coming of our great God and Savior, Jesus Christ" (Tit. 2:13) "who will refashion the body of our lowliness, conforming it to the body of his glory" (Phil. 3:21) and who will come "to be glorified in his saints, and to be marveled at in all those who have believed" (2 Th. 1:10).

This coming proclaims a joyous triumph, a sign of hope for us who continue to believe in the fulfillment of this promise. The day of the Lord is also the day of triumph for those who believed in Christ and who recognized his presence in their brothers and sisters. It will be the day of the revelation of the deeper significance of all we have constructed as great and marvellous in our existence. Thus, "the parousia is the event which concludes history by making the final truth of all things manifest to all."[3]

The "Parousia": The Return of the Lord in Glory

Parousia is a Greek word which signifies presence, coming (entering). It represents a triumphant coming, solemn and joyous, a coming which is the starting point of a total reversal, and of a new reality.

In the Greco-Roman context it signified the solemn entry of an emperor, which was a day set aside as a demarcation point for a new reckoning of time, or a day of special importance. Under this understanding the *parousia*, applied to Christ, "signifies the beginning of the new 'year' of God, the eternal wedding-feast which he celebrates with his own."[4]

Therefore, the return of Christ represents the ultimate self-revelation of the risen Lord. This triumphal and victorious return is connected with the end of the present world and belief in a new creation, the resurrection of the dead and the last judgment. In 1 Thessalonians 4:13-18, Paul gives us the most complete biblical description of the *parousia:*

> But we do not want you to be uninformed, brothers and sisters, about those who have died, so that you may not grieve as others do who have no hope. For since we believe that Jesus died and rose again, even so, through Jesus, God will bring with him those who have died. For this we declare to you by the word of the Lord, that we who are alive, who are left until the coming of the Lord, will by no means precede those who have died. For the Lord himself, with a cry of command, with the archangel's call and with the sound of God's trumpet, will descend from heaven, and the dead in Christ will rise first. Then we who are alive, who are left, will be caught up in the clouds together with them to meet the Lord in the air; and so we will be with the Lord forever. Therefore encourage one another with these words.

As Paul indicated, the *parousia* is related to the events which fulfill our hope, the gaining of final salvation. All this should fill hearers with comfort and joy.

The Day of the Lord

The return of the Lord in glory, as seen above, joined with the awaiting of the fulfillment of salvation, was expressed in the Old Testament by the phrase the day of the Lord. The New Testament presents Christ to us as one in whom the promises of God are fulfilled:

> I give thanks to my God always for you because of the grace of God that has been given you in Christ Jesus, for in every way you have been enriched in him, in speech and knowledge of every kind—just as the testimony of Christ has been strengthened

LIFE BEYOND DEATH

among you—so that you are not lacking in any spiritual gift as you wait for the revealing of our Lord Jesus Christ. He will also strengthen you to the end, so that you may be blameless on the day of our Lord Jesus Christ. God is faithful; by him you were called into the fellowship of his Son, Jesus Christ our Lord. (1 Cor. 1:4-9)

The second coming of the Lord in glory finally accomplishes the saving plan of God initiated with the people of the old covenant and which, in Jesus Christ, is made present among us. What was announced in the Old Testament becomes a reality achieved in the day of the Lord, in his return in glory. It is an event that is awaited, but also one that has already begun in and with Jesus Christ: "'Your ancestor Abraham rejoiced that he would see my day; he saw it and was glad'" (Jn. 8:56).

It is also important to consider the apocalyptic context which surrounds the day of the Lord in both the Old and New Testaments. The catastrophic context which enfolds the day of the Lord is aimed at encouraging believers in the midst of persecution.[5] In this regard, one understands better the signs which, according to the New Testament, precede the return of the Lord, such as it is expressed in the Gospel of Mark:

"But in those days, after that suffering, the sun will be darkened, and the moon will not give its light, and the stars will be falling from heaven, and the powers in the heavens will be shaken. Then they will see 'the Son of Man coming in clouds' with great power and glory. Then he will send out the angels, and gather his elect from the four winds, from the ends of the earth to the ends of heaven." (Mk. 13:24-27)

The cooling of the faith (Lk. 18:8), the appearance of the antichrist (2 Thess. 2:1-12; 1 Jn. 2:18-28), the preaching of the gospel to all nations (Mt. 24:14), and the salvation of all Israel (Rom. 11:25-36) are some of the signs[6] which were intended to give strength and courage to Christians who might be persecuted or weak in their faith. Therefore, these signs actually prevent us from becoming indifferent insofar as they lead all to a triumphant event and are the announcement of a joyous reality, the victorious coming of the Lord.

Within this context of resistance to difficulty, we understand that one of the essential elements of the day of the Lord is its unpredictability: "'For as the lightning flashes and lights up the sky from one side to the other, so will the Son of Man be in his day'" (Lk. 17:24). Consequently, one should be ready: "'Beware, keep alert; for you do not know when the time will come'" (Mk. 13:33). And also be vigilant, because, as Paul wrote to the Thessalonians, "the day of the Lord will come like a thief in the night" (1 Thess. 5:2). The intention was not to frighten the first Christians but rather to give them hope in the midst of persecutions and to invite them to be strong and remain faithful to Jesus Christ.

The Faith of the Church in the Second Coming of Christ

The Church has always seen the fulfillment of the faith in the return of Christ in glory. Since the early centuries, the Church saw the depth of this mystery. The glory which Jesus Christ had received from God in his first coming would be shown in all its splendour. That will be the moment of the manifestation, of the ultimate unfolding of what was hidden. It will be the moment where those who "suffer today as Christ has suffered, will reign with him, as he reigns."[7]

Faith in the *parousia* is already contained in the first symbols or creeds of faith, in the statement that Christ "shall come again to judge the living and the dead."[8] The juxtaposition of the words coming and judgment is explained as flowing from the biblical sense of the last judgment as a manifestation of the liberating power of God and not, primarily, as a juridical action of judgment.[9]

The day of the return of Christ was awaited as a day of salvation (2 Cor. 6:2) and a day of redemption (Eph. 4:30). It is the day when the full solidarity between Christ and those who believed in him will be manifested:

> So if you have been raised with Christ, seek the things that are above, where Christ is, seated at the right hand of God. Set your minds on things that are above, not on things that are on earth,

LIFE BEYOND DEATH

for you have died, and your life is hidden with Christ in God. When Christ who is your life is revealed, then you also will be revealed with him in glory. (Col. 3:1-4)

The day of the Lord is also our day!

The expectation of the early Christian community of the *parousia* of the Lord and of the coming of the day of those who believe in him does not remove human responsibility for the transformation of the world. On the contrary, as has been pointed out in chapter 3, regarding the relationship between hope and human responsibility,

> Far from alienating man from his mission of transforming the world, Christian hope stimulates him to carry out his intramundane task and integrates his commitment to the world in his responsibility before God and before men, who are his brothers in the firstborn among men, Christ. The Christian lives according to the hope (founded in faith) that man's action in the world will neither end in failure nor lose itself in an endless search for a fulfilment sustains him in his worldly activity. Moreover, the grace of the Absolute Future does not remove but on the contrary radicalizes his responsibility as an actor with a part in history (just as the gift of justification does not suppress but is on the contrary fulfilled in the free response of faith); the salvation of man and of the world come about in the dialogue between the Absolute Freedom of God in his self-communication to man and man's responsible freedom before the call of the God-Love. Charity, the fullness of hope, demands from the Christian a radical involvement in the tasks of the world for the good of mankind. Precisely in the fulfilment of his responsibility to mankind, the world and history, Christian hope anticipates the coming of the Kingdom of God in Christ.[10]

The first Christian communities reached this anticipation of faith in joy, in the midst of their liturgical celebrations. The early Christian community was oriented toward the coming of the day of the Lord.

2. A Joyful Event

In its very waiting, the early Church was filled with the joy of triumph, expressed in the active desire for the ultimate meeting with the spouse. It was with just such anticipation that the community proclaimed its *Maranatha:* "Come, Lord Jesus!" (Rev. 22:20).

Moreover, the early Christian community would not only invoke the return of the Lord; it actually lived with the conviction that Christ was coming, which was made present in its midst each day in the celebration of the sacraments. The liturgical celebration represented an occasion to rejoice at Christ's coming, an event regularly made real in the midst of the assembly.

The return of Christ is not only for tomorrow. Through faith, through life and prayer, the *parousia* is already celebrated in the present.[11] The Church highlights this with a particular intensity in the celebration of the Eucharist. The Eucharist is celebrated as a memorial of Christ: "For as often as you eat this bread and drink the cup, you proclaim the Lord's death until he comes" (1 Cor. 11:26). The liturgical celebration—the Eucharist—would be seen as an anticipation of the kingdom of God. It was for this reason that early Christians—on a daily basis and in communion with one another—frequented the Temple and broke bread in their homes (Acts 2:46).

In the Eucharist the Christian community celebrates the presence of Christ in its midst and proclaims its desire for his return in glory. As Cardinal Ratzinger writes: "Every Eucharist is Parousia, the Lord's coming, and yet the Eucharist is even more truly the tensed yearning that he would reveal his hidden Glory."[12]

Awaiting Christ's return was seen as a liberation. The concerns of the present world were vital because of the immediate expectation of the Lord, although this did not lead to any contempt of the world. Paul shows magnificently the return of Christ and its joy:

> Rejoice in the Lord always; again I will say, Rejoice. Let your gentleness be known to everyone. The Lord is near. Do not worry about anything, but in everything by prayer and supplication with thanksgiving let your requests be made known to God. And the

peace of God, which surpasses all understanding, will guard your hearts and your minds in Christ Jesus. (Phil. 4:4-7)

The freedom from all oppression, already set in motion through the death and resurrection of Jesus Christ, is awaited, for its final accomplishment, through the joy of triumphant liberation.[13]

3. A Liberating Experience

Parousia and the last judgment are aspects of the same reality of salvation, as we proclaim in faith: Jesus Christ "shall come again to judge the living and the dead."[14] Nonetheless, there is hardly any aspect of our faith which generates fear more than the theme of the last judgment. The idea of the last judgment presented in the religious culture of our infancy has often evoked catastrophes and terror. Fear is intertwined in our lives, and, most probably, will continue to accompany us.

Jean Delumeau has underlined how the idea of the last judgment has often been united in preaching with the idea of divine vengeance. The good God becomes, on the day of the last judgment, a vengeful God. Thus, "Early modern preaching often portrayed both the end of the world and the Last Judgment as the supreme 'vengeance' of the Almighty against stubbornly sinful earth and all humanity."[15] Without doubt, the intention of this pastoral practice of fear, as highlighted in the first and second chapters above, was to bring about conversion. But the means used by the preachers of past times did not always lead to conversion. Sadly enough, they were often the cause of a lot of anguish and produced a kind of "collective guilt complex." As Delumeau writes,

> A terrible God, more a judge than a father, despite the mercy with which He was almost accidentally credited; a divine justice connected to vengeance; the conviction that, despite Redemption, there would remain only a chosen few, all humanity having deserved hellfire because of Original Sin; the certainty that each sin is both insult and injury to God; the rejection of any amusement or concession to human nature, since these remove one from salvation.[16]

The concept of an infinitely good God becomes radically changed to one of a God who severely punishes our faults at the end of our lives.[17]

Nevertheless, and in line with the second coming of Jesus Christ in glory, when the Church confessed faith in him as the one who is coming to judge the living and the dead, what resonated at the foundation of this article of faith was the comforting message of the victorious grace such as the one proclaimed in 1 John 4:16-18:

> God is love, and those who abide in love abide in God, and God abides in them. Love has been perfected among us in this: that we may have boldness on the day of judgment, because as he is, so are we in this world. There is no fear in love, but perfect love casts out fear; for fear has to do with punishment, and whoever fears has not reached perfection in love.

It is true that much later, and probably under the pressure of the juridical mentality typical of Latin culture, this attitude of hope in the face of the final judgment would diminish and greater emphasis would be put on understanding judgment as a juridical sentence. At the end of this whole evolutionary process, we see that the concept of the day of the Lord had become transformed into a *dies irae*, namely, a "day of anger," due in great part to the influence of medieval thought on its development.[18] The *parousia* was then absorbed by a last judgment strongly accentuating a juridical point of view. This viewpoint no longer evoked a sense of confidence and the certitude of triumph. One lived in anguish and insecurity in the face of an uncertain juridical sentence, already situated at the end of one's very life.

There is no doubt that the idea of a juridical judgment was also influenced by a series of biblical texts whose content is mostly symbolic and flowed from an oriental culture less rational in approach than ours. A literal interpretation of some of these biblical texts that developed in a Western culture, more conceptual than symbolic, contributed to the idea of a last judgment in which the vision of salvation was diminished in favour of a purely juridical vision. The last judgment, then, becomes the moment in which God, through Jesus Christ, demands that we account for our lives.

LIFE BEYOND DEATH

Nevertheless, before the last judgment was reduced to a purely juridical concept, it had been seen as the triumph of the salvific plan of God in all its glory and splendour. It is therefore necessary for us to recover the biblical sense of the last judgment as the Good News of our final salvation.

The Day of Liberation

The notion of a day of Yahweh is already present in the Old Testament. The history of the people of the old covenant, and later of the early Church, is oriented toward the future, toward the final accomplishment of the faith of the people. The day of Yahweh recaptures all that Israel had ever hoped for as fulfillment of the divine promises and a fully happy life. It is the day of the complete manifestation of the kingdom of God with all the connotations presented in chapter 6 above. Thus, the prophets, in speaking of this event present it in these terms:

> They gave it different names: the Day of Yahweh, the Judgment, the coming of the Messiah, the kingdom of God, the new Jerusalem, the Resurrection. And to describe these events which far surpassed the present state of things, they drew their images from the wondrous deeds of past salvation history, from the mythical cosmology of surrounding nations, and from their experience of an encounter with God.[19]

To come to an understanding of God as judge and to an appreciation of the judgment of God, it becomes necessary to ask ourselves first of all just what was the meaning of the words judge and to judge in the Old Testament.[20]

The verb to judge (and its derivative *judgment*) as applied to God as subject or to other persons is a translation of the Hebrew verb *šāpaṭ* whose primary meaning is to *save* or provide salvation (liberation), which implies as a consequence a liberation from injustice. While it also refers to a legal or judiciary institution, "most of the time its meaning is that of *saving*."[21] Thus, in the book of Judges, the judges are liberators, saviours whom God brought forth to save the people from oppression by their enemies.

In the Old Testament there are contexts where the verb *šâpaṭ* (to judge) totally excludes the idea of judgment (in a juridical sense) and solely signifies the idea of saving. Thus, for example 2 Sam. 18:19, 31 speaks of David whom Yahweh has liberated from the hand *(šᵉpâṭô miyyad)* of his enemies. One is able to say the same thing of other passages about the liberation or the saving of orphans and the poor (and not their judgment): "to do justice for [to liberate] the orphan and the oppressed, so that those from earth may strike terror no more" (Ps. 10:18). The world rejoices that Yahweh will come to save it (not that it rejoices because God has come to judge it):

> Let the heavens be glad, and let the earth rejoice; let the sea roar, and all that fills it; let the field exult, and everything in it. Then shall all the trees of the forest sing for joy before the Lord; for he is coming, for he is coming to judge [to liberate] the earth. He will judge the world with righteousness, and the peoples with his truth. (Ps. 96:11-13; see also Ps. 98)

Many times, the verb *šâpaṭ* (to judge) is used synonymously with the verb to save: "May he defend the cause of the poor of the people, give deliverance to the needy, and crush the oppressor" (Ps. 72:4).

There is no doubt that certain translations of the Bible do not respect this idea of judgment as a liberation. Nonetheless, it is necessary to remember that

> it is true that "to save or to liberate from injustice", including at the same time an action against the injustice and the oppressor, was a *judgment* between two parties, and this is able to explain the slow semantic evolution giving to the word "judgment," the juridical sense which it did not have, at least explicitly, in the beginning. The verb *šâpaṭ* [to judge] has fundamentally the sense of "saving or liberating from the injustice" and the word *mišpât (judgment)* signifies, properly speaking, "salvation" or liberation of the one who is unjustly oppressed, with different nuances according to the original signification.[22]

In this way one is able to understand a certain progressive tendency from judgment, as liberation, to judgment as a juridical action.

LIFE BEYOND DEATH

But even within this evolution, the primary meaning of "to judge" is the action in favour of a person who is unjustly oppressed, that is to say, judgment was a liberating action. This is also the meaning of the day of Yahweh, as is presented by the prophets who describe it "with apocalyptic images."[23]

According to Augustin George, in the Old Testament there are several elements which refer to the idea of judgment. Presenting a survey of some of these elements, he underlines:

1. The sober nature of these portraits of the future. They are painted with a few brief images, as if to respect the mysteriousness of God's future intervention [see, for example, Am. 5:18-20; Isa. 2:12-16; 10:20-21; 28:5-6; Zeph. 3:11-13; and the whole book of Joel].

2. Certitude about an imminent intervention that will reestablish justice and provide salvation.

3. This certainty is rooted in the sacred history of Israel, in God's election, covenant and promises that already find a guarantee in his past interventions into the nation's history.

4. These prophetic proclamations about the future always seek to inspire faith, conversion and hope. Right now the people must turn to God, and the eschatological oracles attempt to stress the acute urgency of this decisive step. The imminent nature of the events described is a by-product of this sense of urgency. Israel never lost sight of this, because it never abandoned this hope, even though the Lord's Day was put off time and again.[24]

These descriptions of the day of Yahweh have as their goal the stimulation of faith, conversion, and the perseverance and hope of the people, especially in difficult moments. The idea of judgment as releasing the liberating power of God is maintained in the New Testament. Thus, texts like Mt. 25:31-46, 1 Cor. 15:24-28 and 2 Thess. 2:8 show us that the judgment will be the final victory and suppression by Christ of all hostile powers.[25] Beyond the difficulty of interpreting the meaning of certain texts,[26] the evangelists present Jesus in the last day as one who gathers the elect: "'Then he will send out the angels, and gather his elect from the four winds, from the ends of the earth to the ends of heaven'" (Mk. 13:27). He has not come to judge, to condemn, but rather to gather together those who have believed in him in order to bring about the saving plan of God.

The originality of Jesus is to place himself at the centre of the judgment, as one to whom it is necessary to have recourse in order to accomplish the will of God:

> "Indeed, God did not send the Son into the world to condemn the world, but in order that the world might be saved through him. Those who believe in him are not condemned; but those who do not believe are condemned already, because they have not believed in the name of the only Son of God. And this is the judgment, that the light has come into the world, and people loved darkness rather than light because their deeds were evil." (Jn. 3:18-19; see also 5:24)

One is therefore able to say that the judgment of God, both in its biblical dimension and in the life of the Church before it was reduced to a juridical concept, was first of all a saving and final action of God brought about by Jesus Christ through the power of the Spirit in favour of his people. It is the triumph of God's saving plan in all its glory and splendour. It is the annihilation of all that is negative in history and the fulfillment of that which was already begun with the death and resurrection of Christ, namely, the final establishment of the kingdom of God. It is in this that the traditional theme of the judgment reaches its fullness.[27]

The Day of Anger

Both in the Old and in the New Testaments, the last judgment, even understood as the day of the liberation of the Lord, evoked something terrible: it was a day of anger. Nevertheless this was not the primary sense, but a derived meaning. What prevailed was the liberation, the final establishment of the plan of salvation, even though, for those who refuse it, it would be a day of anger. However, it is true that some announcements of the judgment, such

LIFE BEYOND DEATH

as those presented previously in note 26, that were expressed in a symbolic language, have been interpreted in a literal sense.[28]

If in the first Christian communities there resonated the proclamation of the return of Christ and of the last judgment, it did this as the encouraging message of a final victory which prevailed over evil, as announced in 1 John 4:17-18. Later, this attitude of hope in the face of the last judgment as an act of salvation will be transformed into the terrible moment when we will be judged by a pitiless judge. The day of the Lord would become the day of anger. In the Middle Ages, this idea of the last judgment as a "rendering of accounts," where Jesus Christ will come to examine our lives, became more important. Thus, confidence in facing the day of the Lord gave way to fear when it was seen as a day of anger. Delumeau has underlined the influence of fear in Western preaching from the thirteenth to the eighteenth centuries, and one is able to follow its consequences up to the twentieth century.

There was such a strong insistence on the juridical aspect of the last judgment that the fear of it intruded itself into Western culture until only recently. One is able to see a good representation of this idea of the last judgment in art, for example, in Michelangelo's fresco presenting the last judgment in the Sistine Chapel.

It seems to me that we have remained mentally and culturally locked into the mediaeval representation of the second coming of Christ and of the last judgment. As Müller-Goldkuhle underlines, regarding this period,

> Besides the prolific depictions of heaven, hell and purgatory, the second coming of Christ was a major theme. The end of the world and the general judgment were vividly portrayed, while the antichrist was personified in the changing events of history. The *Dies irae,* which may well date from the turn of the 12th century, gives us a glimpse of the ideas that characterized contemporary popular piety: individual salvation or damnation, fear and trembling before the judgment, punishment or reward for one's deeds with the resultant stress on justification by works and ethical conversion. This may well explain why that age was later designated as the "Dark Ages".[29]

The Church has always proclaimed its faith in the second coming of Jesus Christ in glory united with the last judgment. After the first declaration, which only affirmed the fact that Jesus Christ "shall come again to judge the living and the dead,"[30] as established in the Nicean creed by the First General Council of Nicaea (in 325), the notion of a last judgment with juridical connotations gradually began to develop:

> He [Jesus Christ] shall come at the end of time to judge the living and the dead and to render to each one according to his works, to the reprobate *(reprobis)* as well as to the elect. All of them will rise again with their own bodies which they now bear, to receive according to their works, whether these have been good or evil, the ones perpetual punishment with the devil and the others everlasting glory with Christ.[31]

In the "Profession of Faith of Michael Palaeologus," the Second General Council of Lyons (in 1274) proclaimed: "The same most Holy Roman Church firmly believes and firmly asserts that nevertheless on the day of Judgment all men will appear with their bodies before the judgment-seat of Christ, to render an account of their own deeds [cf. Rom. 14:1-12]."[32]

For its part, the already-mentioned Dogmatic Constitution on the Church (*Lumen Gentium*) of the Second Vatican Council confined itself, in number 48, to citing some very symbolic texts and tracing a kind of parallel between the last judgment and the retribution at the death of each one of us:

> Since we know not the day nor the hour, on our Lord's advice we must constantly stand guard. Thus when we have finished the one and only course of our earthly life (cf. Heb. 9:27) we may merit to enter into the marriage feast with Him and to be numbered among the blessed (cf. Mt. 25:31-46). Thus we may not be commanded to go into eternal fire (cf. Mt. 25:41) like the wicked and slothful servant (cf. Mt. 25:26), into the exterior darkness where "there will be the weeping and the gnashing of teeth" (Mt. 22:13; 25:30). For before we reign with the glorious Christ, all of us will be made manifest "before the tribunal of

Christ, so that each one may receive what he has won through the body, according to his works, whether good or evil" (2 Cor. 5:10). At the end of the world, "they who have done good shall come forth unto resurrection of life; but who have done evil unto resurrection of judgment" (Jn. 5:29; cf. Mt. 25:46).

Nevertheless, a little farther on, in that same number 48, the Constitution cites Philippians 3:21 where, in speaking of the expectation of the return of the Lord, Paul says that "He will transform the body of our humiliation that it may be conformed to the body of his glory." In addition, number 48 ends by quoting 2 Thessalonians 1:10 where Paul speaks again of the second coming of Jesus Christ, "when he comes to be glorified by his saints and to be marvelled at on that day among all who have believed, because our testimony to you was believed." Here, the advent of Christ coincides with the triumph of the divine saving plan, with the glorification of the Lord in and with the saints. This shows how difficult it is to attempt to cite certain texts in a literal fashion without putting into a global context.

The Second Vatican Council is a good example of two tendencies which have not completely disappeared: 1) a tradition marked by the medieval juridical sense of judgment and fear; and 2) the rediscovering of the saving dimension of judgment as a liberating action in Jesus Christ, as expressed in the Bible.

The same idea of the last judgment as a process to be celebrated in a future moment is found in number 17 of the Pastoral Constitution on the Church in the Modern World (*Gaudium et Spes*): "Before the judgment seat of God each man must render an account of his own life, whether he has done good or evil." A little farther on, in number 45, one is able to read: "The Lord Himself speaks: 'Behold, I come quickly! And my reward is with me, to render to each one according to his works. I am the Alpha and the Omega, the first and the last, the beginning and the end' (Apoc. 22:12-13)." Likewise, at the end of the same Constitution, in number 93, which speaks of building up the world and fulfilling its purpose, one reads: "Therefore, holding faithfully to the gospel and benefiting from its resources, and united with every man who loves and practices justice, Christians have shouldered a gigantic task demanding fulfilment in this world. Concerning this task they must give a reckoning to Him who will judge every man on the last day." The last judgment is viewed here from a juridical context. But by that very fact, the idea is put aside of judgment as a liberating action of God through Jesus Christ and in the power of the Spirit, as a final triumph of the saving plan of God.

Finally, Bauckham and Hart have given an excellent summary about the evolution of the understanding of last judgment from its appearance in the Old Testament until now. As they say,

> The notion of eschatological judgement is conveyed in Scripture by two main images: judgement by military victory [a symbolic way of presenting the judgment of God as *a liberation* from oppression] and judgement in a court of law. The latter is what has traditionally been called 'the last judgement', and it is to this that the Creeds refer (Jesus Christ 'will come to judge the living and the dead'). A long tradition of Christian art once depicted it, with Christ the Judge consigning the damned to hell and the redeemed to paradise. It must have been one of the most familiar religious scenes for medieval Christians. However, in the modern period, for a variety of reasons, including both a sense that judgement is inconsistent with the love of God and the growth of an expectation that all will be saved in the end, the last judgement has become one of the most neglected of the major eschatological images.[33]

We need to rediscover the liberating message of the last judgment without eliminating the challenge that it presents to us, even if—and specifically because—this challenge has been traditionally expressed in an imaginative and symbolic way that should not be taken literally.

Re-Actualizing the Meaning of the Last Judgment

The last judgment, seen as God's liberating action through Jesus Christ, ought to lead us to renew our pastoral language in a more imaginative way. Furthermore, even taking into account the challenge that this judgment presents to us, interpreting it in more

LIFE BEYOND DEATH

juridical terms, this judgment can be understood from a personal point of view as a decision of the person. It is a question of one's attitude before the word of God, before Jesus Christ. If one presents the last judgment as the accomplishment of a saving action of God already present in the death and resurrection of Jesus Christ, then the salvation of God becomes a gracious offering and not an imposition. It is an invitation we are free either to accept or refuse throughout our existence.

According to Boros, at the point of judgment our deepest deeds will be fully revealed. "The judgment is the revelation of the essence of things, of the true orientation of the human heart, and therefore is the encounter with the ultimate ground, with Jesus Christ."[34] The last judgment, finally "amounts to no more than the message of joy."[35] It is the ultimate revelation of God, when everything will be manifested, unveiled. Consequently, the judgment is not a divine sentence which will come from the outside. Rather it should be understood in its personal dimension as a self-judgment.

One can certainly find in John the idea that Jesus Christ, as the Son of Man, receives the power to judge from God (Jn. 5:22, 27; 9:39). Nevertheless, the main idea that John develops in his Gospel is that one has to understand the judgment as an option of the person, a negative attitude vis-à-vis faith in Jesus Christ.

The last judgment is the self-condemnation of a human being who refuses to accept the salvation brought by Jesus, and who refuses to believe in his word:

"Indeed, God did not send the Son into the world to condemn the world, but in order that the world might be saved through him. Those who believe in him are not condemned; but those who do not believe are condemned already, because they have not believed in the name of the only Son of God. And this is the judgment, that the light has come into the world, and people loved darkness rather than light because their deeds were evil. For all who do evil hate the light and do not come to the light, so that their deeds many not be exposed. But those who do what is true come to the light, so that it may be clearly seen

197

that their deeds have been done in God."(Jn. 3:17-21; see also 5:24; 8:12-20)

Once again, John repeats that Jesus has not come to condemn the world, nor to judge it, but to save it:

> Then Jesus cried aloud: "Whoever believes in me believes not in me but in him who sent me. And whoever sees me sees him who sent me. I have come as light into the world, so that everyone who believes in me should not remain in the darkness. I do not judge anyone who hears my words and does not keep them, for I came not to judge the world, but to save the world. The one who rejects me and does not receive my word has a judge; on the last day the word that I have spoken will serve as judge, for I have not spoken on my own, but the Father who sent me has himself given me a commandment about what to say and what to speak. And I know that his commandment is eternal life. What I speak, therefore, I speak just as the Father has told me." (Jn. 12:44-50)

However, Jesus Christ established a shared concern with his brothers and sisters (see the judgment of the nations in Matthew 25:31-46). That is why the judgment, as a personal decision for or against Jesus Christ, for or against our sisters and brothers, for or against the transformation of our universe, is something that is happening now, in our engagement in our present time.

In summary, the judgment-decision or self-judgment is not a juridical process that is to take place in the hereafter; rather it is realized continually by the response of human beings to their living responsibilities.[36]

⸭

I believe in the return of Christ in glory and in the last judgment because I believe in the full accomplishment of salvation: the gift of life in its fullness. I believe in the last judgment as a day of liberation, of a revelation of all that has been hidden, of the unveiling of the depth of human beings. I believe in the last judgment as a full revelation of the love which is in us. I do not believe in the

LIFE BEYOND DEATH

last judgment as a juridical process where I must give an account to a heavenly judge.

The Swiss theologian Maurice Zundel writes in 1951: "The judgment will not be finally a balance sheet; the judgement will not be God weighing our actions; at the judgement it will be ourselves in a state of accepting or refusing, and it is not God who will judge us, it is we who will judge God."[37] We judge God because, in our depths, we are able to open or to close ourselves to God's saving action. We are able to say yes or no to the gift which God offers us through Jesus Christ in the power of the Spirit. That is the meaning of the responsibility that derives from the greatness of the freedom to which God invites us, from the freedom that, according to Zundel, can lead us to judge God:

> There is, at the main entrance of Notre Dame [the Roman Catholic Cathedral of Paris], a representation of the last judgment where we see Christ displaying his wounds; it is not a judgment of man by God, but of God by man: God is judged, condemned, crucified by man, he died for those who do not love him. Therefore hell is a hell for God, it is God who is the victim. . . . It is our infinite responsibility, for we are responsible for the life of God. It is freedom, because we decide the destiny of God in the universe.[38]

The God whom Jesus Christ reveals to us banishes the image of a God who waits for us at the last judgment, presented sometimes as an avenger of our evil actions. To the contrary, God is able to be killed by us. Here resides one of the greatest originalities of Zundel's thought. From the beginning, Jesus Christ reveals a fragile, compassionate and innocent God, who depends on us since we have the power of killing God each time, as Zundel wrote in 1937, that we do not witness to God with the transparency of our own life: "We have, therefore, this frightening power of judging God, of condemning him, of bringing about his death. And we have inverted all the terms of this truth, however so obvious, and we have wondered whether God will not condemn us and would reject us as if these very words had any meaning."[39] God is the only one who is able to fail; therein resides God's fragility. God accepts completely the consequences of human freedom which enables one to open oneself to the gift of life, yet also enables one to refuse it eternally.

If salvation is not imposed but offered to us, to be open to the judgment, understanding it as the accomplishment of God's covenant with humanity signifies our accepting the resurrection and eternal life. Nevertheless, as will be presented in next chapter, "The possibility of perdition is given only with a creature's persistent refusal to recognize truth and justice, to accept the mercy of forgiveness, and to participate in the reconciled communion of God's reign. . . . Divine judgement is the dead-end of sin."[40] Consequently, at least as a possibility, one is able to close oneself off from the divine offering; one is able to refuse the gift of eternal life, of the everlasting communion with God, with others and with a transformed universe. This is the meaning of hell!

LIFE BEYOND DEATH

Notes to Chapter 8

1   The First General Council of Nicaea (325): Symbol of Nicaea, *CF*, n° 7.

2   See Ratzinger, *op. cit.*, pp. 194–214.

3   Bauckham and Hart, *Hope against Hope*, p. 121; see also pp. 117–120, 122.

4   Ratzinger, *op. cit.*, p. 202.

5   See chapter 4 above where I presented the origin and characteristics of the Apocalyptic literature.

6   See Ratzinger, *op. cit.*, pp. 196–197.

7   Sesboüé, *op. cit.*, p. 70.

8   *CF*, n° 7.

9   See Ruíz de la Peña, *op. cit.*, p. 167.

10   Alfaro, *op. cit.*, p. 69.

11   See Dagens, *op. cit.*, p. 12.

12   Ratzinger, *op. cit.*, p. 203.

13   See Ruíz de la Peña, *op. cit.*, p. 166. The delay of the *parousia*, as it was highlighted in chapter 2 above, tended to move the early Christian community to deepen its liturgical life, notably its sacramental life, and to interpret the delay as a sign of the mercy of God, who awaited the conversion of all people. From this one can dwell with benefit on the unpredictable character of the return, rather than on its precise moment. The delay of the *parousia* is therefore accompanied by the development of the sacrament of penance as a special way of being ready, of being liberated from all sin, when Jesus Christ's *parousia* will happen. However the expectation of the coming of Christ himself gradually began to dissipate. The result was an almost exclusive concern for the personal destiny of each individual and the beginning of the institutionalization of the Church.

14   *CF*, n° 7.

15   Delumeau, *Sin and Fear*, pp. 401–402.

16   *Ibid.*, p. 296.

17   See *ibid.*, pp. 401–410.

18   See chapter 2 above, and in particular its note 24.

19   A. George, "The Judgment of God," in *Concilium*, 41 (1969), p. 9.

20   I follow here the interpretation given to the biblical terms of *to judge* and *judgment* by J. Alonso Díaz in his book *Términos bíblicos de "justicia social" y traducción de "equivalencia dinámica"*, Madrid: EDICABI/PPC (Fascículos bíblicos, 1), 1978, pp. 6–11.

21   *Ibid.*, p. 6.

22   *Ibid.*, p. 8.

23   Sesboüé, *op. cit.*, p. 75.

24   George, *op. cit.*, p. 17.

25   See Ruíz de la Peña, *op. cit.*, pp. 184–186.

26   In the Gospels, we find Jesus makes several announcements about judgment. There are short announcements to the individuals (Mt. 7:2, 21–23; 12:36: 23:33) or to collectivities (Mt. 11:21–24; 12:38–42; Lk. 19:41–44); announcements of damnation (Mt. 5:22; 10:15, 33; Mk. 12:40) or of rewarding (Mt. 6:4, 6, 18; Lk. 14:14). There is also the eschatological discourse of Mark 13 that is the result of a literal elaboration of Mark, and the famous discourse on the last judgment of Matthew 25:31–46.

27   See George, *op. cit.*, pp. 22–23; Ratzinger, *op. cit.*, pp. 194–214.

28   See chapter 4 above where I underlined the importance of hermeneutics for the understanding of biblical texts, particularly those regarding the eschatological dimension of Christian faith, which are more symbolic than conceptual.

29   Müller-Goldkuhle, *op. cit.*, p. 32.

30   *CF*, n° 7.

31   IV Lateran Council (1215): Symbol of Lateran, *CF*, n° 20.

32   *CF*, n° 27.

33   Bauckham and Hart, *Hope against Hope*, pp. 139–140; see also pp. 141–144.

34   Boros, "Some Thoughts on the Four Last Things," p. 41.

35   *Ibid.*, p. 42.

36   See *The Gospel According to John: Introduction, Translation, and Notes* (by R. E. Brown), Garden City: Doubleday (The Anchor Bible, 29), 1966, vol. 1, p. 345; Ruíz de la Peña, *op. cit.*, pp. 187–189.

37   M. Zundel, unpublished text of 1951, quoted in M. Donzé, *Témoin d'une présence: Inédits de Maurice Zundel (vol. 2)*, Geneva: Éd. du Tricorne (Buisson Ardent), 1987, p. 60.

38   M. Zundel, unpublished text of 1951, quoted in Donzé, *Témoin d'une présence*, p. 61.

39   M. Zundel, unpublished text of 1937, quoted in M. Donzé, *L'humble présence*, p. 163.

40   N. H. Gregersen, "The Final Crucible: Last Judgement and the Dead-End of Sin," in Fergusson and Sarot (Eds.), *The Future as God's Gift*, p. 172; see also pp. 169–171, 173–177.

LIFE BEYOND DEATH

9

Is an Unending Hell Possible?

Salvation is not a road leading in two directions: life or death. God's offer is an invitation to live fully. The Gospel is the proclamation of a final salvation, of the accomplishment of the covenant of God with humanity through Jesus Christ, his Son, and the Holy Spirit. Thus, the Good News is not the presentation of a doctrine of two alternate paths.

In giving us life, God introduces us into a rich adventure, to a human life called to unfold in all of its richness. Furthermore, humanity is called to surpass itself and to enter into a relationship with the God who created human beings who are to develop in God's own image and likeness. Finally, in Jesus Christ, God invites us to become God's adoptive children.

But a gift is not imposed; it reaches its depth only when accepted. Love respects the freedom of the loved person. That is why love implies suffering, for there is a risk of refusal. Encountering a closed or hardened heart, love becomes totally powerless. The response to this offered love is not theoretical but must involve a fourfold engagement: toward the person who offers love, toward ourselves, toward others and toward creation. A gift can only become a reality when it is placed at the service of others through the acceptance of our responsibilities toward them.

Therefore, the gift that God offers us can be refused. God invites us to live in communion with God, through Jesus Christ and in the Holy Spirit, with others and with the rest of creation. The God of love cannot pressure us to accept this gift of salvation. This is God's "fragility": we can refuse God's love. God is as powerless as we are in the face of a heart which closes itself off from receiving our love.

Nevertheless, if our life can uniquely find its fullness in communion with God, with others and with the transformed universe for eternity, I personally believe that refusing to enter into this communion means that one forever accepts death—an eternal death. The result would be a life absolutely wasted, a life limited by its complete selfishness, and by its finitude, a life which has refused to evolve into the image and likeness of God. In this way the individual refuses to become a child of God and, in consequence, accepts everlasting death. The sacred Scripture and the Church both acknowledge the possibility of this refusal on the part of human beings.

If the theme of the last judgment has already alerted us to the danger of a literal interpretation of certain biblical texts where the content is expressed in symbolic language, we should be aware of a greater danger when we examine texts presenting the possibility of an eternal damnation. How can we understand damnation? How can we comprehend the eternity of damnation? How should we interpret the meaning of suffering associated with it? What is the import of the declarations of the magisterium of the Church in regard to hell? These are the questions to which I shall attempt a reply in this chapter.

What can one say about hell? The hypothesis that I will develop in this chapter is that hell symbolizes the individual who has refused to love forever and, consequently, does not accept life for all eternity. Only one who loves is able to open the self to the gift of eternal life. There is no greater pain than this: in the face of the gift of eternal life offered by God, the one who rejects it remains mired forever in the most radical solitude. He or she is forever dying!

1. *God Offers Us the Fullness of Life*

God, in Jesus Christ, offers us life in its fullness. The originality of Jesus' preaching about the kingdom of God, in accord with the prophets who preceded him, consisted in his announcement of a promise of salvation rather than in a proposal of a choice between salvation and damnation: "From that time Jesus began to proclaim, 'Repent, for the kingdom of heaven has come near'" (Mt. 4:17). In him, in his incarnation, life, death and resurrection, the promises of God are accomplished.

The God that Jesus Christ reveals to us appears in all his nobility and goodness. God does not try to intimidate us in order to entice us to him. He does not say to us, "You had better do this or you will be lost!" Jesus Christ presents not a code of moral laws which one must obey but a person who loves us and who invites us to live always with him. Eternal death does not appear as an essential element of the Gospel, which literally signifies Good News: the announcement of salvation.

Having dealt with the concept of eternal life, we should now avoid the notion of eternal death as if both were situated at the same level in the Christian message. As Karl Rahner highlights:

> Thus Christian eschatology is not the *parallel* prolongation of a 'doctrine of the two ways' (which is rather Old Testament than Christian) to reach the two termini of these two ways. Its central affirmation is concerned only with the victorious grace of Christ which brings the world to its fulfilment.[1]

Consequently, God does not place us before the possibility of a choice between life and death. In Jesus Christ he offers us life—the fulfillment of salvation. This leads us to become aware of the riches of this invitation. The first account of creation presents us as created beings, dependent and finite, yet created nevertheless to be the image and likeness of God (Gen. 1:26-27). Therein we are already called to exceed the limits of human finitude. Furthermore, in Jesus Christ God invites us to become God's adoptive children, as Paul writes to the Galatians:

> So with us; while we were minors, we were enslaved to the elemental spirits of the world. But when the fullness of time had come, God sent his Son, born of a woman, born under the law, in order to redeem those who were under the law, so that we might receive adoption as children. And because you are children, God has sent the Spirit of his Son into our hearts, crying, "Abba!

Father!" So you are no longer a slave but a child, and if a child then also an heir, through God. (Gal. 4:3-7)

The heritage which God offers is the full realization of our most noble and magnificent dreams, the achievement of our humanization and of our freedom, full communion with God, with others, and with a transformed universe. In summary, God offers us the fullness of life!

To Be a Creature: Contingency and Finitude

The human person is a created being, as is illustrated in the two accounts of creation (Gen. 1:27; 2:7). Perfection is not given to the individual at birth; it is a continuing realization, a "work-in-progress" as an arrow which points always toward the future.

Fragility, dependence and death form part of human nature; they are constituent dimensions of our existence. Thus, human beings as finite beings are incomplete, fragile, and limited. Death is the ultimate manifestation of the fragility of this created reality called the human person.

Yet, although a created reality, the human person is open to transcendence—*capax Dei*, namely, capable of God. Men and women carry within themselves a desire for the infinite which can only be fulfilled in communion with God. It is not in oneself that the key for our understanding lies. Rather the key to our complete understanding lies outside oneself: "That the individual person is not self-sufficient, and is not able to be fulfilled without turning toward the Unknown who created and who summons her, is enclosed in this fundamental affirmation of faith: we are created, we are creatures."[2]

As created beings, women and men are in solidarity with the rest of creation, for each is part of the universal fragility, and each seeks the integration of all the dimensions of his or her earthly existence. The greatest sadness in one's life lies in the tension between the individual's desires for infinity and the experience of one's own fragility. Nevertheless, it is as a created being that one refers to the Creator. A human being does not exist as a pure nature, without any relationship to transcendence. Each one is already borne by grace:

"The only truly natural human is one who recognizes oneself as a creature carried by grace, called into union with one's creator."[3] Even as a creature, a human being is already divinely oriented "*to enter into a dialogue with* her or his personal God."[4] God does not abandon the human person following her or his creation. Rather that person is invited to become God's own image and likeness.

Called to Become the Image and Likeness of God

A human being is not tied solely to the earth. Though established in solidarity with the rest of creation, the human person is created to be the image of God (Gen. 1:27). After forming the human being from the dust of the earth, God breathed into his nostrils the breath of life and the human became a living being (Gen. 2:7). This idea of the image and likeness of God "has come to be since Genesis a criterion of the special dignity, almost sacredness, of the human person."[5] Our mission consists in making it possible that this image and likeness shine forth in the midst of creation. Accordingly, a human being is "projected, thought and placed within the world, in order to play the role of the image of God."[6] It is for this reason that, as it was already indicated in chapter 7 above, God says in Exodus: "You shall not make for yourself an idol [image/likeness], whether in the form of anything that is in heaven above, or that is on the earth beneath, or that is in the water under the earth" (20:4). Only the human person is called to represent God.

God goes to the encounter of the person, wishing to enter into a dialogue and a covenant with him or her, even beyond the person's possible refusal of the invitation (Isa. 5:1-7; Hos. 2:2-23). Therefore "all that God does appears as an appeal to which he invites an ever more perfect human response."[7] God does not create a human being as a marionette but as "a freedom who is able to decide against God, to exclude him from his creation, and able to endanger the fulfillment of it [creation]."[8] In a word, a human being is called to respond freely to God.

We should not assume that, when one is called to become the image and likeness of God, one is already what one has been called to become as if it were a seal imprinted on the human being at creation. Rather, the call is instead an invitation continuously awaiting a response throughout one's entire life. In reality, at the end of life is one able to say: here exists a person who has become the image and likeness of God. That is why the Roman Catholic Church does not canonize any living person.

This call to become the image and the likeness of God occurs in a process aided by grace. However, it is in Jesus Christ that this invitation, addressed to human beings by God, reaches its summit. In Jesus a human person is invited to become an adoptive child of God and, at the same time, to rediscover the calling to be the image achieving the pinnacle of reality in Christ, the likeness of God par excellence (Col. 1:15-23; Heb. 1:1-4). Thus, "that the man is at the image of God signifies therefore that he is at the image of Christ. It is only in Christ that the man finds his truth."[9] Through our incorporation into the death and resurrection of Christ in baptism, the image of God becomes, according to Brinkman, an eschatological concept:

> the reference to humans as God's image not only shows us our place in a restrictive sense but also in a 'glorifying' aggrandizing sense. The expression 'God's image' constantly reminds us not to think too little of ourselves. After all, in this 'resembling God' lies our greatness as well. It gives us a unique position among all God's creatures and indicates our 'holiness' in the sense of inviolability (Genesis 9:6).

> Thus the expression 'image of God' is an indication of both our smallness and our greatness, since the reference to a God who is constitutive for our human existence preserves us from overestimating as well as underestimating ourselves (Psalm 8). Consequently, in the expression 'image of God' we are given the freedom not too [sic] think too little or too much of ourselves. This conclusion creates an enormous latitude (= responsibility) which is constantly explored by high and low points in the Old Testament.

> Explicitly, however, the concept of God's image plays only a relatively minor role in the Old Testament. It is only in the New

LIFE BEYOND DEATH

Testament that the term acquires a further substantive meaning through the notion of being reborn in the image of Christ by dying and risen with him through baptism. It is only there that it becomes an eschatological concept which indicates our destiny. It constitutes a bridge between protology and eschatology, between our whence and our whither.[10]

As an eschatological concept indicating our final destiny, the concept "image of God" arrives at it full realization with the call to become adoptive children of God in Jesus Christ.

Invited to Be Children of God in Jesus Christ

In number 22 of the Pastoral Constitution on the Church in the Modern World (*Gaudium et Spes*) of the Second Vatican Council, Jesus Christ is presented as the new human being in a beautiful text, which it seems appropriate here to cite in its entirety:

> The truth is that only in the mystery of the incarnate Word does the mystery of man take on light. For Adam, the first man, was a figure of Him who was to come, namely, Christ the Lord. Christ, the final Adam, by the revelation of the mystery of the Father and His love, fully reveals man to man himself and makes his supreme calling clear. It is not surprising, then, that in Him all the aforementioned truths find their root and attain their crown.

> He who is "the image of the invisible God" (Col. 1:15), is Himself the perfect man. To the sons of Adam He restores the divine likeness which had been disfigured from the first sin onward. Since human nature as He assumed it was not annulled, by that very fact it has been raised up to a divine dignity in our respect too. For by His incarnation the Son of God has united Himself in some fashion with every man. He worked with human hands, He thought with a human mind, acted by human choice, and loved with a human heart. Born of the Virgin Mary, He has truly been made one of us, like us in all things except sin.

> As an innocent lamb He merited for us life by the free shedding of His own blood. In Him God reconciled us to Himself and among ourselves. From bondage to the devil and sin, He deliv-

ered us, so that each one of us can say with the Apostle: The Son of God "loved me and gave himself up for me" (Gal. 2:20). By suffering for us He not only provided us with an example for our imitation. He blazed a trail, and if we follow it, life and death are made holy and take on a new meaning.

The Christian man, conformed to the likeness of that Son who is the firstborn of many brothers, receives "the first-fruits of the Spirit" (Rom. 8:23) by which he becomes capable of discharging the new law of love. Through this Spirit, who is "the pledge of our inheritance" (Eph. 1:14), the whole man is renewed from within, even to the achievement of "the redemption of the body" (Rom. 8:23): "If the Spirit of him who raised Jesus from the death dwells in you, then he who raised Jesus Christ from the dead will also bring to life your mortal bodies because of his Spirit who dwells in you" (Rom. 8:11).

Pressing upon the Christian, to be sure, are the need and the duty to battle against evil through manifold tribulations and even to suffer death. But, linked with the paschal mystery and patterned on the dying Christ, he will hasten forward to resurrection in the strength which comes from hope.

All this holds true not only for Christians, but for all men of good will in whose hearts grace works in an unseen way. For, since Christ died for all men, and since the ultimate vocation of man is in fact one, and divine, we ought to believe that the Holy Spirit in a manner known only to God offers to every man the possibility of being associated with this paschal mystery.

Such is the mystery of man, and it is a great one, as seen by believers in the light of Christian revelation. Through Christ and in Christ, the riddles of sorrow and death grow meaningful. Apart from His Gospel, they overwhelm us. Christ has risen, destroying death by His death. He has lavished life upon us so that, as sons in the Son, we can cry out in the Spirit: Abba, Father!

Christ is the key to the understanding of the human person. With him, we take part in an ontological transformation: from being created, the person is called to become a child of God. This invita-

LIFE BEYOND DEATH

tion surpasses the desire for the infinite, that is to say, the openness to transcendence. Furthermore, this is an invitation extended to every human person.

In Jesus Christ, the divine orientation which is present in the human being is fully unveiled. Christ, the complete manifestation of God, also reveals to us in his fullness what it means to be human and to be called to become a child of God through the Spirit of Jesus Christ:

> So then, brothers and sisters, we are debtors, not to the flesh, to live according to the flesh—for if you live according to the flesh, you will die; but if by the Spirit you put to death the deeds of the body, you will live. For all who are led by the Spirit of God are children of God. For you did not receive a spirit of slavery to fall back into fear, but you have received a spirit of adoption. When we cry, "Abba! Father!" it is that very Spirit bearing witness with our spirit that we are children of God, and if children, then heirs, heirs of God and joint heirs with Christ—if, in fact, we suffer with him so that we may also be glorified with him. (Rom. 8:12-17)

The Holy Spirit, who also becomes gift of the risen Christ, is the one who communicates his life (1 Cor. 15:45), the one who "attests" our divine kinship. Divine adoptive filiation unites us to the sonship of Jesus Christ as children of God by faith in him. As such, we share his relationship with the Father (Gal. 4:4-7). Therefore, for John, the presence of Christ in human beings refers, as a direct consequence, to the presence of God: "'Those who love me will keep my word, and my Father will love them, and we will come to them and make our home with them'" (Jn. 14:23).

The divine filiation in humans is comparable to a new birth, the ultimate birth to life eternal. This new life has become already now a reality in our present life through baptism, given us a new birth from God: "You have been born anew, not of perishable but of imperishable seed, through the living and enduring word of God" (1 Pet. 1:23). This, for us, is new life through the power of the Holy Spirit.

This is the full revelation of the gift which God offers us in Christ: life in its fullness. This gift leads us to be glorified with Jesus Christ and to live forever in communion with God, with others and with a transformed creation. This gift awaits a human response.

2. A Gift Waiting for an Answer

One of the most difficult dimensions of our existence is the understanding of the profound meaning of this so-called gift, present, or offering. One is sometimes so constrained to accept a gift that the meaning of what is pure grace can be lost. Yet, to discover that grace is very important for us in order to live life in all its depth.

Grace has several implications. Primarily, on the part of the one who offers something, it implies that what is freely given cannot be imposed, since an imposed gift loses all its value. God offers us the gift of eternal life, a gift which awaits our response indicating our readiness to enter into an interpersonal relationship with him. But God does not wish to impose this gift on a human being. He makes an offer and waits for the answer.

In consequence, the only worthy attitude in the offering of a gift is respect for the freedom of the one who receives it. It is important to recognize the difficulty involved in respecting the freedom of another. How many times has one felt obliged to accept a gift? And how many times have we heard this expression: "But my dear, this is for your own good!?" Nevertheless, our own good does not always coincide with the good of the one who wishes to do us well!

God also respects the freedom of the person when offering that person this gift of eternal life. God did not create puppets or marionettes but human beings called to live in freedom.

A gift therefore has implications for the person who accepts it. Accepting a gift signifies involvement in a loving relationship with the one who offers the gift. To recognize this proffered love is to become responsible for the one who loves us, who is offering us her or his friendship and life itself. Accepting the gift of God calls us to become responsible for ourselves, for others, and for all of creation.

LIFE BEYOND DEATH

A Gift Which Is Not Imposed

What is free has a value that can neither be sold nor imposed. It is most difficult today for us, living in a world where almost everything can be bought or sold, to recognize the true value of something which is graciously and freely offered. We can often hear parents warning their children about those who offer them something free. In human interaction, we frequently have the experience of receiving a bill for services rendered, yet become rather suspicious of anything received "for free." As it may also happen, people often give with one hand in order to receive with the other.

Nonetheless, love, friendship, solidarity, support, and recognition can be neither bought nor sold. Each time that one is forced to buy love, friendship or recognition, it becomes an empty gift and one's self-esteem is all the more diminished. Whenever someone wants to sell us a gift, the gift loses its meaning. It is the extent of the grace which gives value to the gift, which makes it important for human life, which helps us to overcome mediocrity in our relationships, and which gives a special flavour to life. This is why a gift which is founded in love—in life, friendship and solidarity—is always so fragile. This fragility is not a synonym for weakness but is rather a synonym for respect and for responsibility, which prevents us from trying to control the loved person and from imposing our own wish on her or him.

Children understand how difficult it is to refuse a gift from their parents, especially if they sometimes do not wish to receive it. This can also be the case of employees in their relationships with their employers and, basically, it is true of all of those who find themselves in a relationship of subordination toward someone else. The non-imposition of a gift frees one from paternalistic relationships which are often established between human beings. Showing respect for other persons is a way of recognizing their value as unique beings and of recognizing that their desires are not to be violated, reduced, or presumed by others.

In this way God offers us the gift of life in its fullness. God places a value on creation by respecting human autonomy, freedom, and responsibility. This is God's greatness. It is in this sense that God reveals his magnanimity. God is a Father or Mother, so to speak, who withdraws from the scene once the gift has been offered so as not to influence the receiver either to accept or reject the offering.

An Offer Which Respects Human Freedom

Who is not tempted to control human freedom? Whether it will be in the home, at school or church, in the village, city or in any other area of public activity, there are always groups trying to limit, control, or "dole freedom out in driblets." I like very much what Zundel said during a retreat in 1959:

> The human being has always had fear of freedom because he did not know what it was, he did not understand what it signified and he often judged that it was more prudent to restrict it, and to allow it only to trickle forth, and to monitor it in all ways, because he trusted neither the group nor himself. And that is where we are.[11]

There is no doubt that we can have a false idea of freedom when it is simply identified as an arbitrary power to do whatever we wish. Nonetheless, we have already seen in chapter 6 above how freedom is the result of the process which goes from the liberation from all external constraints to a liberation from internal ones in order to discover that freedom is acquired, finally, in the gift of oneself to others, in giving up the tendency to possess everything around us. Freedom consists in giving one's self to the other/Other.

It is here that the inviolability of the human being is displayed. For even if one is capable of forcing acceptance of a gift on someone by means of some external pressure, there are still large unassailable areas within the human person. No one, for example, is able to violate the interiority of another being; no one is able to penetrate the sanctuary of his or her conscience; no one can oblige another human being to open himself or herself, without her or his own consent, in a voluntary and free way, to the love which has been offered.

God also respects human freedom because God created it. God does not wish a servile love, an obligatory response or a forced

LIFE BEYOND DEATH

consent motivated by the fear of eternal punishment. Servile love is not able to be eternal; it does not deserve the name of love. A forced response is never able to be free; freedom conditioned in such a way is not permitted in our relationship with God.

Responsibility toward Ourselves, Others and Creation

Accepting from someone a gift which flows from love, from affection or solidarity implies an involvement and a responsibility on the part of the person who accepts the gift. But most of all, one who accepts a gift permits another person to enter into his or her life, that is, one becomes vulnerable. One understands how a person must be at ease to permit another to enter and live within one's own life.

Permitting another to dwell within becomes a way of discovering ourselves as human beings and leads us to accept a new responsibility toward ourselves wherein we allow another to be welcomed into our lives where she or he can feel at home. This of course must be done with regard for one's privacy, leaving the dignity of the other intact and respected.

We need to develop a sense of responsibility vis-à-vis the rights of the other in situations when we risk falling into the temptation of appropriating that person, of making the individual our possession or an echo of our own voices and desires. Only another human being is truly capable of leading us outside ourselves. As I have already expressed it,[12] people can discover their gifts, their talents, and who they are in the eyes of those who recognize and receive them, particularly in the eyes of those who love them.[13] Only in the presence of another human being can people discover themselves as human, as Adam did in the presence of Eve, according to one of the two symbolic creation accounts in the book of Genesis (2:23). Other people are not potential enemies but are a reflection, as in a mirror, of one's very self. This mirroring of others is essential for human development[14] and for our spiritual journey. It allows for the sharing of one's innermost feelings and emotions with someone else.

There is also a responsibility toward our "mother earth" that enables us to recognize a welcoming space within her. It reminds us of the great expanding universe from which we originate, always calling us to be a part of herself and to make it possible that creation will be transformed into the image of the image. Finally, accepting the gift of eternal life that God offers to us implies also our own responsibility: to recognize in God someone who loves us, who awaits our response. In short, we are called to respond to God's gift in our own life, totally, throughout our whole existence. There is no closed horizon which is outside of the dynamic of human life. God's offer is always present: God does not withdraw love for human beings.

Therefore, if this gift awaits a response which is rooted in our autonomy, freedom and in our sense of responsibility, this response is not forced, but is awaited in love and respect. And most of all, there is no doubt that this invitation can be refused.

3. An Invitation that Can Be Refused

The love of God is not imposed on us. As Sesboüé says: "It is offered in order to be recognized and welcomed."[15] This recognition and welcoming demand a free act from us, a response which is able to be negative. In that denial lies the foundation of the notion and reality of hell.

God does not force us to accept love, and therein is God's fragility. God respects our decision, our power to refuse it. The Bible and the magisterium of the Church proclaim the possibility of this refusal. Now we should try to see how to understand this difficult possibility.

The "Fragility" of God: We Are Able to Refuse God's Love

Fragility is not synonymous with weakness. Thus, the fragility of God does not indicate any kind of weakness in God's constitution. Fragility expresses the graciousness of God's love and respect of creatures. God does not like an obligatory and servile love, or a forced response, or a *yes* given under pressure. "It is in this dimension," said Zundel in 1965, "that God is fragile and disarmed in the face of our refusal to enter into a dialogue that radically excludes any constraint."[16] God always accepts the refusal of the human person to be open so that God might establish a relationship of love, of becoming a free person. That is why, as in all free relationships, the possibility of refusal is present. It is, in effect, a rejection of the love offered by God. According to Maurice Zundel, it is there that one finds the meaning of hell—in the refusal of God: "Hell, is essentially the refusal of God by us, the condemnation which the free creature is able to inflict on God, the eternal crucifixion of Love in a heart which does not love him."[17] Even though God always offers his love, we are able to reject it; we are able to destroy, definitively, this relationship to God, to enclose ourselves in our own great solitude.

All people who love experience this fragility, the possibility of a definite rejection of their love. The donor becomes the first victim of the love that is refused. Therein is the meaning of the suffering of compassion, of the suffering which constitutes the fragility of God:

> God undergoes a suffering of compassion in identifying with us, like that displayed by the image of the mother who identifies with her child and suffers in him, through him, and even more so than the child himself because she feels in her love the extent of the misery of her child more profoundly than the child himself who is deprived of this high enlightenment.[18]

How could we conceive of hell as God's creation, or a God who places us in hell, knowing the compassion of His love? God is like a mother who suffers the refusal of her children. Hell is the suffering of God, a suffering which is born out of his own compassion.

A Refusal Which Is Able to Become a Reality

The theme of eternal death can be traced back to the Old Testament following the evolution of *Sheol*, as we have seen in chapter 5. *Sheol* is the dwelling place of all the dead. Much later it will become, with the appearance of faith in the resurrection of the dead, a place of waiting, before finally becoming the place of perdition. Thus Scripture envisages the possibility of a total disaster, namely, the eternal damnation of the human being:

> And they shall go out and look at the dead bodies of the people who have rebelled against me; for their worm shall not die, their fire shall not be quenched, and they shall be an abhorrence to all flesh. (Isa. 66:24)

For its part, the Book of Daniel, in speaking about the resurrection, says: "'Many of those who sleep in the dust of the earth shall awake, some to everlasting life, and some to shame and everlasting contempt'" (Dan. 12:2).

In the New Testament, this condemnation is formulated as the negation of the communion with God, which constitutes beatitude:

> For those who want to save their life will lose it, and those who lose their life for my sake, and for the sake of the gospel, will save it. For what will it profit them to gain the whole world and forfeit their life? Indeed, what can they give in return for their life? (Mk. 8:35-37)

In the parable of the banquet, which is an image of the kingdom, one sees that sinners are excluded from the table:

> There will be weeping and gnashing of teeth when you see Abraham and Isaac and Jacob and all the prophets in the kingdom of God, and you yourselves thrown out. Then people will come from east and west, from north and south, and will eat in the kingdom of God. Indeed, some are last who will be first, and some are first who will be last. (Lk. 13:28-30; see also Mt. 22:13-14)

Besides, there were the foolish bridesmaids to whom the door was not opened at the wedding feast; they were not recognized by the bridegroom, as were the wise virgins who entered with the spouse (Mt. 25:1-13). For his part, Paul speaks of the possibility of not inheriting the kingdom (1 Cor. 6:9-10; Gal. 5:21) while John uses the expression to *not see life:* "Whoever believes in the Son has eternal life; whoever disobeys the Son will not see life, but must endure God's wrath" (Jn. 3:36).

All of these statements present a possibility of condemnation consisting principally in an exclusion from immediate access to God or to Christ through whom human beings attain eternal life. Hell is not described as such, but damnation is inferred indirectly from the refusal of salvation.

Other statements describe hell first of all as the opposite of glory or eternal life. Thus, hell represents a lost life which goes nowhere and is therefore meaningless. Consequently, hell finds its most real sense in the idea of death, or of eternal death.[19]

There is, in the New Testament, a series of images describing hell directly. These descriptions, using a symbolic language, underline the fact that hell represents the eternal loss of God on the part of the one for whom life becomes a tragic disaster. Furthermore, it is this separation from God which constitutes the essence of physical suffering. Thus, among the images which describe hell, one finds: the unquenchable fire (Mk. 9:43; Mt. 13;42; Rev. 19:20); the weeping and gnashing of teeth (Mt. 8:12; 13:42; Lk. 13:28); the outer darkness (Mt. 8:12); "the lake of fire that burns with sulfur" (Rev. 19:20); the worm that will never die (Mk. 9:48); the prison (1 Pet. 3:19).[20]

Nevertheless, in speaking of the last judgment in the preceding chapter, I suggested that one should not interpret, in a rigorously literal fashion, all of a series of texts with their own unique symbolic import and which were usually written in an apocalyptic context. One cannot interpret the images and symbols which describe hell in a literal way.

As an example, one can see the need for interpreting the meaning of fire, which is used in several images describing damnation. To understand fire in an empirical and literal sense as constituting one of the punishments of hell would be as unacceptable as believing that a messianic banquet of food and drink would become one of the elements of beatitude. In the synoptic vocabulary of the state of perdition, fire is symbolic of that state in its entirety and not solely one of its elements. The symbol of fire is not used to illustrate a physical suffering accompanying the exclusion from the kingdom but rather the emptiness of a life lacking communion with God. Outside of this communion, human existence remains completely frustrated, useless, and without any meaning, like a tree without fruit or a stalk without grain. What is useless, such as a tree without fruit or a stalk without grain, is burnt. Burning signifies uselessness symbolically, but the fire is not real.[21]

The doctrine on hell appears in the most ancient documents of the patristic era and in texts of the magisterium of the Church up to the Second Vatican II Council. The magisterium defines the existence of a state of mortal sin or enmity with God. Thus, in the declarations of the magisterium on hell there is mention of its existence, its eternal duration, hell immediately after death for the rejected; the distinction between the pain of loss (the privation of the vision of God) and the pains of the senses, that is to say, the physical sufferings.[22]

Number 48 of the Dogmatic Constitution on the Church (*Lumen Gentium*), of the Second Vatican Council, in speaking of retribution at the end of our earthly life, refers also to hell:

> Since we know not the day nor the hour, on our Lord's advice we must constantly stand guard. Thus when we have finished the one and only course of our earthly life (cf. Heb. 9:27) we may merit to enter into the marriage feast with Him and to be numbered among the blessed (cf. Mt. 25:31-46). Thus we may not be commanded to go into eternal fire (cf. Mt. 25:41) like the wicked and slothful servant (cf. Mt. 25:26), into the exterior darkness where "there will be the weeping and the gnashing of teeth" (Mt. 22:13; 25:30).

The texts of the magisterium of the Church speak of the existence of a state of eternal damnation which includes the privation of the vision of God and the undergoing of physical pains. Therefore, how is it possible to understand the scope of these statements? What is the real meaning of this which is defined as a dogma of faith? How are we able to understand, basically, the meaning of eternal death?

LIFE BEYOND DEATH

The Meaning of "Eternal Death"

The deepest meaning of the biblical texts and of the magisterium of the Church is to place before us human responsibility in the face of God's love. It treats of the responsibility that accompanies freedom and which is mediated by an involvement of respect for oneself, others and creation. A human being is able to refuse the love God offers and to refuse to enter into communion with God for all eternity. In that refusal there emerges a deprived life which has not been a positive response to the call of God, which has not accepted the invitation to develop into the image and likeness of God, which has refused to live as an adoptive child of God. Briefly, it is a life which remains bound to its own self-dependence, to its own finitude.

Hell is a real possibility connected with the freedom of the human being. In this sense, one is able to say "that hell is no longer a punishment from God, but rather a creation of the human being. God did not make hell. Hell arises when love is totally refused."[23] That is why no one is authorized to use the fear of hell as a means of conversion. Regardless of the affirmation of hell, "anyone who considers the possibility that even only one other, besides oneself, is damned, that one will probably find difficult to love without reservation."[24] As Christians, we are called to hope for all.

The Church defines two kinds of sufferings attached to hell: the pain of loss and the pain of the senses. The pain of loss consists in the privation of the vision of God, that is to say, in being separated from communion with God. The pain of the senses refers to bodily pains, to physical suffering without specifying them, and indicates only a variety among them. Thus, in the Second General Council of Lyons (in 1274), in the "Profession of Faith of Michael Palaeologus," it is professed: "As for the souls of those who die in mortal sin or with original sin only, they go down immediately *(mox)* to hell *(in infernum),* to be punished however with different punishments."[25]

Nevertheless, the most difficult question to interpret is that of the eternity of hell, as was proclaimed, for example, in the Provincial Synod of Constantinople (in 543), in the anathemas against the

Origenists when it was affirmed that, "If anyone says or holds that the punishment of the demons and of impious human beings is temporary, and that it will have an end at some time, or that there will be a complete restoration *(apokatasasis)* of demons and impious human beings, *anathema sit [let her or him be an anathema]*."[26]

How are we able to interpret the pains of hell and its eternity? This is the most difficult question about hell. I believe that to say, as did Sesboüé, "the eternity of hell is a corollary of the love of God and of the freedom of the human being"[27] no longer makes sense. That the foundation of hell lies in the refusal of God's love, that it is a consequence of human freedom, is evident; but to say that its eternity derives from this is difficult to understand.

One possible explanation, in our attempt to understand damnation and its related suffering, might be to see such a destiny as a real eternal death. If the human being is, by creation, dependent and finite, then death must be part of one's nature. If the gift of eternal life truly represents an invitation from God to become God's image and likeness, then logically death must represent, for any who reject such a gift, the end of life forever. In this sense, one can employ the expression eternal death to refer to hell: death is truly eternal! As Gregersen says, "Finally, I propose an annihilation theory, according to which perdition is interpreted as eternal nothingness rather than as eternal torment."[28] Edward Schillebeeckx expressed it in the same way:

> The evildoers do not have eternal life, their death is the end of everything: they have excluded themselves from God and from the community of the righteous. They will not know the new heaven and the new earth. They have ceased to exist, incapable as they are of understanding the good which renders people happy and righteous. But a hell which is the opposite of the eternal joy of the Kingdom of God, that does not exist.[29]

On the other hand, is it possible to imagine pains greater than those which come from the fact of remaining dead forever? Death implies the absence of communion with God (the pain of the loss), isolation from others and from a renewed universe. Thus, it seems

LIFE BEYOND DEATH

to me that there is no greater suffering (suffering of the senses) than to remain cemented to one's finitude forever, to die for ever!

Eternity is not united to the contingency and finitude of the human being. Eternity is an invitation, an offer which God makes to human beings, but which may be accepted or rejected. It is in this way that one is able to safeguard, on the one hand, the declarations of the magisterium of the Church regarding hell and, on the other hand, to try to understand a little more fully this sad possibility.

Hell is not a creation of God; it is not a place where one goes. Hell is the end of the one who should have preferred, in a clear and reflective manner, to build her or his life in communion with God, with our sisters and brothers and with the new heaven and the new earth (Rev. 21).

⁑

In the light of a real possibility of damnation, as expressed both in Scripture and in the magisterium of the Roman Catholic Church, and apart from the symbolic expressions of certain biblical texts and of the language often used in the magisterial declarations and in preaching, "the Church, which has declared saints of so many, has never expressed herself regarding the perdition of a single one among them."[30] That is why one is not justified in using the fear of hell or of damnation as a means of conversion, of subjugation. The end never justifies the means.

God offers us life and final salvation, forever, for all eternity; it is only in God that one finds one's full human development. But all are called to respond to this gift from God; a human being is free to accept the offer or to reject it. That is each one's responsibility! Nevertheless, we are invited to hope for the salvation of all.

Notes to Chapter 9

1   Rahner, *More Recent Writings*, p. 340.

2   Clément, *op. cit.*, p. 29; see also Vogels, *Nos origines*, pp. 41–89.

3   Clément, *op. cit.*, p. 31.

4   M. Flick and Z. Alszeghy, *L'homme dans la théologie* (M. Lionnet, trans.), Paris/Sherbrooke: Apostolat des Éditions/Paulines (Le Point, 20), 1972, p. 77.

5   *Ibid.*, p. 68.

6   *Ibid.*, p. 70.

7   *Ibid.*, 82.

8   Clément, *op. cit.*, p. 45.

9   *Ibid.*, p. 49.

10   M. E. Brinkman, *The Tragedy of Human Freedom: The Failure and Promise of the Christian Concept of Freedom in Western Culture* (H. Flecken and H. Jansen, trans.), Amsterdam/New York: Rodopi B. V. (Currents of Encounter: Studies on the Contact between Christianity and Other Religions, Beliefs, and Cultures, 20), 2003, p. 36; see also pp. 27–35.

11   M. Zundel, *Je parlerai à ton coeur*, (Retreat preached to the Franciscan sisters of Lebanon, in August 3 to 10, 1959), Quebec: Anne Sigier, 1990, p. 48.

12   See my book *Death by Despair*, pp. 76–78.

13   See S. Chance, *Stronger than Death*, New York/London: W. W. Norton & Company, Inc., 1992, p. 101; H. B. Mokros, "Suicide and Shame," in *American Behavioral Scientist*, 38/8 (1995), pp. 1091–1103; H. J. M. Nouwen, *Reaching Out: The Three Movements of the Spiritual Life*, Garden City: Doubleday & Company, Inc., 1975, p. 61; see also pp. 46–78.

14   See S. Feshbach, B. Weiner and A. Bohart, *Personality* (4th ed.), Lexington: Health and Company, 1996, pp. 146–147, 547–548.

15   Sesboüé, *op. cit.*, p. 153.

16   M. Zundel, *Hymne à la joie*, Paris: Ouvrières (Points d'appui), 1965, p. 41.

17   *Id.*, unpublished text of 1950, quoted in Donzé, *Témoin d'une présence*, p. 62.

18   *Id.*, unpublished text of 1963, quoted in M. Donzé, *L'humble présence*, p. 167. Maurice Zundel spoke often of the experience of a mother who suffered in silence and in patience, contemplating her son's separation and his return home as a sick person: "Finally, after thirty years and more of this life, he came back, ill with tuberculosis. Even the sanatoria no longer wanted to keep him. And it

is here that this dialogue I spoke to you about is set, the dialogue of this woman faced with her son doomed to die, this marvellous dialogue in which she begged God for one thing alone: that her son should not die without casting a look at Him. She asked nothing for herself, but she prayed that this life might not come to an end without a glance toward God.

"She said nothing. She watched him day and night in a heroic silence. And it was then that this son met a priest who kept the same kind of silence as that of the mother. One day, the son told the priest the whole story of his life and said to him: 'It is true, I have never had any religion, but now I want my mother's religion.' And to his mother, he said: 'Mama, if you had spoken of God to me, I would never have converted. Because you never spoke of him to me, I understood because of you, through you.'

"He had made out the face of God, the silence of God, for he had felt it in his mother's silence, and this woman saved her son without uttering a word, simply because she had become the monstrance of Jesus. She had prayed that her son die on All Saints' Day and he did. She really gave him back to the Lord without asking anything for herself." (M. Zundel, *With God in Our Daily Life*, [Retreat preached to the sisters of the Saint-Augustine Work at Saint-Maurice, Valais, Switzerland, in November 1953] [F. Audette, trans.], Sherbrooke: Paulines, 1933, p. 169)

19   See Lk. 13:3; Jn. 5:24; 6:50; 8:51; Rom. 5:12; 6:21; 1 Cor. 15:21; Eph. 2:1-5; 1 Tim. 5:6; 1 Jn. 3:14; 5:16-17; Rev. 20:14.

20   See Sesboüé, *op. cit.*, pp. 150–152; Ruíz de la Peña, *op. cit.*, pp. 267–288; Ratzinger, *op. cit.*, pp. 215–218; Schmaus, *op. cit.*, pp. 249–259. According to Bauckham and Hart, "What is clear from the use of all the images of final condemnation is that at least they depict the unimaginable horror of rejection by God and its finality. They do not suggest a limited judgement or purgatorial experience from which people may eventually emerge to salvation. They represent the final loss of salvation. It may be that beyond this we cannot go. The traditional doctrine of hell took the images of eternally experienced punishment literally, but was thereby obliged to take the images of final destruction less literally. Our contention that eschatological language is irreducible imaginative suggests that we should be content to let the various images stand, not reducing one to another, though we must also avoid understanding them in a way that is inconsistent with what we know of God and God's purposes in Christ. The literal reading of these images has in the past sometimes exercised a seriously distorting effect on believers' images of God, while conversely the modern tendency to exclude them altogether has helped to sap the seriousness from the biblical account of God's judgement." (Bauckham and Hart, *Hope against Hope*, pp. 146–147; see also p. 145)

21   See Ruíz de la Peña, *op. cit.*, pp. 273–275; H. U. von Balthasar, *L'enfer: Une question* (J. L. Schlegel, trans.), Paris: Desclée de Brouwer (DDB), 1988, pp. 23–33.

22   See *CF*, nᵒˢ 17, 20, 26, 506, 2301, 2303, 2317.

23   Sesboüé, *op. cit.*, p. 154; see also Boros, "Some Thoughts on the Four Last Things," p. 42.

24   Balthasar, *op. cit.*, p. 60.

25   *CF*, n° 26.

26   *CF*, n° 2301. See chapter 2 above where, in its note 15, I have referred to the theory of an universal restoration which is linked to Origen.

27   Sesboüé, *op. cit.*, p. 158.

28   Gregersen, *op. cit.*, p. 172; see also pp. 178–180.

29   E. Schillebeeckx, *L'histoire des hommes, récit de Dieu* (H. Cornelis-Gevaert, trans.), Paris: Éd. du Cerf (Cogitatio Fidei, 166), 1992, p. 215; see also pp. 211–216.

30   Balthasar, *op. cit.*, p. 32.

Is There a Life Between Death and Resurrection?

We have already seen how the first Christians expected the early return of the Lord. Some even believed that they would be alive when the *parousia* of Christ—his second coming in glory—was to take place. With it, Christian hope would arrive at its fulfillment: in the resurrection of the dead, along with life everlasting, a renewed humanity, a new heaven and a new earth. However, Christians still waited for the return of Christ, and death continued to be a part of human existence. What would take place between the individual's death and the resurrection at the end of time? Do we wait in some place, in the meantime? Is there an individual judgment?

At the moment of death each one of us is confronted with the ultimate. Death is also the stage where how we actually lived our very personal life is revealed, the point at which so-called retribution comes to pass. Then rejoicing in the presence of God forever shall truly take place. All this will occur despite the possibility of our need to be "purified" in order to enter into eternal communion with the Holy One (this is the meaning of *purgatory*), or the extreme and sad possibility of dying forever.

This chapter will also address the question of the relationship and/or difference between the immortality of the soul and the resurrection of the body. Between personal death and the final resurrection, does the soul, separated from the body, rejoice in the presence of God? Or, does the resurrection come about at the moment of the death of each of us?

According to the Christian understanding of hope, after death we definitively become one with Christ. In effect, from the moment of our death we also become members of the body of the risen Christ. In the New Testament, this way of dying is called *dying in the Lord*. If through baptism we already participate in the resurrection of the Lord, by death, we also participate in the body of the risen Christ. These important points will be discussed throughout this chapter.

1. Final Retribution: Particular Judgment and the Question of Purgatory

The idea of an intermediate state between death and final resurrection is born in Judaism with the belief in the resurrection of the dead at the end of time. I have noted in chapters 5 and 9 how, before faith in the resurrection emerged, *Sheol* was considered to be the residing place of the dead. With the belief in the resurrection, *Sheol* became an intermediate state, a waiting place until the resurrection and the final retribution. It would ultimately become identified with hell.

There, in *Sheol*, we can already perceive a certain recompense for the righteous and, later, also for the evildoer. The Hellenistic world view presented a dualistic anthropology: a human being is composed of body and of soul. The soul, separated from the body, becomes the recipient of the retribution. What is defined as a dogma of faith is that after our death each one of us will enter into a final state, that is, the ultimate retribution.[1] At death the individual's ultimate destiny is realized. This is the basis of what has been called the particular (personal) judgment. However, particular judgment has not been declared as a dogma of faith by the Roman Catholic Church.

If at death one enters into communion with God, that is to say, one rejoices in the sight of God in a definitive way, this excludes any limitation. We understand how difficult it is to hold that each of us is able to attain such perfection. The theological meaning of purgatory underlines this dimension of purification which proceeds throughout our existence and which, at death, arrives at its summit.

From a "Waiting Time" to a Final Retribution

In the Old Testament, from the time when belief in the resurrection of the dead began, death ushers in a period of waiting, with *Sheol* as the place where both the righteous and the evildoer await resurrection in order to receive their retribution. Later on in the apocryphal literature,[2] under the influence of Greek culture and its world view, the idea of retribution after death evolved. In the First book of Enoch, in chapter 22, in speaking about the sojourn of the spirits awaiting the judgment Enoch refers to *Sheol* where the righteous and sinners are kept separated. The sinners, plunged into obscurity, await the final judgment in order to receive the punishment which they have not received during their lives, but the righteous (including among others the martyrs who hold a privileged position), who did not receive a proper recompense during their lifetime, have assembled together close to a fountain and are living in the light: they have already started to enjoy their reward. First Enoch is influenced by Hellenistic dualistic anthropology: the soul, separated from the body, is the subject of immortality and awaits the final (general) judgment and the resurrection of the body:

> Then I went to another place, and he showed me on the west side a great and high mountain of hard rock and inside it four beautiful corners; it had [in it] a deep, wide, and smooth (thing) which was rolling over; and it (the place) was deep and dark to look at. At that moment, Rufael, one of the holy angels, who was with me, responded to me; and he said to me, "These beautiful corners (are here) in order that the spirits of the souls of the dead should assemble into them—they are created so that the souls of the children of the people should gather here. They prepared these places in order to put them (i.e. the souls of the people) there until the day of their judgment and the appointed time of the great judgment upon them." I saw the spirits of the children of the people who were dead, and their voices were reaching unto heaven until this very moment. I asked Rufael, the angel who was with me, and said to him, "This spirit, the voice of which is

reaching (into heaven) like this and is making suit, whose (spirit) is it?" And he answered me, saying, "This is the spirit which had left Abel, whom Cain, his brother, had killed; it (continues to) sue him until all of (Cain's) seed is exterminated from the face of the earth, and his seed has disintegrated from among the seed of the people." At that moment, I raised a question regarding him and regarding the judgment of all, "For what reason is one separated from the other?" And he replied and said to me, "These three have been made in order that the spirits of the dead might be separated. And in the manner in which the souls of the righteous are separated (by) this spring of water with light upon it, in like manner, the sinners are set apart when they die and are buried in the earth and judgment has not been executed upon them in their lifetime, upon this great pain, until the great day of judgment—and to those who curse (there will be) plague and pain forever, and the retribution of their spirits. They will bind them there forever—even if from the beginning of the world. And in this manner is a separation made for the souls of those who make the suit (and) those who disclose concerning destruction, as they were killed in the days of the sinners. Such has been made for the souls of the people who are not righteous, but sinners and perfect criminals; they shall be together with (other) criminals who are like them, (whose) souls will not be killed on the day of judgment but will not rise from there." At that moment I blessed the Lord of Glory and I said, "Blessed be my Lord, the Lord of righteousness who rules forever."[3]

From then on death is presented in Scripture in a double perspective. It is the end of the time of trial and the beginning of the ultimate retribution. That is, death is the end of a stage during which the person is able to merit or to demerit, to decide in favour of God or against God, to say yes or no to the friendship that God offers. After death, a human being no longer has any possibility of making a new decision for or against God (see Wis. 2–5).

Death is portrayed in the same way in the New Testament: "For all of us must appear before the judgment seat of Christ, so that each may receive recompense for what has been done in the body, whether good or evil" (2 Cor. 5:10; see also Mt. 25:31-46).

LIFE BEYOND DEATH

For the New Testament, final salvation is not purely a future reality but a reality which has immediate consequences for those who opt for Christ:

> For to me, living is Christ and dying is gain. If I am to live in the flesh, that means fruitful labor for me; and I do not know which I prefer. I am hard pressed between the two: my desire is to depart and be with Christ, for that is far better; but to remain in the flesh is more necessary for you. (Phil. 1:21-24)

In Luke's description of the two criminals who were crucified with Jesus Christ (Lk. 23:42-43), the one popularly called the "good thief" presents the same reality to us: after death there is communion with God through Jesus Christ (see also 2 Cor. 5:6-8). These texts teach us that, through Christ, with him and in him, those who die in him already enjoy this perfect communion with him, namely, eternal life.

In theology one does not find any clear statement on this subject before the fourteenth century. As Ruíz de la Peña writes, "the fact that a final state of life or of eternal death immediately following death, without waiting the end of history, became the object of many controversies even after the beginning of the XIVth century."[4] Yet, during the Patristic era, death was regarded as the end of life's journey. All of which goes to establish the urgent necessity of living in a Christian manner during the brief time given us to accept the friendship which God offers to us.

During the second and third centuries the predominant view was that death led to a "beginning" of retribution until the moment of the final judgment. Nevertheless, while the idea of a definite retribution did not appear clearly before the fourteenth century, the liturgical practice showed something else, for example in the cult of the martyrs, and later of saints generally. This cult would have had no meaning if there were not already a question of a definite glorification.[5]

As noted in chapter 2, the magisterium of the Church made a pronouncement on the question of a definite retribution at the moment of death in its reply to the problem created by the *Sermon of All Souls* of Pope John XXII in 1331. The Constitution *Benedictus Deus* of Pope Benedict XII (in 1336) responded:

> By this Constitution which is to remain in force for ever, we, with apostolic authority, define the following: According to the general disposition of God, the souls of all the saints who departed from this world before the passion of our Lord Jesus Christ and also of the holy apostles, martyrs, confessors, virgins and other faithful who died after receiving the holy baptism of Christ—provided they were not in need of any purification when they died, or will not be in need of any when they die in the future, or else, if they then needed or will need some purification, after they have been purified after death—and again the souls of children who have been reborn by the same baptism of Christ or will be when baptism is conferred on them, if they die before attaining the use of free will: all these souls, immediately (*mox*) after death and, in the case of those in need of purification, after the purification mentioned above, since the ascension of our Lord and Saviour Jesus Christ into heaven, already before they take up their bodies again and before the general judgment, have been, are and will be with Christ in heaven, in the heavenly kingdom and paradise, joined to the company of the holy angels. Since the passion and death of the Lord Jesus Christ, these souls have seen and see the divine essence with an intuitive vision and even face to face, without the mediation of any creature by way of object of vision; rather the divine essence immediately manifests itself to them, plainly, clearly and openly, and in this vision they enjoy the divine essence. Moreover, by this vision and enjoyment the souls of those who have already died are truly blessed and have eternal life and rest. Also the souls of those who will die in the future will see the same divine essence and will enjoy it before the general judgment.

> Such a vision and enjoyment of the divine essence do away with the acts of faith and hope in these souls, inasmuch as faith and hope are properly theological virtues. And after such intuitive and face-to-face vision and enjoyment has or will have begun for these souls, the same vision and enjoyment has continued and

LIFE BEYOND DEATH

will continue without any interruption and without end until the last Judgment and from then on forever.

Moreover we define that according to the general disposition of God, the souls of those who die in actual mortal sin go down into hell immediately (*mox*) after death and there suffer the pain of hell. Nevertheless, on the day of judgment all will appear with their bodies "before the judgment seat of Christ" to give an account of their personal deeds, "so that each one may receive good or evil, according to what one has done in the body" [*2 Cor. 5:10*].[6]

In number 49 of the Dogmatic Constitution on the Church (*Lumen Gentium*) of the Second Vatican Council, the same doctrine is repeated: the righteous dead and already purified "are in glory, beholding 'clearly God Himself triune and one, as He is.'"[7]

If death is the culmination of our earthly journey, then it is also through death that a person enters into the fullness of life which God offers us through Jesus Christ and in the Holy Spirit.

A Particular Judgment?

In reality, Scripture refers only to the last (general) judgment which the magisterium of the Church has defined as a dogma of the faith. What is commonly called individual (personal) judgment denotes the conviction that, at death, there is established a final state for each individual. Consequently, it is not correct to understand it as a legal judgment where the person undergoes a process and awaits sentence, as was presented in some preaching and in a certain religious tradition that engendered fear and became the source of much self-abnegation and repression.[8]

The magisterium of the Church defines the final retribution after death. While preaching currently speaks clearly of an individual judgment, the official Church definitions treat only of the final state immediately after death, namely, of the conviction, attested in Scripture, that a human being is recompensed by God according to their deeds (Ps. 62:12; Eccl. 3:17; 11:9; 12:14; Jer. 32:19; Mt. 16:27; Rom. 2:6; 2 Cor. 5:10; Rev. 20:12). Furthermore, the Bible, while recognizing that retribution is a function of earthly merits, only speaks of a universal judgment at the end of time. That a judgment takes place immediately after the death of each person is not mentioned anywhere in Scripture.

Today the best way to understand what is popularly called a particular (personal) judgment is to say that at death each one is faced with a definite outcome. At death the deepest dimension of our existence is manifested, and at that time there is no longer the possibility of hiding this. It is the moment of supreme clarity which permits us to see if we have constructed our life in communion with God, with others, and in solidarity with creation. It is therefore the moment of one's total self-revelation. In this sense one is able to speak of a self-judgment to which I have referred in chapter 8 above. Finally, a human being will either feel worthy of the eternal life that God offers in Jesus Christ and in the Holly Spirit, or will see life simply as an existence built on the greatest of solitudes and on the eternity of death itself—that is, that the person dies forever. The moment of one's ultimate retribution therefore begins immediately after death.

The Question of Purgatory

If eternal life begins immediately after death, there is another point of which Scripture speaks: only a person freed from all limitations, by a fully accomplished human life, is worthy of eternal communion with God. Consequently, one is able to say that only a person whose life is characterized by absolute purity is worthy to be admitted to the presence of God (Ex. 20:18-21; Isa. 35:8; 52:1; Mt. 5:8, 48). This is the rational for the doctrine of purgatory.

The "official birth" of purgatory did not occur until the twelfth century.[9] In order to understand the development of the doctrine, according to Sesboüé, one must consider two dimensions: "The value of the prayer for the dead and the conviction of the need for most of the departed to have a purifying sanctification, before they might be able to appear in the presence of God. The two themes are connected and each depends on the other."[10]

In the Old Testament, when faith in the resurrection at the end of time finally appears, Judas Maccabee and his people offered prayers for those killed in battle and upon whom were found forbidden objects:

> Then Judas assembled his army and went to the city of A·dul'lam. As the seventh day was coming on, they purified themselves according to the custom, and kept the sabbath there.
>
> On the next day, as had now become necessary, Judas and his men went to take up the bodies of the fallen and to bring them back to lie with their kindred in the sepulchres of their ancestors. Then under the tunic of each one of the dead they found sacred tokens of the idols of Jam'ni·a, which the law forbids the Jews to wear. And it became clear to all that this was the reason these men had fallen. So they all blessed the ways of the Lord, the righteous judge, who reveals the things that are hidden; and they turned to supplication, praying that the sin that had been committed might be wholly blotted out. The noble Judas exhorted the people to keep themselves free from sin, for they had seen with their own eyes what had happened as the result of the sin of those who had fallen. He also took up a collection, man by man, to the amount of two thousand drachmas of silver, and sent it to Jerusalem to provide for a sin offering. In doing this he acted very well and honorably, taking account of the resurrection. For if he were not expecting that those who had fallen would rise again, it would have been superfluous and foolish to pray for the dead. But if he was looking to the splendid reward that is laid up for those who fall asleep in godliness, it was a holy and pious thought. Therefore he made atonement for the dead, so that they might be delivered from their sin. (2 Macc. 12:38-45)

For its part, the Christian community prays for its brothers and sisters who "have finished with this life and are being purified."[11] The community is aware that not all have reached the end of life with full perfection already attained.

In reality, the doctrine of purgatory is united to the development of the doctrine of justification, which places in evidence the importance of assuming human responsibility for acquiring one's own salvation.[12] There is a difference between the guilt (fault) itself and the debt (penance) for the sin committed. If pardon of sins removes the guilt (fault), there still remains the debt (penance) from which it is necessary to be purified.[13] The meaning and purpose for indulgences is to intercede for ourselves or for someone else in order to remove, or decrease, the debt (penance) due to sins. Such intercession may also be applied on behalf of the dead in the event that they may have died without having paid the full debt (penance) due to their sins.

The magisterium of the Roman Catholic Church defined the existence of a state of punishment and of purification where souls are cleansed of venial faults, or who still have to pay a certain temporal penance for their sins.[14] What is the extent of these declarations?

In the first place, what appears to be defined and accepted by both Eastern and Western churches is the existence of a state where the dead who may not have been fully purified at the end of their earthly existence must still undergo this purification. In the second place, one notes the penal and expiational character of this state, and, finally, the value of the intercessions of the living for the dead, such as prayers, alms, good works, indulgences and, especially, the sacrifice of the mass.

The possibility of offering this assistance is founded in the doctrine of the communion of saints. All those who are united to Christ are intimately united among themselves. All that they do, they do as members of the community that unites them. The whole community is therefore affected by the deeds of each of its members. All members together as one take a mysterious part in the action of the individual and speak in his or her words. In the same way, according to the traditional doctrine of the Roman Catholic Church, the souls who undergo this process of purification (in so-called purgatory) are comforted by the love of their brothers and sisters on earth. Death does not destroy the community formed in Christ but brings it to perfection.[15]

At the same time, it is very important to avoid representing purgatory as a kind of temporary hell rather than as a transitory state of purification. This risk appears in the style of some of the official declarations of the magisterium of the Church when speaking about the penal character of purgatory. Delumeau refers to

LIFE BEYOND DEATH

the process of *infernalization* of purgatory, even in contrast to the best intentions of the magisterium of the Church. Certain works on purgatory are nevertheless an exception to this process, such as those of Catherine of Genoa (1447–1510). Finally, purgatory will be conceived as a state in which one is placed in order to be punished for sins committed: "This place [purgatory] is thus a punishment more than a purification. It is a scene of expiation, of execution of the 'judgments of God,' who 'avenges' Himself on guilty men, no matter if they have been pardoned."[16] In this sense, even if one is not able to find a single mention of the fire of purgatory in the solemn declarations of the magisterium of the Church, the fire of purgatory was presented in preaching as one of the physical punishments. For example,

> During the Counter-Reformation, Bellarmine was convinced that the primary physical pain of Purgatory is that of fire. Like many experts, however, he wonders whether this fire is actual or metaphoric. Without formally committing himself, he argues that, on the general opinion of the theologians, it is a real fire.[17]

Consequently, as Cardinal Ratzinger highlights, we have to recover the deep theological meaning of purgatory as a process of purifying transformation and not as a kind of "concentration camp":

> The essential Christian understanding of Purgatory has now become clear. Purgatory is not, as Tertullian thought, some kind of supra-worldly concentration camp where man is forced to undergo punishment in a more or less arbitrary fashion. Rather is it the inwardly necessary process of transformation in which a person becomes capable of Christ, capable of God and thus capable of unity with the whole communion of saints. Simply to look at people with any degree of realism at all is to grasp the necessity of such a process. It does not replace grace by works, but allows the former to achieve its full victory precisely as grace. What actually saves is the full assent of faith. But in most of us, that basic option is buried under a great deal of wood, hay and straw. Only with difficulty can it peer out from behind the latticework of an egoism we are powerless to pull down with our

own hands. Man is the recipient of the divine mercy, yet this does not exonerate him from the need to be transformed. Encounter with the Lord *is* this transformation. It is the fire [in a symbolic way] that burns away our dross and re-forms us to be vessels of eternal joy.[18]

This process of human maturation which permits us to enjoy the presence of the Lord and the communion with our brothers and sisters for eternity is undoubtedly not easy to obtain. Most of us will reach the end of life not as a finely carved statue but as a rough outline. Notwithstanding, in order to live with God it is necessary to belong totally to God. God grants the human person the possibility and necessity of maturing during life up to the moment of death. At death, the human person is confronted with what he or she truly is, with what will be eternally stable in his or her being. This is a painful process because a human being can no longer make excuses for her or his life. Thus, as Boros underlines,

> We call this state purgatory. It is the process of ultimate submission that every lover knows. Purgatory is man's encounter with his true self, the consolidation of total existence into essence, the instantaneous passage to total selfhood that is the essence of death, the anthropological and existential aspect of the death process. But because a man cannot be so utterly "himself" without at the same time experiencing, in his own process of becoming truly man, the reality of the incarnation, his self-encounter develops through Christ into an encounter with God. This is not an additional aspect of the death process but rather the revelation of the integration of the human reality with the being of Christ that comes about through grace. Through encountering himself in total honesty, which means himself divested of all existential irrelevancies, man meets Christ.[19]

This process begins on earth. The sufferings, the frustrations and the tragedies of life can be transformed in strong and precious sources of interiorization and of purification. Maurice Zundel uses a beautiful image to describe the process of purifying transformation as similar to a ripening:

And purgatory is that! Look, the purgatory is nothing other than an immense hope! There is a crowd of people who have not been models! My goodness. Without doubt, they have done what they could, but they have not achieved their best. They perhaps could have done more, but they have not done the maximum. They might perhaps have achieved a better earthly existence. There are even those who, because they knew very little, failed to accomplish much! Purgatory is like a big incubator where all souls who have not developed in the sunlight of Love will be able to hatch and grow.[20]

No doubt we have often experienced at certain privileged moments a sense of standing before ourselves without any protective screen, and how these moments can be painful, even though they are also magnificent! We are then completely ourselves with all that we have created and developed throughout life: before us is the image which we have formed! Nevertheless we are dependent and finite beings. Perfection comes after a long voyage which does not always lead to a good port. That is our purgatory! There are painful passages, but we are able to open ourselves to the sunlight of the love of God in order to come, at the end of the journey, to the perfect light, our meeting with God. If there is an indissoluble solidarity between our becoming human and our encounter with God, the stage of purification permits us to die and to reach the accomplishment of this communion. Those who love are well acquainted with this purifying and maturing dimension of life.

I have already suggested elsewhere[21] what I would do if I were God, whenever someone comes into my presence after death, and I had to decide whether he or she deserves to live forever in Paradise. If I were God, I would ask everyone to write an essay before he or she were allowed to enter heaven. However, I would not ask them to write about their personal misdeeds, faults or limitations. The sins that we commit in life are, after all, pretty much the same for everyone. There is no originality in defining or listing our moral shortcomings. I would rather ask them to write about those talents and gifts which they had received in life but, for various reasons, were not able to make blossom fully in this world.

Paradise, heaven, is life everlasting. One has to "enter alive" into death. Therefore, such an essay might help people become reconciled with all the wonderful gifts they have had in their lives yet may not have been able to explore as a way of becoming fully alive in eternal life. This is the way in which I conceive purgatory.

2. Immortality of the Soul and Resurrection of the Body

I have already spoken of the immortality of the soul. There is a certain view reflected in a particular language that holds that it is the soul separated from the body which enjoys the presence of God and awaits a final resurrection. However, what does this mean for us today within a scientific view of the universe?[22] How may we interpret this in a non-dualistic language? When we speak of the immortality of the soul and the resurrection of the body, are we referring to two different realities?

The Problem

The human person is destined to earn either merit or demerit. The unique subject of retribution is this same person in his or her own integrity and identity. Biblical anthropology is not dualistic. The creation of the human being, like that of matter, is a very good work of God (Gen. 1:31). Matter and spirit are equally part of God's creation and are called to a re-creation in Christ. That is why corporeality, as noted in chapter 7, where we spoke about biblical anthropology, is an essential dimension of the human person. Insofar as the person is a created being, the human individual, both in this world and in the next, ought to be open to others and to the world. Consequently, in the ultimate plenitude, there will also be this opening to others, not as a restriction to limit one, but as the full realization of being human. Corporeality is therefore essential to this opening.

On the other hand, according to the dogma of faith, if after death a human being reaches a definitive retribution (eternal life, death forever, or a state of purification in view of salvation), how may we understand the intermediary state between personal death and resurrection? And what becomes of the human person in all

240

of that? Does our faith in the fulfillment of salvation lie in the immortality of the soul, or in the resurrection of the body? If our faith rests in the resurrection of the body, how may we reconcile ultimate salvation with this intermediary state?

As we already know, Paul, grounding himself in the resurrection of the Lord as the first fruits of our own (1 Cor. 15:20-23; Rom. 8:11), speaks of the hope of resurrection for all who die in Christ. Nevertheless, he is aware of the difficulty of the delay of the promised rebirth. This difficulty is also ours, and it is not easy to find an answer in revelation to it. This is what gives rise to several questions:

> What are we to understand by this "intermediate state" in which the Christian is placed between his death and his resurrection? Does biblical anthropology allow us to hold that there is real life without the body? How are we to regard man's state during this long period of waiting? Is it one of full spiritual activity for his "separated" soul or of "sleep" for all its powers?[23]

The Platonic idea of the immortality of the soul influenced Judaism in the Hellenistic period, precisely when faith in the final resurrection of the dead began to be spread in apocalyptic circles (about the second century before Christ). Moreover, this Platonic understanding will affect Christian hope from the first centuries. Nevertheless,

> The witness of the early Church is at least quite clear in this respect. It presents us with not just the possibility but the necessity of the resurrection of the dead as an eschatological event already inaugurated in the resurrection of Jesus. This was, in the earliest tradition, not just an event for Jesus alone but the first and decisive phase of the *eschaton* as prefigured in the apocalyptic circles to which the first followers of Christ belonged (see Acts 2. 16-36; 1 Thess. 4. 15, 17; 1 Cor. 15. 20; Mt. 27. 52-53).[24]

It was therefore the delay of the second coming of Jesus Christ which gave rise to the problem concerning what is very inappropriately called the intermediate state. Thus, "The need to reconsider and reformulate the character of the primitive Christian hope rooted in the Easter faith arose only with the delay in the Lord's coming which threatened to detach the resurrection of Jesus from the antecedent religious postulate of the resurrection of the dead."[25] One thing is certain: according to the Christian tradition, matter and spirit form a unity. In consequence, the body and matter are not evil prisons from which we must be liberated but gifts which proceed from God.

Interpretations

I have previously noted how biblical faith, both in the Old and in the New Testaments, is faith in the resurrection of the body.[26] Only the Book of Wisdom of Solomon employs a dualistic terminology, soul-body, postulating a soul separated from the body as the recipient of immortality.

Tradition interprets this book as written under the influence of the Hellenistic culture of that time. With it appeared in the Old Testament a different anthropological language. For example, "As a child I was naturally gifted, and a good soul fell to my lot; or rather, being good, I entered an undefiled body"(Wis. 8:19-20). And also: "a perishable body weighs down the soul, and this earthly tent burdens the thoughtful mind" (Wis. 9:15; see also 2:22; 3:1-9; 4:7–5:23).

The contrast is seen by referring to the books of Daniel and 2 Maccabees. As has been presented in chapter 5, these two books shortly preceded the book of the Wisdom of Solomon. Faith in the resurrection of the dead first appears Daniel and 2 Maccabees. The anthropology of the book of the Wisdom of Solomon can be summarized as follows:

a) The human being is composed of a soul and of a body. The soul (pre-existent?) is immortal, while the body, as corruptible, obstructs its natural operations.

b) The *soma-psychic* (body-soul) tension is resolved with death which implies the survival of the dis-incarnated soul and its retribution according to its proper merits.

c) There is no reference to the resurrection of the body.[27]

LIFE BEYOND DEATH

This anthropological dualism—soul-body—is also found in certain apocryphal books, for example in the first book of Enoch, and the fourth book of Ezra (late first century of the Christian era).[28] In the latter book, speaking of the state of the departed before the judgment, the souls of the dead lived in distinct rooms, awaiting the resurrection, but they have already started to received their retribution:

> I answered and said, "If I have found favor in your sight, my lord, show this also to your servant: whether after death, as soon as every one of us yields up his soul, we shall be kept in rest until those times come when you will renew the creation, or whether we shall be tormented at once?"

> He answered me and said, "I will show you that also, but do not be associated with those who have shown scorn, nor number yourself among those who are tormented. For you have a treasure of works laid up with the Most High; but it will not be shown to you until last times. Now, concerning death, the teaching is: When the decisive decree has gone forth from the Most High that a man shall die, as the spirit leaves the body to return again to him who gave it, first of all it adores the glory of the Most High. And if it is one of those who have shown scorn and have not kept the way of the Most High, and who have despised his Law, and who have hated those who fear God—such spirits shall not enter into habitations, but shall immediately wander about in torments, ever grieving and sad, in seven ways. The first way, because they have scorned the Law of the Most High. The second way, because they cannot now make a good repentance that they may live. The third way, they shall see the reward laid up for those who have trusted the covenants of the Most High. The fourth way, they shall consider the torment laid up for themselves in the last days. The fifth way, they shall see how the habitations of the others are guarded by angels in profound quiet. The sixth way, they shall see how some of them will pass over into torments. The seventh way, which is worse than all the ways that have been mentioned, because they shall utterly waste away in confusion and be consumed with shame, and shall wither with fear at seeing the glory of the Most High before whom they

sinned while they were alive, and before whom they are to be judged in the last times.

"Now this is the order of those who have kept the ways of the Most High, when they shall be separated from their mortal body. During the time that they lived in it, they laboriously served the Most High, and withstood danger every hour, that they might keep the Law of the Lawgiver perfectly. Therefore this is the teaching concerning them: First of all, they shall see with great joy the glory of him who receives them, for they shall have rest in seven orders. The first order, because they have striven with great effort to overcome the evil thought which was formed with them, that it might not lead them astray from life into death. The second order, because they see the perplexity in which the souls of the ungodly wander, and the punishment that waits them. The third order, they see the witness which he who formed them bears concerning them, that while they were alive they kept the Law which was given them in trust. The fourth order, they understand the rest which they now enjoy, being gathered into their chambers and guarded by angels in profound quiet, and the glory which awaits them in the last days. The fifth orders, they rejoice that they have now escaped what is mortal, and shall inherit what is to come; and besides they see the straits and toil from which they have been delivered, and the spacious liberty which they are to receive and enjoy in immortality. The sixth order, when it is shown to them how their face is to shine like the sun, and how they are to be made like the light of the stars, being incorruptible from then on. The seventh order, which is greater than all that have been mentioned, because they shall rejoice with boldness, and shall be confident without confusion, and shall be glad without fear, for they hasten to behold the face of him whom they served in life and from whom they are to receive their reward when glorified. This is the order of the souls of the righteous, as henceforth is announced, and the aforesaid are the ways of torment which those who would not give heed shall suffer hereafter."

LIFE BEYOND DEATH

I answered and said, "Will time therefore be given to the souls after they have been separated from the bodies, to see what you have described to me?"

He said to me, "They shall have freedom for seven days, so that during these seven days they may see the things of which you have been told, and afterward they shall be gathered in their habitations."[29]

Among Catholics, certain theologians, such as Michael Schmaus, interpret the soul-body component in a rather dualistic sense. For Schmaus the spirit of a human being enjoys divine participation at the end of life. The soul leaves the body as one liberated from the catastrophe of a corporeal existence, even if Schmaus recognizes that the soul is ordered to an existence in the body, with the body, and through the body. Death represents the dissolution of the unity of the human being; it implies a profound transformation for the human person. The purely spiritual functions which the soul accomplishes by means of the body during its earthly life will be, without the body, abandoned by the soul after death. It is the all-powerfulness of God that makes possible the survival of the soul separated from the body while awaiting the resurrection.[30]

Nevertheless, today one underscores the unity of the human person, as was manifested in both the Old and in the New Testaments, even while one recognizes that the problem of the subject of retribution—that is, of the corporeal situation after death—was not so important. One stresses that eternal life begins with the death of the righteous, though revelation does not give any concrete answer to the mode of this beatific existence after death.

A quite different interpretation comes to us from Cardinal Ratzinger. For him, the idea of the soul as presented in Christian tradition has nothing to do with the dualistic philosophy issue of Platonism:

The idea of the soul as found in Catholic liturgy and theology up to the Second Vatican Council has as little to do with antiquity as has the idea of resurrection. It is a strictly Christian idea, and could only be formulated on the basis of Christian faith whose vision of God, the world and human nature it expresses in the realm of anthropology.[31]

According to Ratzinger, we are using the word "soul" in two different anthropological senses: one, dualistic, flowing from Hellenism and the other, Christian, which expresses a different theological reality: the human person, as a created being, is related and connected to God and to others:

> We agreed earlier that it is not a relationless being oneself that makes a human being immortal, but precisely his relatedness, or capacity for relatedness, to God. We must now add that such an opening of one's existence is not a trimming, an addition to a being which really might subsist in an independent fashion. On the contrary, it constitutes what is deepest in man's being. It is nothing other than what we call "soul."[32]

The relational dimension, essential to human beings, continues after death. That is the meaning of the immortality of the soul, namely, that the human person, who is created in relationship with God, with others, and with the universe, in accepting eternal life continues to live in this relational dimension.

Notwithstanding the opinion of Cardinal Ratzinger, other theologians continue to hold that the idea of a soul separated from the body is not Christian. In order to resolve the difficulties presented by the distinction between immortality of the soul and resurrection of the body they ask themselves the question whether or not we could know if resurrection might occur for each of us immediately after death. Pierre Benoît, facing the difficulties that the idea of an intermediate state raises, says:

> And if none of these solutions is satisfactory will it not be necessary to revise the statement causing the difficulty, that is, the postponement of the resurrection until the end of time and the parousia? Would it not be easier to regard the resurrection as taking place for each individual directly after death?[33]

On his side, Ladislaus Boros proposes a hypothesis which maintains that there might be a sense of a resurrection for each

LIFE BEYOND DEATH

person after death, while recognizing that a human being needs a transformed universe in order to reach its fulfillment:

> As a hypothetical resolution, I suggest the following: resurrection happens immediately upon dying; nevertheless it does not occur then in full. The resurrected body needs the transformed and transfigured world as its natural environment. Hence immortality and resurrection would be one and the same reality.[34]

It seems to me that there is another position which is more adequate and without doubt less hypothetical. We believe in a God of life, a God who is saviour and liberator, a God whose promises are accomplished in Jesus Christ through whom eternal life is already present among us. This saving God who is the creator is also the One who is the origin of the gift of eternal life. Words used to express this conviction are less important. The Christian community believes that after death we continue to live in the presence of God. That is why I very much like the text of an exegete which states:

> Believers today have reached a higher degree of maturity and see no need to exercise their imaginations on details of "how" God acts from the culminating moment of each person's death. They believe in a God who saves and are prepared to give him a "blank check" to act in the form and manner in which he thinks best.[35]

The God of Christians—the God of Abraham, of Isaac and of Jacob—is the God of life; "this God is not a God of the dead, but of the living."[36] God awaits us beyond the fragility of death, without our knowing exactly how this transformed existence will be.[37]

Therefore, in spite of differing linguistic influences, when we speak of the immortality of the soul and of the resurrection of the body, from a Christian point of view we do not adopt a Platonic dualism. A human being, created to be the image and likeness of God, is invited to eternity. Death inaugurates a different kind of life which will reach its complete fulfillment in the *parousia* of Christ.

The Same Faith Expressed in a Different Language?

Much has been written on the difference and similitude between immortality and resurrection. Nevertheless, beyond any discussion, the issue is whether or not the same reality is actually being expressed through different concepts. Karl Rahner, for example, arrived at the following conclusion: "In the Christian doctrine proposed by the Church of the 'immortality of the soul' and of the 'resurrection of the flesh' the whole man in his unity is always envisaged."[38]

According to the Christian faith, one cannot accept an immortality that inevitably leads to dualism, nor understand the resurrection as a simple revival of a dead body. It seems to me that, when we speak of immortality or resurrection, people always think in the category of incarnated beings. After death, we are in communion with God, with those who are our loved ones and our friends, without insisting strongly on an intermediate state. At the pastoral level, in spite of dualistic language, the Christian who speaks of immortality of the soul interprets it in the sense of an incarnated reality.

When the word "soul" appears in the New Testament, it refers to the entire human person and not only to a part of one's being in opposition to the body (Mk. 8:35). The word "soul" expresses the fact that we are created to become the image and likeness of God, in relation with God, with others, and with creation. Thus, for those who have fully accepted to become the image and likeness of God, to be adopted children of God in Jesus Christ, death is not the end of life but, rather, the beginning of its fullness. Consequently, the word "soul" expresses the relational dimension of the person—a dimension that cannot disappear with death. Even after death we will continue to be relational beings.

It seems to me that the problem of the intermediate state has been created by the Greek notions of soul and immortality.[39] Recognizing this, it is not really accurate to speak of an intermediary state, since the one who has accepted the gift of eternal life has already gone through death into a definitive new life. The same might be said for those who die forever.

Even if we accept that there is no real opposition in Christianity between immortality and resurrection, the fact is that the concepts of soul and body have been interpreted in a dualistic way. Perhaps the best way to avoid the risk of dualistic interpretation is to abandon such dualistic concepts. The human being is a bodily being, a relational person, and this reality will not cease with death.

How is one to understand corporeality after our death? The answer is that in dying in the Lord we become part of the body of the resurrected Christ and we are in relationship with all those who share the same body of glory.

3. Being with Christ

Paul, as was presented in chapter 7, had to fight against the despair of those for whom death meant an end to all hope. What does the resurrection of Jesus Christ provide, if we must die forever? If we accept the final resurrection at the second coming of Jesus Christ in glory, what happens to those already dead? Paul's response is that they will be resurrected on the last day (see 1 Thess. 4:13-18). Furthermore, those who are dead in the Lord are already in his presence forever. They are part of the body of the risen Christ, the body which awaits its fullness at the final resurrection, when Jesus Christ will return in his glory and when the transformed humanity will live in a renewed world.

To Die in the Lord

Although death continues to present a sad face, Jesus Christ has destroyed the power of sin and of death which, even if it is a consequence of being created, Paul considers a consequence of sin (Rom. 5:12). Death is compared with being unclothed, to a departure (2 Pet. 1:13-15; 2 Cor. 5:4) or with being "away from the body and at home with the Lord" (2 Cor. 5:8). For Paul, "The main thing is that he takes confidence from the belief that even without his body and in a state of 'nakedness' he will already be 'with the Lord.'"[40]

The New Testament speaks in particular of a death in the Lord: "I heard a voice from heaven saying: 'Write this: Blessed are the dead who from now on die in the Lord.' 'Yes,' says the Spirit, 'they will rest from their labors, for their deeds follow them'" (Rev. 14:13). By baptism, we die to sin and we are thus destined to this mode of ultimate life that Jesus Christ inaugurated and which will continue, transformed, after our death (Rom. 6:8-11). Jesus also referred to death as a baptism: "But Jesus said to them [James and John], 'You do not know what you are asking. Are you able to drink the cup that I drink, or to be baptized with the baptism that I am baptized with?'" (Mk. 10: 38) For Paul, more than by our physical death, it is by baptism that we die in the Lord. The Christian life, as a preparation for death in the Lord, ought to be a continual death, namely, "always carrying in the body the death of Jesus, so that the life of Jesus may also be made visible in our bodies. For while we live, we are always being given up to death for Jesus' sake, so that the life of Jesus may be made visible in our mortal flesh" (2 Cor. 4:10-11). That is why Paul is convinced

> that even now the Christian possesses, after a spiritual and hidden, but none the less real, manner, the life of Christ. And this comes about through the union contracted at baptism. Further, the more the final phase of full and definitive union in the risen body is delayed, the stronger is the apostle's assertion that the essential is given even now. In his explanation of baptism (Rom. 6. 1-11) he shows that the Christian's death is already accomplished according to the mystical manner of the sacrament, and that already he lives the new life of Christ in God.[41]

Referring to Paul's argument, Benoît continues,

> In saying this Paul maintains that this new life remains hidden with Christ in God and will only appear with the manifestation of Christ, that is, with the parousia (Col. 3. 1-4). But he gives the impression that while he abided by the traditional affirmation of the last resurrection, he regards it as less and less important and believes that the essential has already come to pass. His eschatology, which at the outset was "futurist", has become increasingly one that has already been affected. This might well give us cause for reflection, since we live in a time when the delay in the parousia is far greater than in St Paul's day.[42]

LIFE BEYOND DEATH

Immediately after death, one is already with Christ in an ultimate fashion: "I am hard pressed between the two: my desire is to depart and be with Christ, for that is better" (Phil. 1:23). All of this is similar and expressed in the Pauline hope to be with the Lord at the time of his second coming in glory: "Then we who are alive, who are left, will be caught up in the clouds together with them to meet the Lord in the air; and so we will be with the Lord forever" (1 Thess. 4:17). To be with the Lord from death is compared to being with him at the time of the *parousia*. There is no indication of a life that is less blessed immediately after death than it will be when the return of Christ in glory will happen—and with it the final accomplishment of everything.[43] Those who lived and are dead in the Lord are already members of the risen body of Christ.

Members of the Risen Body of Christ

Paul does not conceive an immortal soul according to a Hellenistic world view. In the new life entered into at baptism, for Paul death signifies being "at home with the Lord" (2 Cor. 5:8). By incorporation into the death and resurrection of Christ, those who are dead live in their celestial home: "For we know that if this earthly tent we live in is destroyed, we have a building from God, a house not made with hands, eternal in the heaven" (2 Cor. 5:1). This heavenly dwelling is "the very body of the risen Christ, already established in the glory of heaven, which is waiting to be joined fully and definitely with his chosen ones. This body of Christ which unites to itself all the bodies of Christians as its members, we have already mystically put on by baptism (Gal. 3. 27; Rom. 13. 14)."[44] We will join it, definitively, immediately after death.

The Pauline conviction that I have been presenting in this book is that, from baptism, the Christian already lives the ultimate. In this sense, one is not able to separate being with Christ after death from being with him at the time of the final resurrection in an ultimate accomplishment. These are two dimensions of the same reality—of our transformed existence. From now, even before death, we are enveloped in the glorious body of Jesus Christ.

A Body Which Awaits Its Fullness

This vision does not make the *parousia* superfluous. The second coming of Christ in glory is the event which completes the process. The resurrection of the body is an essential dimension of our faith: "not only the creation, but we ourselves, who have the first fruits of the Spirit, groan inwardly while we wait for adoption, the redemption of our bodies" (Rom. 8:23). It is not only a question of the resurrection of the body, but also of the hope for a transformed creation which presently "has been groaning in labor pains until now" (Rom. 8:22) and which "waits with eager longing for the revealing of the children of God" (Rom. 8:19) in order that creation also may be liberated from all constraint and from all slavery.

At the moment of death, the Christian enjoys eternal life which he or she began to live from the moment of baptism.

> This approach, does not exempt us from looking forward to the final resurrection of the body as the definitive redemption of the whole human being (Rom. 8. 25), but it enables us to conceive in the interval an already essential possession of heavenly life because it is in union with him who even now possesses this life to the full in the whole of his risen being, body and soul.[45]

It is therefore a celestial body which grows through the progressive incorporation of all who die in the Lord and which will reach its fulfillment at the moment of the *parousia* of Christ, when all humanity, with creation, will be transformed for eternity. This transformation is the final plenitude!

It is necessary to remember that, while one speaks of the end of time, it treats of our present time. Then, as in the beyond, in ultimate existence, there will be another form of temporality which it is difficult for us to grasp. Temporality is a part of being created and is an essential dimension of humanity; it will not completely disappear in the ultimate state of salvation. Accordingly, while still believing in the resurrection of the body and in the transformation of the world,

> at the same time we must acknowledge that we have no idea at all of what this end of our times corresponds with in the new and

LIFE BEYOND DEATH

already present world in which the risen Christ lives. And since, in addition, we know that we are already united here below in the Holy Spirit with the body of the risen Christ, we are able to believe that directly after death we shall find in this uninterrupted union the source and means of our essential blessedness.[46]

Within this union we will find the very centre of Christian hope in human beings and their final connection with an ultimate fulfillment. It is a hope which immediately fills us with joy. We know in effect "that neither death, nor life, nor angels, nor rulers, nor things present, nor things to come, nor powers, nor height, nor depth, nor anything else in all creation, will be able to separate us from the love of God in Christ Jesus our Lord" (Rom. 8:38-39). In Christ, no horizon is completely closed. Therein is the source of our Christian hope!

※

And after death? We will live in ultimate communion with God. This communion is initiated by the death and resurrection of Jesus Christ and by the Holy Spirit continues to be a reality in our lives through baptism, calling us to extend it to all of God's creation.

This communion with God is also a communion with brothers and sisters who are already in the presence of God through death. It is a communion as well with those incorporated into the body of Christ through baptism and who, consequently, form part of the Christian community travelling toward the celestial home. That is what is called the communion of saints.[47] This communion awaits its fullness at the return of Christ in his glory, with the resurrection of the body and the ultimate transformation of creation. The vision of the book of Revelation will then become a reality:

> Then I saw a new heaven and a new earth; for the first heaven and the first earth had passed away, and the sea was no more. And I saw the holy city, the new Jerusalem, coming down out of heaven from God, prepared as a bride adorned for her husband. And I heard a loud voice from the throne saying, "See, the home of God is among mortals. He will dwell with them

as their God; they will be his peoples, and God himself will be with them; he will wipe every tear from their eyes. Death will be no more; mourning and crying and pain will be no more, for the first things have passed away." (Rev. 21:1-4)

Our life will not finish in absurdity if we accept the gift of eternal life that God offers us. At the heart of our existence we are invited to prepare ourselves to wear with dignity the white garment which we received on the day of our baptism. We know how easy it is to soil it; we know how difficult fidelity is. We recognize the extent of our own limits. However, the experience of our fragility actually enables us to grow. It is the purgatorial dimension to our purification bringing us through the process of becoming fully open and transparent beings. This is the way that we carve the statue of our humanity and of our liberation. This is the way that we come to dwell in the heavenly tent, the body of Christ glorified.

LIFE BEYOND DEATH

Notes to Chapter 10

1   See *CF*, n°s 2305-2309. In May 17, 1979, the Sacred Congregation for the Doctrine of the Faith published a letter on "Certain Questions Concerning Eschatology." It is important to refer to what is said there regarding the condition of the human person after death to know the "traditional" position of the Roman Catholic Church on the subject of the eschatological dimension of Christian faith: "The Sacred Congregation, whose task is to advance and protect the doctrine of the faith, here wishes to recall what the Church teaches in the name of Christ, especially concerning what happens between the death of the Christian and the general resurrection.

"1. The Church believes (cf. the Creed) in the resurrection of the dead.

"2. The Church understands this resurrection as referring to the whole person; for the elect it is nothing other than the extension to human beings of the resurrection of Christ himself.

"3. The Church affirms that a spiritual element survives and subsists after death, an element endowed with consciousness and will, so that the 'human self' subsists, *though deprived for the present of the complement of its body*. To designate this element, the Church uses the word 'soul', the accepted term in the usage of scripture and tradition. Although not unaware that this term has various meanings in the Bible, the Church thinks that there is no valid reason for rejecting it; moreover she considers that the use of some word as a vehicle is absolutely indispensable in order to support the faith of Christians.

"4. The Church excludes every way of thinking or speaking that would render meaningless or unintelligible her prayers, her funeral rites and religious acts offered for the dead. All these are, in their substance, *loci theologici*.

"5. In accordance with the Scriptures, the Church looks for 'the glorious manifestation of our Lord Jesus Christ' (*DV 4 [Dogmatic Constitution on Divine Revelation*, Dei Verbum*, of the Second Vatican Council]*), believing it to be distinct and deferred with respect to the situation of people immediately after death.

"6. In teaching her doctrine about the human person's destiny after death, the Church excludes any explanation that would deprive the assumption of the Virgin Mary of its unique meaning, namely the fact that the bodily glorification of the virgin [*sic*] is an anticipation of the glorification that is the destiny of all the other elect.

"7. In fidelity to the New Testament and tradition, the Church believes in the happiness of the just who will one day be with Christ. She believes that there will be eternal punishment for the sinner, who will be deprived of the sight of God, and that this punishment will have a repercussion on the whole being of the sinner. She believes in the possibility of a purification for the elect before they see God, a purification altogether different from the punishment of the damned. This is what the Church means when speaking of hell and purgatory.

"When dealing with the situation of the human being after death, one must especially beware of arbitrary imaginative representations: excess of this kind is a major cause of the difficulties that Christian faith often encounters. Respect must, however, be given to the images employed in the Scriptures. Their profound meaning must be discerned, while avoiding the risk of over-attenuating them, since this often empties of substance the realities designated by the images.

"Neither Scripture nor theology provides sufficient light for a proper picture of life after death. Christians must firmly hold the two following essential points: on the one hand, they must believe in the fundamental continuity, thanks to the power of the Holy Spirit, between our present life in Christ and the future life (charity is the law of the Kingdom of God and our charity on earth will be the measure of our sharing in God's glory in heaven); on the other hand, they must be clearly aware of the radical difference between the present life and the future one, due to the fact that the economy of faith will be replaced by the economy of fulness of life; we shall be with Christ and 'we shall see God' [cf. 1 Jn. 3:2], and it is in these promises and marvellous mysteries that our hope essentially consists. Our imagination may be incapable of reaching these heights, but our heart does so instinctively and completely." (CF, n° 2317)

2   The apocryphal literature develops between the second century before and the first century after Christ. These apocrypha represent a number of writings, Jewish or Christian, close to the biblical style, or which try to imitate it.

3   1 Enoch 22 (in *1 [Ethiopic Apocalypse of] Enoch [Second Century B.C. – First Century A.D.]: A New Translation and Introduction by E. Isaac*, in J. H. Charlesworth [Ed.], *The Old Testament Pseudepigrapha: Volume 1, Apocalyptic Literature and Testaments*, Garden City: Doubleday & Company, Inc., 1983, pp. 24–25).

4   Ruíz de la Peña, *op. cit.*, p. 301; see also pp. 291–300; Ratzinger, *op. cit.*, pp. 119–161, 189–190.

5   See Ruíz de la Peña, *op. cit.*, pp. 301–304.

6   CF, n°° 2305–2307. J. Neuner and J. Dupuis, in the introduction to this text of the Constitution *Benedictus Deus* of Pope Benedict XII, say the following regarding the context that motivated this official proclamation of the Church: *"The common teaching of the Church on immediate retribution after death held that the blessed on entering the heavenly state were introduced to the immediate and eternal vision of God. Departing from this traditional opinion, Pope John XXII, in a series of sermons preached in 1331, asserted, as a private theologian, that soon after death the blessed enjoy only the vision of Christ's glorified humanity, while the access to the vision of the Triune God will be opened to them only after the resurrection, on the day of judgment. The following year, he adapted this opinion of a progressive retribution to the condition of the*

LIFE BEYOND DEATH

damned. The Pope's opinion led to a fierce controversy, notably between the Franciscans who supported the Pope and the Dominicans who opposed him. The university of Paris requested the Pope to settle the dispute authoritatively. Though he intended to heed the request, John XXII was able only to retract his own former opinion on the eve of his death and to submit personally to the traditional doctrine of the Church. His successor Benedict XII, after a thorough enquiry, issued in 1336 the Constitution Benedictus Deus *by which he meant to bring the controversy to an end. According to this Constitution the souls of the blessed departed see the Triune God face to face immediately after death and prior to the resurrection. But the nature of their intermediate state between death and resurrection, which is conceived as that of bodiless souls, is presupposed by the Constitution rather than directly taught."* (CF, p. 942)

7   The Second Vatican Council repeats here the doctrine of the Bull *Laetentur Coeli*, the Decree for the Greeks, proclaimed by Pope Eugene IV in the General Council of Florence (in July 6, 1439), which is inspired by the previously cited Constitution *Benedictus Deus*. See *CF*, n°s 2308–2309.

8   See, for example, how Delumeau, in his book *Sin and Fear* (pp. 296–303, 372–410), to which I have already oftentimes referred in my work, describes a collective guilt complex, the tortures of afterlife, and a "lynx-eyed" God that generate a lot of anxiety.

9   See chapter 2 above where, in its note 23, I refer to the historical emergence of purgatory and its importance for the medieval Church. However, as Schwarz indicates, the doctrine of purgatory was not accepted easily by other Christian churches: "The doctrine of purgatory presupposes an intermediate state between death and resurrection and is often viewed as a divisive issue between Roman Catholicism and the rest of Christendom. With the Council of Trent (1545–63) the final separation occurred between Roman Catholics and Protestants. One of the main arguments was the doctrine of purgatory." (Schwarz, *op. cit.*, p. 352; see also pp. 353–364)

There is no doubt that Jacques Le Goff, in his already-cited book, *The Birth of Purgatory*, represents an authority on this subject. According to him, besides the "highly sophisticated legal and penal system" (p. 5) that the doctrine of purgatory requires, "Purgatory brought to the Church not only new spiritual power but also, to put it bluntly, considerable profit, as we shall see. Much of this profit went to the mendicant orders, ardent propagandists of the new doctrine. And finally, the 'infernal' system of indulgences found powerful support in the idea of Purgatory" (p. 12). Nevertheless, the notion of purgatory "took hold" beyond theological ideas, such as "the relationship between belief and society, about mental structures, and about the historical role of imagination" (p. 13).

Despite its limited biblical roots and historical development, "The Christian doctrine of Purgatory was not finally worked out until the sixteenth century by the Council of Trent. Rejected by Protestants, it was an exclusively Catholic doctrine" (p. 41). Furthermore, "the history of Purgatory is an affair of the Latin

West" (p. 52). The twelfth century, as it was indicated above, is the century of the birth of purgatory (see p. 130), and "[i]t was the century of the great Crusades. . . . In short, Purgatory was part of a comprehensive system involving both the social structure and the way it was conceived, and this system was an achievement of the twelfth century" (p. 132).

The profit that the Church obtained from the doctrine of purgatory refers, particularly, to the power acquired by the Church through this doctrine. "In any case," says Le Goff, "the Church, in the ecclesiastical, clerical sense, drew considerable power from the new system of the hereafter. It administered or supervised prayers, alms, masses, and offerings of all kinds made by the living on behalf of the dead and reaped the benefits thereof. Thanks to Purgatory the Church developed the system of indulgences, a source of great power and profit until it became a dangerous weapon that was ultimately turned back against the Church" (p. 249). Finally, "The most fervent, most 'glorious' moments in the history of Purgatory belong to the period between the fifteenth and nineteenth centuries. Besides the traditional means of publicity, such as sermons and pamphlets and, later, books, images played an important part in propagating the new doctrine. Frescoes, miniatures, engravings, chapel and altar decorations all served to crystallize the images surrounding the idea of Purgatory" (p. 356). It is interesting to know, by contrast, as Le Goff indicates, how "Paradise has aroused surprisingly little interest among historians" (p. 358).

10   Sesboüé, *op. cit.*, p. 136; see also pp. 137–147.

11   Dogmatic Constitution on the Church (*Lumen Gentium*), n° 49.

12   See the General Council of Trent Decree on Justification (1547), in *CF*, n°s 1924–1983.

13   See Le Goff, *op. cit.*, pp. 213–218.

14   See *CF*, n°s 26, 35, 39/21, 1980, 2304, 2308, 2310, 2317.

15   See the already-mentioned Dogmatic Constitution of the Church (*Lumen Gentium*), n°s 48–51.

16   Delumeau, *Sin and Fear*, p. 388; see also Le Goff, *op. cit.*, p. 205.

17   Delumeau, *Sin and Fear*, p. 391.

18   Ratzinger, *op. cit.*, pp. 230–231; see also Ruíz de la Peña, *op. cit.*, pp. 327–343.

19   Boros, "Some Thoughts on the Four Last Things," p. 40.

20   M. Zundel, *Ta parole comme une source: 85 sermons inédits de Maurice Zundel*, Quebec: Anne Sigier/Desclée, 1987, p. 411.

21   See my book *Death by Despair*, pp. 96–97.

22   There is an interesting discussion regarding "subjective immortality" and "subjectivity" in the framework of the process-relational metaphysics of

Alfred North Whitehead (1861–1947). This discussion originated with Marjorie Hewitt Suchocki's "reconstruction" of Whitehead's metaphysics as leading to a possible "subjective immortality," in *The End of Evil: Process Eschatology in Historical Context*, Albany: State University of New York Press, 1988. Reactions of some philosophers and theologians to Marjorie Hewitt Suchocki's position are included in Bracken (Ed.), *World without End*. See, for example, L. S. Ford, "An Alternative Theory of Subjective Immortality," pp. 112–127; Clayton, *op. cit.*, pp. 137–145; J. H. Haught, "Behind the Veil: Evolutionary Naturalism and the Question of Immortality," pp. 150–176.

23   P. Benoît, "Resurrection: At the End of Time or Immediately After Death?" in *Concilium*, 10/6 (1970), p. 104.

24   J. Blenkinsopp, "Theological Synthesis and Hermeneutical Conclusions," in *Concilium*, 10/6 (1970), p. 117; see also Schwarz, *op. cit.*, pp. 280–301.

25   Blenkinsopp, *op. cit.*, p. 117.

26   See Schillebeeckx, "The Interpretation of Eschatology," p. 56.

27   See Ruíz de la Peña, *op. cit.*, pp. 360–383.

28   For the content of the fourth book of Ezra, see *The Fourth Book of Ezra (Late First Century A.D.). With the Four Additional Chapters: A New Translation and Introduction by B. M. Metzger*, in Charlesworth (Ed.), *op. cit.*, pp. 517–559.

29   IV Ezra 7:75–101 (in *ibid.*, pp. 539–540).

30   See Schmaus, *op. cit.*, pp. 225–248.

31   Ratzinger, *op. cit.*, p. 150; see also Schwarz, *op. cit.*, pp. 272–280.

32   Ratzinger, *op. cit.*, p. 155.

33   Benoît, *op. cit.*, p. 104.

34   L. Boros, "Has Life a Meaning?" in *Concilium*, 10/6 (1970), p. 18.

35   J. M. González-Ruíz, "Should We De-Mythologize the 'Separated Soul'?" in *Concilium*, 41 (1969), p. 95.

36   *Ibid.*, p. 95.

37   I think that this is the way in which we should interpret the official declarations of the magisterium of the Church (see, for example, the General Council of Vienna [1311–1312] which proclaimed that the spiritual soul is the form of the body [*CF*, n° 405], and the already-mentioned Constitution *Benedictus Deus* [1336] of Pope Benedict XII [*CF*, n°ˢ 2305–2307]). Through an apparently dualistic language, in which the soul is the recipient of retribution after death, theology tries to demonstrate that in any of these official declarations of the Church it is proved that the doctrine defined as dogma of faith by these texts formally imposes the theses of an intermediate state and of a separated soul. It is a question of defending the personal immortality of each human being, that is

to say, the imperishability of the person after death. I believe that this imperishability does not apply to those who have not accepted the gift of eternal life (see Ruíz de la Peña, *op. cit.*, pp. 391–395).

38   Rahner, *More Recent Writings*, p. 352.

39   See Schwarz, *op. cit.*, pp. 269–272.

40   Benoît, *op. cit.*, p. 107.

41   *Ibid.*, p. 108.

42   *Ibid.*, p. 109.

43   See Ruíz de la Peña, *op. cit.*, p. 299.

44   Benoît, *op. cit.*, pp. 112–113.

45   *Ibid.*, p. 113.

46   *Ibid.*, p. 114.

47   See Bregman, *Death and Dying, Spirituality and Religions*, pp. 217–219.

LIFE BEYOND DEATH

Conclusion

I believe that Jesus Christ "shall come again to judge [to liberate] the living and the dead." I believe in the communion of saints, in the resurrection of the body and in eternal life. I also believe that a transformed humanity shall live in a renewed earth, in total harmony with every human being and with creation, as the prophet Isaiah prophesied beautifully and with great imagination:

> The wolf shall live with the lamb, the leopard shall lie down with the kid, the calf and the lion and the fatling together, and a little child shall lead them. The cow and the bear shall graze, their young shall lie down together; and the lion shall eat straw like the ox. The nursing child shall play over the hole of the asp, and the weaned child shall put its hand on the adder's den. They will not hurt or destroy on all my holy mountain; for the earth will be full of the knowledge of the Lord as the waters cover the sea. (Isa. 11:6-9)

My belief is rooted in the Christian creed. However, as has been highlighted several times in this book, I further believe that the new heaven and the new earth (Rev. 21:1-8) are already among us through the incarnation, life, death and resurrection of Jesus Christ. Through him, with him and in him the ultimate is present among us, even if it has not yet been fully completed, namely, the new creation has become a task to be accomplished with our own engagement, too.

The fulfillment of our faith is a future already working in our present. In this regard, it is impossible to speak about a Christian future disconnected from human history. I am not speaking here about history in general, but about the history we continue to live on a moment-to-moment basis through the daily realities of our lives.

Consequently, from the Introduction of this book on, I have stressed that Christian hope does not imply a contempt of the world, nor a contemplation of what lies beyond life that might somehow cut us off from our own responsibility for the transformation of our world. Contemplation does not consist in the seeing of a distant heaven, a dream of a utopian illusion meant to separate us from this earth. Contemplation invites us to discover the advent of something different in our existence that lies in the inmost dimension of life: goodness, beauty, love, solidarity. In summary, Christian contemplation consists in discovering the presence of the Holy Spirit in the midst of all human endeavour, namely, to recognize among us the signs of the new heaven and the new earth.

The fulfillment of the eschatological dimension of Christian faith cannot be divorced from the search to become fully alive, free, autonomous, and responsible human beings who are also engaged in the transformation of the universe. In fact, the one common theme running throughout this book has been the need to appreciate the gift and meaning of life itself. Life, indeed, is the greatest gift received from God. Thus, we can understand why the most beautiful expression for designating the accomplishment of our faith is life everlasting. To have eternal life, to live forever, coincides with the full realization of human beings and their freedom. Entering into life everlasting is synonymous with becoming fully alive, being in communion with God, through Jesus Christ and the Holy Spirit, with others and with the renewed universe. Then, we will forever be children of God.

Nonetheless, having a full life is inseparable from our discovering a different God. Jesus Christ shows us another image of God. Rather than the "lynx-eyed" God—a God conceived as a despotic monarch—Jesus Christ reveals to us the fragility of a God who is present in human life as a love without any limit. This is in stark contrast to a medieval theocratic image of God that was meant to give a final meaning to our universe, imposing God's will without any further consideration of human beings. In contrast again, the

God of Christians would never oppress women or men by waiting to hand them a statement of account at the end of their lives, or threatening them with eternal punishment in hell. God grounds human freedom, and we are invited to discover the real God who lies in human hands.

This God needs also the response of human beings in order to establish a loving relationship with them, a relationship which holds the promise of eternity. Nevertheless, they can say "no" to God, refusing the invitation to live forever in solidarity with others and with creation. We are then the hope of God. We do not have the right to use fear of eternal damnation in order to bring people to conversion. God is opposed to constraint and punishment. God is a God of freedom and respect for human beings.

The discovery of human greatness and freedom has led people, particularly since Modernity, to reject God because they have for so long perceived divinity as a kind of enemy to all their human aspirations and dreams. Fortunately human beings today are at last beginning to see themselves with the capacity actually to be God's own revelation. Accordingly, far from feeling diminished before God, human beings are called to become fully alive in order to enter life everlasting. The greatness of God is the revelation of human splendour. The only possibility that Jesus Christ's God has for manifesting the divine presence in our world is through our own transformation, by becoming a living gospel. This is the centre of Jesus Christ's revelation: the inseparable solidarity between God and human greatness.

Our faith is full of life and hope for the future because it is also full of hope and life for the present. That is why it is so important to understand how what lies beyond death leads us to contemplate in the present the signs of the new life brought about by Jesus Christ. This journey transforms the signs of death into signs of hope and life, making our own life a parable of life everlasting.

The eschatological dimension of Christian faith deeply affects human beings. Their desire to live forever, their need for a global integration of the different dimensions of human life, their search for harmony and reconciliation with creation, their desire for peace and solidarity among humans, with God, through Jesus Christ and the Holy Spirit, and with a renewed universe for eternity. Indeed, the renewed interest in spirituality shows us this deeply felt need for peace and for a life lived in a holistic fashion. For these reasons, Christian community has a great responsibility in this human search for freedom, peace, and fulfillment. This responsibility consists in presenting our faith, particularly with regard to its ultimate, eschatological dimension, in a renewed way—a way that will recover the fresh novelty of the Good News of our salvation in Christ.

Through this book, we have been confronted with the difficult question of how to present the Christian message on the last things in a language that is always provisional and limited. We have had the opportunity to see how oftentimes the language used for the formulation of this faith has remained fixed to the past, to the culture of the time of its formulation and, in this sense, how the ultimate meaning of Christian faith no longer challenged us. For this reason, I have tried to present the Christian message on eschatology in a way that will be able to engage our life deeply and will help to deepen our faith.

Even so, language is not the only way of expressing our faith. There is also its celebration in the liturgy. Early Christian communities lived in the certainty that Jesus Christ was present among them and, at the same time, they proclaimed the *Maranatha:* "Come, Lord Jesus!" (Rev. 22:20). They lived with the assurance that through him, with him and in him the ultimate dimension of faith was a reality already acting in the present, even if they were also looking forward to its ultimate accomplishment. We must therefore renew and transform our liturgical celebrations in order to experience anew the presence among us of the ultimate dimension of Christian faith. This is also the best way of becoming witnesses to this hope and to the new life present among us. For this is finally what will allow us to enter "alive" into death—to enter "alive" into eternity. As a result, we are called to reintegrate dying and death in our own process of maturation. These are not shameful experiences of life but the way through which we reach our final destination in heaven.

LIFE BEYOND DEATH

Selected Bibliography

Alighieri, D. *Dante, Theologian: The Divine Comedy* (P. Cummins, trans. and commentary), St. Louis: B. Herder Book Co., 1953 (c1948).

Anderson, R. S., *Theology, Death and Dying*, Oxford: B. Blackwell, 1986.

Bauckham, R. and Hart, T., *Hope against Hope: Christian Eschatology at the Turn of the Millennium*, Grand Rapids: W. B. Eerdmans Publishing Co., 1999.

Braaten, C. E. and Jenson, R. W. (Eds.), *The Last Things: Biblical and Theological Perspectives on Eschatology*, Grand Rapids: W. B. Eerdmans Publishing Co., 2002.

Bracken, J. A. (Ed.), *World without End: Christian Eschatology from a Process Perspective*, Grand Rapids/Cambridge: William B. Eerdmans Publishing Company, 2005.

Bregman, L., *Beyond Silence and Denial: Death and Dying Reconsidered*, Louisville: Westminster John Knox Press, 1999.

Bregman, L., *Death and Dying, Spirituality and Religions: A Study of the Death Awareness Movement*, New York: Peter Lang Publishing, Inc. (American University Studies. Series VII: Theology and Religion, 228), 2003.

Bromley, D. G. and Melton, J. G. (Eds.), *Cults, Religion, and Violence*, Cambridge, UK: Cambridge University Press, 2002.

The Christian Faith in the Doctrinal Documents of the Catholic Church (6th revised and enlarged edition, J. Neuner and J. Dupuis: edited by Jacques Dupuis), New York: Alba House, 1998 (c1996).

Cote, R. G., *Lazarus! Come Out! Why Faith Needs Imagination*, Ottawa: Novalis, 2003.

Delumeau, J., *Sin and Fear: The Emergence of a Western Guilt Culture, 13th–18th Centuries* (E. Nicholson, trans.), New York: St. Martin's Press, 1990.

Delumeau, J., *History of Paradise: The Garden of Eden in Myth and Tradition* (M. O'Connell, trans.), Urbana: University of Illinois Press, 2000.

Duquoc, C. (Ed.), *Spirituality: Hope*, London: Burns & Oates (Concilium: Theology in the Age of Renewal, 9/6), 1970.

Fergusson, D. and Sarot, M. (Eds.), *The Future as God's Gift: Exploration in Christian Eschatology*, Edinburgh: T. & T. Clark, 2000.

Fiddes, P. S., *The Promised End: Eschatology in Theology and Literature*, Oxford: Blackwell, 2000.

Fiorenza, E. S., (Ed.), *The Power of Naming: A Concilium Reader in Feminist Liberation Theology*, Maryknoll/London: Orbis Books/SCM Press (Concilium Series), 1996.

Greer, R. A., *Christian Life and Christian Hope: Raids on the Inarticulate*, New York: The Crossroad Publishing Company, 2001.

Gutiérrez, G., *On Job: God-Talk and the Suffering of the Innocent* (M. J. O'Connell, trans.), Maryknoll: Orbis Books, 1987.

Gutiérrez, G., *The God of Life* (M. J. O'Connell, trans.), Maryknoll: Orbis Books, 1991.

Holt, P., *Thirsty for God: A Brief History of Christian Spirituality*, Minneapolis: Augsburg Publishing House, 1993.

Kübler-Ross, E., *Death: The Final Stage of Growth*, Englewood Cliffs: Prentice-Hall, 1975.

Kübler-Ross, E., *On Death and Dying*, New York: Macmillan, 1978.

Le Goff, J., *The Birth of Purgatory* (A. Goldhammer, trans.), Chicago: The University of Chicago Press, 1984.

Logan, F. D., *A History of the Church in the Middle Ages*, London: Routledge, 2002.

Martínez de Pisón, R., *The Religion of Life: The Spirituality of Maurice Zundel*, Sherbrooke: Médiaspaul, 1997.

Martínez de Pisón, R., *Sin and Evil* (R. R. Cooper, trans.), Sherbrooke: Médiaspaul, 2002.

Martínez de Pisón, R., *Death by Despair: Shame and Suicide*, New York: Peter Lang (American University Studies. Series VII: Theology and Religion, 245), 2006.

McFague, S.*, The Body of God: An Ecological Theology*, Minneapolis: Fortress Press, 1993.

McGrath, A. E., *A Brief History of Heaven*, Malden: Blackwell Publishing (Blackwell Brief Histories of Religion), 2003.

McTernan, O., *Violence in God's Name: Religion in an Age of Conflict*, Maryknoll: Orbis Books, 2003.

Moltmann, J., *Theology of Hope: On the Ground and the Implications of a Christian Eschatology* (J. W. Leitch, trans.), London: SCM Press Ltd., 1967.

Obayashi, H. (Ed.), *Death and Afterlife: Perspectives of World Religions*, New York: Praeger, 1992.

Polkinghorne, J. C., *The God of Hope and the End of the World*, New Haven: Yale University Press, 2002.

Rahner, K., *More Recent Writings* (K. Smyth, trans.), London: Darton, Longman & Todd (Theological Investigations, IV), 1966.

Rahner, K., *The Theology of the Spiritual Life* (K. H. and B. Kruger, trans.), Baltimore: Helicon Press (Theological Investigations, III), 1967.

Rahner, K., *Hearers of the Word* (M. Richards, trans.), New York: Herder and Herder, Inc., 1969.

Rahner, K., *Concerning Vatican Council II* (K. H. and B. Kruger, trans.), New York: Crossroad (Theological Investigations, VI), 1982.

Ratzinger, J., *Eschatology: Death and Eternal Life* (M. Waldestein, trans.), Washington, DC: Catholic University of America Press (Dogmatic Theology, 9), 1988.

Ruether, R. R., *Gaia and God: An Ecofeminist Theology of Earth Healing*, San Francisco: HarperSanFrancisco, 1992.

Sauer, V. J., *The Eschatology Handbook: The Bible Speaks to Us Today about Endtimes*, Atlanta: John Knox Press, 1981.

Schillebeeckx, E. and Willems, B. (Eds.), *The Problem of Eschatology*, New York: Paulist Press (Concilium: Theology in the Age of Renewal – Dogma, 41), 1969.

Schmaus, M., *Justification and the Last Things*, Kansas City: Sheed and Ward (Dogma, 6), 1977.

Schwarz, H., *Eschatology*, Grand Rapid: W. B. Eerdmans Publishing Co., 2000.

Toolan, D., *At Home in the Cosmos*, Maryknoll: Orbis Books, 2001.